POSITIVE TRADING PSYCHOLOGY

PRAISE FOR
POSITIVE TRADING PSYCHOLOGY

"Reading *Positive Trading Psychology* by Dr. Brett Steenbarger deeply resonated with me. In this new book, he connects the dots between personal strength and trading performance in a way that feels both practical and inspiring. As a high-altitude climber, I found myself relating to so many of the principles he describes. The mindset and emotional control required to summit peaks like Mount Everest are very similar to what's needed to succeed in trading. Dr. Brett's insights perfectly capture how those same personal qualities can be turned into trading strengths."

—Andrew Aziz, trader, investor, high-altitude mountaineer, and best-selling author of *How to Day Trade for a Living*

"After almost two decades of following Dr. Brett Steenbarger to drive change in my trading performance, this book stands above all the others. If you're ready for transformation—whether you are learning to refine process, build personal strengths, or shift mindset to maximize performance in your life and in trading—this is your blueprint!"

—Anne-Marie Baiynd, creator of the Market Positioning System and author of *The Trading Book*

"When is the last time you focused on your strengths and what you did 'right' to get even better? In his recent groundbreaking work, *Positive Trading Psychology*, Dr. Brett Steenbarger engages us to win by reverse engineering our most successful trading, bringing the rigor of athletic training to our daily process, and introducing trading pods as a method for exponential growth. Brimming with practical advice and actual case studies, this is a refreshing and inspiring must-read for all traders!"

—Eve Boboch, portfolio manager, market strategist, and co-author of *The Lifecycle Trade*

"Over a decade ago, I read my first book on trading psychology by Dr. Brett Steenbarger and began applying his best practices to my own trading. Since then, I've had the privilege of working alongside him and witnessing firsthand the impact his insights have on elite traders. It's incredible to see *Positive Trading Psychology* make decades of hard-earned wisdom accessible to the broader trading community in a way that can elevate both mindset and performance."

—Lance Breitstein, trading trainer and mentor

"Dr. Brett Steenbarger defines intuition as 'what we know but don't know we know.' Positive psychology helps us uncover that implicit knowledge. Successful traders develop the confidence to trust and act on it."

—Jim Dalton, trader and author of *Markets in Profile* and *Mind Over Markets*

"Renowned trading coach and clinical psychologist Dr. Brett Steenbarger offers actionable insights and evidence-based strategies to help traders develop their performance and mindset. Packed with practical tools, real-world case studies and contributions from successful trading mentors, this book is a comprehensive guide to mastering the mental game of trading and building a fulfilling and profitable career."

—Brian Shannon, founder of Alphatrends and author of *Technical Analysis Using Multiple Timeframes* and *Maximum Trading Gains With Anchored VWAP*

"Drawing from diverse settings like hedge funds and proprietary firms, Dr. Brett Steenbarger reveals the underappreciated significance of teamwork in developing successful traders and investors. He compellingly shows how fostering interdependence and leveraging shared psychological strengths are key drivers of adaptability and consistent performance in today's complex markets."

—Steven Spencer, co-founder and partner, SMB Capital.

POSITIVE TRADING PSYCHOLOGY

TURNING PERSONAL STRENGTHS INTO TRADING STRENGTHS

BRETT N. STEENBARGER, PH.D.

Harriman House

HARRIMAN HOUSE LTD
Website: harriman.house

First published in 2026 by Harriman House, an imprint of Pan Macmillan
Associated companies throughout the world
www.panmacmillan.com
www.panmacmillan.com/ai-at-pan-macmillan

Copyright © Brett N. Steenbarger 2026

The right of Brett N. Steenbarger to be identified as the author has been asserted in accordance with the Copyright, Design and Patents Act 1988.

Paperback ISBN: 978-1-80409-185-2
eBook ISBN: 978-1-80409-186-9
audiobook ISBN: 978-1-80409-431-0

All rights reserved. No part of this publication may be reproduced, stored in a retrieval system, or transmitted in any form or by any means (including without limitation electronic, mechanical, photocopying, recording, or otherwise) without the prior written permission of the publisher. This book is sold subject to the condition that it shall not, by way of trade or otherwise, be lent, hired out, or otherwise circulated without the publisher's prior consent. This work is reserved from text and data mining (Article 4(3) Directive (EU) 2019/790).

Harriman House does not have any control over, or any responsibility for, any author or third-party websites (including without limitation URLs, emails and QR codes) referred to in or on this book. This book is for informational purposes only. Readers are advised to consult an appropriate professional in light of their relevant circumstances and requirements before acting on any information in this book.

No responsibility or liability for loss occasioned to any person or corporate body acting or refraining to act as a result of reading material in this book can be accepted by the publisher, by the author, or by the employers of the author.

Cover design by Charlotte Smith. Adobe Stock images used in cover design.

01

Printed in the United States of America.

CONTENTS

Prologue ... ix

Introduction ... 1

1 Trading Is a Performance Field ... 7
2 The Unique Performance Challenges of Trading ... 53
3 The Role of Psychology in Trading Success ... 95
4 Changing Our Trading Psychology ... 123
5 Evolving Frontiers in Positive Psychology ... 170
6 The Positive Psychology of Mentoring—Brett Steenbarger and Jeff Holden ... 212
7 Therapy for the Mentally Well: New Directions for Trading Psychology ... 245

Conclusion ... 272

Acknowledgments ... 274

Notes ... 275

Index ... 289

About the Author ... 294

"The world you desire can be won. It exists…it is real…it is possible…it's yours."
—*Ayn Rand, Atlas Shrugged*

PROLOGUE

YOU ARE THE entrepreneur of your life.

From the moment you awaken each day—from the start of each week—your life's enterprise can flourish in the excitement of startup mode.

What is your life's mission and purpose? (If I asked you, right here and now, to write out a mission statement for your life, could you do that?)

Who is part of the team that moves your life's mission forward?

Whose teams do you belong to that fuel your life's efforts?

What role does trading play in your life's venture?

How do your life activities support the growth of your trading?

These are a few questions posed by the rapidly growing field of positive psychology.

Applied properly, positive psychology can be an incubator of your life's success, helping you coach yourself to ever greater achievement and fulfillment.

How you lead your life shapes the leadership of your trading business.

Know this: *Your life is not meant to be a trade*.

When we leverage our strengths, our lives become profitable investments.

Success in trading requires investing in ourselves.

How are you raising your personal venture capital today?

INTRODUCTION

It was a bit over two decades ago that I sat in a Wegmans café in DeWitt, New York writing my first book on the topic of trading psychology. I'm sitting here now writing this book and, sure enough, I'm in a Wegmans café—this time in Mt. Laurel, New Jersey. Some things never change!

One thing that does change, however, is science. Ongoing research and discoveries bring fresh understanding. The field of psychology has grown tremendously in the last 20 years, especially in the area known as *positive psychology*. Positive psychology is a branch of applied psychology that focuses on personal strengths and well-being. The key idea behind positive psychology is that we can further our development by building upon our strengths, not just by correcting our weaknesses.

In their review of positive psychology research, Compton and Hoffman report that well over 1,000 peer-reviewed studies of positive psychology are being published every year![1] Many of these studies have led to innovations in practice, including techniques for identifying and building personality strengths, processes for improving quality of thinking and creativity, methods for developing fulfilling personal and professional relationships, and powerful practices for sustaining individual and team well-being.

Through an understanding of psychological research, we uncover promising tools and techniques that can revolutionize our trading psychology. Two decades ago, writing my first book in the field, I never dreamt of drawing upon spiritual methods to expand our ability to identify opportunities in markets. I also never envisioned novel applications of teamwork that can help us rapidly adapt to changes in market environments. Indeed, my work today as a trading psychologist looks very little like it did early in my career. As a faculty member at a medical school for approximately four decades, I've learned the importance of continually improving our practice by drawing upon the latest theory and research. It is in that spirit that this book updates our understanding of trading psychology by building upon the innovations of positive psychology.

An early review of the field of positive psychology from Ed Diener and Robert Biswas-Diener is subtitled "Unlocking the Mysteries of Psychological Wealth."[2] That's a good way to think of positive psychology. The positive psychologist does not simply attempt to lessen problems and conflicts. Rather, the positive practitioner helps us draw upon and expand strengths that we already possess.

The overarching theme of this book is that we are much more likely to achieve financial wealth in markets when we operate from a foundation of psychological wealth.

Trading success requires more than fighting our fear of missing market moves (FOMO) and minimizing impulsive trading. Rather, success requires that we:

1. figure out how we best process market-related information;
2. build processes that leverage our cognitive/emotional/social strengths in making decisions under conditions of complexity and uncertainty; and
3. flexibly adapt those processes to ever-changing market conditions.

The goal of a positive trading psychology is to draw upon our psychological wealth in pursuing favorable market returns.

INTRODUCTION

This book is intended as a guide to building your trading by recognizing, developing, and applying your personality, cognitive, and social strengths. In growing our personal assets, we evolve as people—and as traders. Like any entrepreneurial effort, that requires effort and practice. As we shall see, what comes naturally and automatically will not change your life, and it will not make you successful in financial markets.

Positive psychology makes us more of who we already are when we are at our best.

We know that we are on the right path to performance when the effort of self-development *gives* us energy.

What you'll find in *Positive Trading Psychology*

The pages ahead emphasize perspectives on trading performance grounded in research and evidence-based practice. Over the years, I've had the honor of working with remarkably successful short-term traders, portfolio managers, and trading teams. One thing that experience has taught me is that trading success is invariably grounded in—and preceded by—success in other areas of life. This is because our personal strengths form the foundation of our trading strengths.

Readers will find three unique features in this book:

1. Perspectives from successful professional traders

Because my work has focused on professional traders in proprietary and hedge fund settings, I share insights from a broad cross section of trading experience and success. If there has been a weakness in the trading psychology literature, it has been that it largely addresses issues faced by beginning traders. Those hurdles are indeed important early in a trader's learning curve, but experienced traders seeking mastery of their craft undergo very different challenges. For example, I often go for weeks of daily meetings with hedge fund managers, traders, and teams and never once encounter problems with emotional trading. Instead, our meetings focus on such things as maximizing productive interactions with colleagues; reviewing recent trading to uncover hidden strengths and weaknesses; creating better forms of mentoring to accelerate growth; optimizing work-life balance during periods of unusual risk and reward; and developing creative ways of viewing markets that uncover fresh opportunities. I worked with one successful trader on ways of better identifying and trading 'choppy' markets. By studying his successful trades during periods of low market volatility, we were able to identify *his* ways of succeeding when trend and momentum were low. Interestingly, we found that when he improved his trading by playing to his hidden strengths, his mindset became much more engaged and energized. That, in turn, led him to uncover fresh opportunities and expand his profitability.

2. Perspectives from successful traders and trading coaches

Over the years, many insightful books have been written about trading psychology by coaches and traders with significant experience. One goal in writing this book is to capture the wisdom and state-of-the-art practice across the field to both cement what we know and identify fresh areas of challenge and opportunity. A framework in psychology that has informed much of what I do is known as a 'solution-focused' approach. As I explored in my book *Enhancing Trader Performance*, the solution-focused coach is particularly interested in what traders are doing when problems are *not* occurring.[3] For instance, a trader might find themselves becoming overconfident and then oversizing positions following a period of profitability. This pattern may play out many times for the trader, but there also are occasions when it *doesn't* occur. The solution-focused coach is open to the possibility that, when problems aren't occurring, the trader might be doing something right; i.e., might be enacting their own solution to their dilemma. The challenge becomes doing more of what works and not just attempting to eliminate problems.

This book takes a solution-focused approach to the entire field of trading psychology.

Across the broad range of writings and practices from various coaches and traders, we can identify patterns of success and 'best practices.' This book is not simply written to describe what I do, but to capture the state of the art—and the positive psychology—embedded in the work of many talented professionals in the financial markets.

3. Perspectives from my own trading

A third distinctive feature of this book is that I open the kimono on my own trading and share some of my trading experience. I make no claims to being a 'market wizard,' but I think it will be helpful to see positive psychology practices applied to the actual trading of someone who has followed and traded markets since the late 1970s. These examples illustrate that the applications of psychology to markets are far richer than we commonly recognize. For instance, a major innovation in my trading has been daily work on techniques that sustain intense cognitive focus. Instead of simply meditating to clear my mind and relax, I enter a prolonged state of concentration aided by brain wave biofeedback and allow ideas to come to me when I'm in 'the zone.' Very often, these ideas reflect insights that lead to promising trades.

An important purpose of such exercises is to uncover what we know, but don't know that we know.

By improving our access to intuition, we become able to generate ideas and trades that separate us from the crowd. Positive psychology practices that have been found to be effective in the research literature have inspired techniques for my own self-coaching. My hope is that they also spur your efforts at developing your success, helping you incubate your own best practices.

Viewing trading psychology through the lens of positive psychology, we can appreciate that there is no hard-and-fast distinction between what we do in markets and what we do in life. The quality of our friendships and romantic relationships; the optimization of our physical health; the development of our cognitive strengths; the pursuit of meaning and fulfillment outside of market hours—all of these make us better people. For that reason, they also fuel our development as traders.

Everything we do to maintain a positive psychology in life—to achieve psychological wealth—is relevant to our trading psychology and success.

It is in that context that we are always training. If we live mindlessly, we train distraction and lack of purpose. If we live purposefully, we turn every day into a workout that expands who we are and what we do. That is the essence of positive psychology and the ultimate foundation of a winning trading psychology.

Growing ourselves and growing our trading are two sides of a single coin. When we cultivate our strengths, every part of life becomes stronger. Small, frequent, evolutionary changes in what we do yield revolutionary changes over time: in life and in trading.

Let's start the journey!

Brett

CHAPTER ONE

TRADING IS A PERFORMANCE FIELD

Let's take a look at two very different traders and some of the psychology that makes them not so different after all. Ruth is a portfolio manager at a large 'multi-strat' hedge fund. A multi-strat fund is one that trades multiple strategies across different financial markets and countries. The fund managers' goal is to achieve superior, unique returns for institutional investors while exposing them to only modest risk.

Ruth's strategy is known as 'global macro,' which means that she invests capital in various markets to take advantage of global patterns of monetary supply, inflation, economic growth, and geopolitics. Her portfolio at any one time will consist of positions in the U.S., Europe, and Asia and can include positions in equity (stock) markets, fixed income (bond) markets, currency markets, and commodities. Her challenge is to assemble a basket of relatively uncorrelated positions that capture strength and weakness in global economies. This diversification of risk helps her sustain profitability even when one or two of her views fail to play out.

Although Ruth's positions typically last weeks to months, she makes trading decisions daily based upon news and market developments.

For example, on a particular day, oil prices might begin to rise due to geopolitical conflicts, which in turn could raise concerns regarding inflation in the U.S. and Europe. Ruth might tactically take profits in her fixed income and equity positions, figuring that she will likely have opportunities later to re-enter at better levels.

By contrast, Shay is a day trader at a proprietary trading firm. He trades the capital of the firm's owners and typically holds positions intraday—often for only a few minutes. He focuses on individual stocks on the U.S. exchanges and trades them based upon patterns of momentum and trend.

The software Shay uses scans a broad range of stocks and identifies those that are trading with above-average volume and volatility. He further scans for news items on these companies, searching for possible catalysts for sustained price action. Thus, for instance, he might notice that a stock has been in a downtrend but has moved significantly higher in the premarket on elevated volume following a positive earnings print. Based upon the company's press release and the comments from analysts on the sell side, Shay believes this could be perceived as a game-changer for the company. He waits for a short-term pullback in the stock to enter a long position early in the morning session. His thesis is that many short-sellers are trapped in the stock and will need to cover their positions over the course of the day.

As the day unfolds, Shay's screening tools identify several other short-term trading opportunities, including breakouts of ranges and sector exchange-traded funds (ETFs) displaying unusual strength and weakness relative to the overall market. Often, he only holds one or two positions at a time and trades those positions actively, using short-term moving averages and technical indicators to identify relatively overbought and oversold levels. Over the course of the day, he may trade many stocks in different directions and for different reasons, achieving diversification sequentially rather than through a single, broad portfolio held over time.

On the surface, what Ruth and Shay do could not be more different. There are, however, important similarities.

At the most basic level, Ruth and Shay are engaged in performance activities. They operate in competitive arenas and take risk to achieve rewards. Like sports teams, Olympic athletes, chess champions, and professional musicians, they spend significant time in preparation to achieve superior performance. They review their work in detail, seeking lessons that will help them become better and better at what they do.

The nature of Ruth and Shay's work in markets reveals important overlaps among trading psychology, sports psychology, and peak performance psychology. To be sure, the specifics of trading are greatly different from the specifics of basketball or chess, but in all of these fields there is an underlying challenge of improving performance under ever-changing conditions of risk and reward.

As we shall see, performance does not simply start with confidence and a positive mindset. Rather, a positive—and durable—mind frame emerges from the well-grounded pursuit of performance mastery across every facet of trading process.[4]

The building blocks of performance

Across performance domains, we can identify three factors responsible for sustained success:

1. Talents

These are largely inborn capabilities that typically appear early in the lifespan. Research in psychology suggests that many of our positive qualities, from intelligence to emotional well-being, have a significant inherited component. We typically find the pursuits of our talents to be intrinsically rewarding, so they often appear in childhood as areas of interest as well as strength. A child could be fascinated with chess or might become absorbed in sports activities.

At a very early age, I devoured every book on Greek and Roman mythology that I could find, enjoying heroic tales and the worlds of the gods. Later, in college, I became fascinated with heroic traditions in philosophy, including the writings of Ayn Rand. As a psychologist, I gravitated to the work of writers such as Abraham Maslow and Martin Seligman, seeking applications of counseling and therapy to our optimal development. My core talent (and passion) was to absorb and integrate large amounts of information—usually through reading—to better understand human potential. Sure enough, that talent has been a driving force in my writing of this book.

As Ed Seykota noted in his *Market Wizards* interview, successful performers not only have talent; the talent has them.[5] For peak performers in art, chess, or competitive sports, their activities are more than personal interests; they are *callings*. It is for this reason that peak performers devote unusually large amounts of time and attention to their craft, fueling impressive learning curves.

2. Skills

We can observe a common process across performance domains: *Skills are developed through ongoing mentoring.* Talents are necessary for success, but rarely are they sufficient. A young adult may display a variety of athletic talents, from foot speed to jumping ability. To become a basketball star, however, those talents must be trained. That is the role of a coach or mentor. Think of all the skills that go into success as a basketball player, from running different plays and implementing various defenses to shot selection, passing, and positioning for rebounds. These require practice, and it is the role of the mentor to structure those practices so that feedback leads to efforts at improvement and steady learning.

As the work of K. Anders Ericsson points out, this deliberate practice is essential to expert performance across fields. Indeed, he estimates that expert performers put in 10,000 or more hours of structured, deliberate practice to reach their level of success.[6] Across a variety of performance fields, such skill development occurs over a period of years.

Among day traders such as Shay, skills are demonstrated and practiced through mentoring offered by experienced traders at proprietary trading firms or within trading communities. Hedge fund portfolio managers like Ruth typically begin as junior members of teams, providing research and support for the risk-takers and learning through observation how senior team members think and act.

An important reason that success rates in trading are notoriously low is that sufficient time is not allotted for the learning curves required for expert performance. Whether it's in sports, theater, or chess, elite levels of skill development cannot be achieved in a year or two. It takes time—and dedicated, well-structured practice—to translate talents into specific skills.

3. Psychology

When we think of elite performers, such as Michael Jordan in basketball, we recognize that a key part of their success lies in their competitive drive and achievement-oriented mindset. In the trading world, with the exception of certain specialized strategies, it's rare to sustain win rates of over 55%. That means that losing trades—and losing periods of trading—are inevitable. It also means that market participants function under ongoing conditions of uncertainty.

The ability to tolerate uncertainty and bounce back from adversity is a form of emotional resilience sometimes called 'grit.'[7]

Not everyone possesses high levels of emotional resilience. Nor is emotional resilience alone sufficient to thrive in the trading world, where an unusual combination of additional characteristics is required for success: the conviction to risk meaningful capital on good ideas and also the open-mindedness to reduce risk if those ideas become less attractive.

Having studied the characteristics of successful traders, another psychological quality that consistently stands out to me is intellectual curiosity. The great traders love to hunt for opportunity and figure out markets in ways that others miss. They dig deeper in finding ideas and they look for ideas in a broader range of places. I have worked with many profitable traders who, at some point in their careers, could no longer sustain success. They possessed clear talent and skills, but lacked the inquisitive mindset and emotional and cognitive flexibility needed to reinvent themselves and adapt to altered market dynamics. Talent and skill are necessary for trading success, but psychological strengths are vital to sustaining that success.

In any performance field, success requires a high level of talent, a prolonged period of skill development, and a flexible, achievement-oriented mindset. I've observed these dynamics among the medical students and residents I've worked with in Syracuse, NY. They begin with the academic talent needed to get into medical school and then they undergo intensive learning of medical science and 'rotations' through various medical specialties where they are mentored by physicians. During those rotations and subsequent specialized clinical experiences, they discover where their calling might lie. It's only after four years of undergraduate medical education that the new physicians actually begin their specialization and, over the next few years of residency, develop true competence and expertise in a specific area of practice. During that time, there are the challenges of dealing with difficult patients and difficult cases, as well as coping with the occasional negative outcomes of treatment. Talent, skill, and psychological fortitude combine to create the elite medical professional.

> **How we develop our trading is how we develop our trading psychology. Confidence and emotional resilience come from the practice and training that generate successful experience.**

Beginning traders often hope that success is around the corner and search for the magic 'edge' that will make them consistent money after a few weeks or months of effort. The reality of success in any true performance field is more sobering. Of all the people who try their hand at acting, few will ever make their living from Broadway or Hollywood. Many others will play baseball, basketball, or football, but only a fraction of these ultimately turn their athletic interests into ongoing careers. The much-desired 'trading for a living' requires the right blend of talents, skills, and mindset. The good news, we shall see, is that if we properly structure our development, we, like the aspiring medical professionals, can greatly improve the odds of our success.

Finding your calling: going broad before you go deep

Let's return to the example of medical education. First medical students study basic science areas such as anatomy, physiology, and biochemistry. Then they begin clinical rotations, observing and participating in medical care across fields as diverse as internal medicine, psychiatry, and surgery. Only after these rotations do the students begin to specialize by pursuing more intensive practical experience in a particular field. From there, medical students receive the M.D. and begin graduate medical education, immersing themselves in their specialty of choice and often seeking a subspecialty. The entire training process may last 8–10 years, as the medical student becomes a physician, then might pursue the work of a surgeon, and then could emerge as a subspecialized back surgeon. Other students choose to remain generalists, offering care to a wide range of patients across a variety of medical concerns, as in family medicine. It is after experiencing various fields of practice during medical school that a student is able to make an intelligent, informed decision as to whether he or she wants to pursue very different disciplines as a radiologist, a psychiatrist, or a cardiologist.

Several factors help determine the ultimate choice of a field of practice, including the student's talents and the influence of mentors. The idea of medical education is to provide a smorgasbord of learning opportunities and hands-on experiences so that aspiring physicians can discover their passion and direct their talents through diverse mentoring. Medical educators recognize that *we first must experience an activity before we can recognize that it might be our calling.*

This same process is extremely important for developing traders. We cannot know if a certain area of trading is our calling unless we experience a wide range of markets and strategies. Think back to Ruth and Shay: High-frequency day trading is very different from the active investing of hedge funds, and both differ considerably from long-term asset management.

There are also great differences between trading equity markets, where there are thousands of stocks and multiple exchanges and sectors, and trading single commodities with distinctive patterns of supply and demand, such as power or soybeans.

The practice environments of traders can also be quite different, ranging from large, interactive team environments to small trading 'pods' to solo trading. Some traders find their niche in researching and trading quantitative systems. Others specialize in actively pricing and trading options; still others enjoy the continuous involvement of market making. Without experiencing a range of markets and roles related to trading and investment, it is very difficult for an aspiring trader to know the kind of market involvement that might best speak to their skills, talents, and personality.

This is why it is vital to pursue markets broadly before immersing ourselves in any particular type of trading. Starting broad and only then going deep allows you to find the kind of market activity you're best suited for and then begin the long process of achieving expertise through deliberate practice and mentoring. One active trading firm I worked with brought on interns from college and had them rotate to several teams over the course of a summer. That way they were able to experience different trading and mentoring styles. If the mentors liked the intern and the intern found their niche in a certain kind of trading, a job offer followed and hands-on training began.

Similarly, an intern at a hedge fund or investment bank might observe and work in several parts of the business to see where there might be an ideal fit. From this perspective, it's not surprising that online trading communities have sprung up for individual, independent traders, allowing them to learn from different mentors and try their hands at different trading styles. A notable feature of such active trading communities as SMB Capital,[8] Investors Underground,[9] TraderLion,[10] Bear Bull Traders,[11] My Investing Club,[12] and Topstep[13] is that traders are exposed to multiple role models and practice trading different strategies—often starting in simulation mode—in order to figure out their eventual specialization.

Our strengths are typically discovered in the process of training and performing.

When developing traders short-circuit this process and don't allow themselves a period of broad experience before learning in depth, the odds are great that they will pursue styles and strategies poorly suited to their talents and personalities. In such cases, they don't find what they are doing in markets to be a calling and indeed can find it frustrating and unfulfilling. When their frustration impacts their subsequent efforts at learning and trading, they blame their performance problems on trading psychology and hope that managing their emotions will bring them success. *In such cases, frustrated, impulsive trading is the result of the problem, not the cause.*

Traders become emotional not simply because they're not playing the game well, but because they are playing the wrong game.

Consider: Before we marry, we typically meet many people and go on many dates. Jumping into marriage prematurely and out of need is likely to result in something less than an ideal match. When we choose a field of work—including a kind of trading—we create a marriage. It makes sense to date before we mate.

Research in positive psychology tells us that we are most likely to perform well when we are flourishing: intellectually, emotionally, and socially.[14] If we are not flourishing in a trading role, the answer is not necessarily to tinker with our psychology, but to find a role that best draws upon who we are and what we do well.

This advice applies not only to young, beginning traders, but also experienced ones who find themselves at a dead end as old strategies lose their edge.

When I first began work with hedge funds, equity 'long/short' strategies were not particularly common. These strategies involve simultaneously identifying strong companies to set up long positions on their stocks while going short on the stocks of weaker firms, generally in the same industry. That way, the overall market could go up or down and the long/short team would make money as long as the basket of stronger companies outperformed the basket of weaker ones.

Fast forward to recent years, and many funds and teams have been pursuing long/short investing in equities. Positions now become quite crowded and it takes deeper and more original research to find long and short opportunities that are not recognized by the crowd. In some cases, portfolio managers and team members have had to step back and reinvent themselves to capture fresh edges in markets. Like new traders, they start with a broad search—checking out a variety of strategies and markets—before pursuing any in depth. One team I worked with transitioned to trading companies involved in litigation, drawing upon the expertise of one of the team members who is an attorney. The strategy was a variant of long/short, but involved selecting longs and shorts across sectors on the basis of litigation risk/reward and not just company fundamentals. This was a much less crowded space, given the specialized experience needed.

There is no path to elite performance that does not involve elite expertise development and a leveraging of talent, mentor-built skills, and personality.[15] If an area of trading is not your passion, it's probably not your path. Without passionate energy, it is impossible to sustain intensive expertise development. Careful listening to our experience allows us to hear our calling. Broad exposure to markets, strategies, and mentors provides us with more to listen to.

Case study: developing performance at a successful proprietary trading firm

In recent months, I have joined experienced trader and Director of Training Jeff Holden at SMB Capital for some of his online training sessions. The calls, held late in the morning Eastern time, typically take a top-down approach, first reviewing what is happening in the overall stock market and then drilling down to areas of the market—and specific stocks—that have shown unique opportunity.

Note how the mentoring starts with a broad look at the market and then goes deep by focusing on individual opportunities. In a very important sense, mentoring models the thought processes behind successful trading

Performance begins with an open mind and making sure that we're fishing in the right ponds. Consideration of what we should be trading precedes how we're to trade it. In the case of Jeff and SMB, they are typically looking for 'stocks in play,' which means opportunities that benefit from unusual movement. Sometimes, perhaps as the result of a catalyst, the entire market is in play. Other times, it will be a sector of the market, such as tech stocks, or individual small-cap names. One of the most important things Jeff models is how to be involved in the most promising opportunities at any given time.

Once the group has focused on what to be trading, the emphasis shifts to finding favorable risk-reward points for participating in the movement.

In a recent session, one of the meme stocks traded weak early in the session, hitting a liquidity refreshment point (LRP) where market makers needed to come in and provide more liquidity. That's a sure sign of market imbalance. Interestingly, the stock bounced nicely and stayed above the level that had triggered the heavy selling. That was a valuable sign of a shift in supply and demand, making it possible for the nimble trader to buy short-term pullbacks. All of this was illustrated via charts and discussion during the online session.

Notice how good mentoring entails role modeling. A different mentor might have a different process for identifying opportunity, focusing on different trading instruments and different time frames. Jeff's mentoring walks the developing trader through:

a. understanding market context;
b. drilling down to how the market is trading now; and
c. identifying specific 'setups' that provide solid reward relative to risk.

At a hedge fund, this process might look like:

a. idea generation based on patterns of economic data, news, and market behavior;
b. tracking the market to identify occasions when market participants are leaning the wrong way; and
c. using short-term market action to execute a trade based on the idea with favorable risk/reward.

What is important to understand is that, at successful programs of trader development, *trading psychology is taught and modeled in the context of real-time, evolving trades.* Trading psychology is not mere advice-giving about 'discipline' and emotional control. Rather, the mindset of the trader is modeled by mentors like Jeff and absorbed by students over the course of many exposures to opportunities. When students learn how a mentor thinks, they naturally absorb the mentor's focus and mind frame. This cannot be accomplished simply by watching videos or reading books. (See

Chapter Six for further discussion of the role of mentoring and learning in the development of a positive trading psychology.)

It is significant that, when a trader at SMB goes into a slump and a negative mindset, the initial guidance from the mentors is *not* psychological advice. Rather, the focus is on placing 'one good trade' by rigorously following the processes of one's best trading.[16] These processes are captured in 'playbooks' that detail precisely how one has been successful in their trading.[17] The takeaway here is that psychology, by itself, cannot generate superior performance. Rather, trading well grows a winning trading psychology—and that fuels our future development.

The role of positive psychology in developing our performance

The explosion of research in positive psychology mentioned in the introduction has opened new perspectives on the development of peak performance. Recent research compiled by Cheavens and Feldman finds that positive experiences, such as life satisfaction, optimism, and social support, significantly contribute to work performance and are negatively correlated with burnout.[18] They cite studies from Barbara Fredrickson and colleagues[19] showing that positive emotional experience broadens our perception and enables us to flourish in many areas of life.[20] Such positive experience can contribute to the quality of our teamwork, our tracking of market opportunities and threats, and our generation of trade ideas.

As Alice Isen has found in her research, positivity also contributes to cognitive flexibility, creativity, and problem-solving.[21] When we enjoy positive experience, we are more likely to engage in healthy behaviors, further contributing to our well-being in an upward spiral.[22] *In other words, how we structure our trading vitally impacts how we think, feel, and make decisions. It isn't simply that a positive mindset helps our trading; the quality of our trading environment and experience help shape our mindset.*

Classic research from Seligman finds that the positive experience that enables us to flourish consists of five elements, known by the acronym PERMA:[23]

> *Positive emotions*: Happiness, joy
> *Engagement*: Active involvement in life
> *Relationships*: Sharing life with romantic partners, family, and friends
> *Meaning*: Living with a sense of purpose and significance
> *Accomplishments*: Appreciating tangible achievements based on our efforts

A later formulation referred to PERMA+, with the plus referring to our physical health and well-being. Indeed, we are unlikely to achieve high levels in the five PERMA categories if we are not well physically and if we are not actively engaged in healthy eating, fulfilling relationships, exercise, and proper sleep.[24] How we live impacts our cognitive and emotional experience and that impacts our abilities to perceive opportunity and our ability to make decisions to capitalize on this opportunity.

It is worth noting that one of the most common problems that traders bring to their meetings with me is burnout. They devote so much time and energy to trading that they run themselves down and impair their future performance.

> **Many traders hope to make money to achieve a happy life. The reality is that a happy life significantly contributes to trading success.**

In a recent talk with a high-performing hedge fund team, I emphasized that how we lead our lives shapes the quality of our performance. The key word, I pointed out, is 'lead.' As we saw at the very beginning of this book, we don't just carry out our lives from day to day; we're the *leaders* of our lives. What we choose to do impacts our energy levels, our focus, and our positivity.

Too often we seek to work on our psychology only when things go wrong, ignoring the more important reality that every hour of every day we are shaping our psychology and our potential for peak performance.

How we engage markets can play to our strengths or frustrate us. How we engage others can stimulate our curiosity and motivation or it can leave us isolated and drained. How we review performance can affirm and expand our strengths or it can bog us down in problems and negativity. *Our trading environments and processes play a central role in shaping our positivity, and that plays a vital role in contributing to our performance.*

Zelenski, in his summary of positive psychology research, identifies character strengths as the basic personality unit of positive psychology.[25] He observes that there is significant overlap between those strengths and what are known as the 'big five' personality traits. This is not surprising: our personalities are expressed through what is most distinctive about us. He also points out that, while our traits characterize us in the long run, we also respond to our immediate circumstances.[26] *Who we are shapes our performance, and our environments impact our experience of who we are. Successful trading comes from developing trading processes that draw upon our strengths and also affirm them, providing us with experiences of fulfillment and meaning.*

Compton and Hoffman, in their positive psychology review, cite research that suggests that our ideals—our 'inner hero'—shape our quest to become our best selves.[27] Who we revere captures our aspirations for ourselves. We find our positive experience in moments of joy and meaning, but particularly in the degree to which we lead lives consistent with our inner heroism. Ayn Rand observed that anyone who fights for tomorrow lives in it today. *An important part of our positive psychology is our sense that we are living a quest that embodies our noblest ideals.*

It is easy to become so bogged down in the ups and downs of performance, as well as profit and loss (P/L), that we lose sight of our ideals. Compton and Hoffman summarize research into the 'sustainable happiness model,'[28] which traces our well-being to three factors:

1. our genetically-determined temperament;
2. our immediate life circumstances, such as recent life events; and
3. our intentional activity in terms of how we spend our time.

Their work finds that actions we take to change our life's activities, such as beginning the pursuit of a new goal, lead to significant improvements in our positivity.[29] *Significantly, however, such goal pursuit only contributes to our well-being if the goals are consistent with our values.*

In other words, just setting a goal to hold a trade longer or size a position differently won't in itself make a meaningful difference in our overall positive psychology. *It is the pursuit of what is most meaningful to us that energizes us and brings out our strengths and best efforts.* From this perspective, we can ask the important question: *To what degree do my trading processes draw upon my values, ideals, and strengths?* Reducing our negative emotionality may help us avoid episodes of 'tilt' (loss of control) but won't in itself inspire our best efforts.

Many developing traders fail because their efforts at development do not bring out the strengths and values needed for peak performance. This is particularly true for independent traders, attempting to learn trading from books and online guidance. Advice about what to trade, when to trade, and how to trade cannot inspire our own 'sustainable happiness model.' In such cases, it is not a failure of psychology that underlies most trading problems. Rather, those problems reflect a larger disconnect between traders and their essential talents, interests, values, and skills. *If we are not actualizing our inner hero, we will inevitably fall short of our potential.* Trading is a performance activity; success vitally depends upon the factors that bring out our best, most consistent performance.

An evolutionary perspective on expertise development

We often think of our development as traders as a linear process, as we progress from our earliest learning phases to ever greater expertise. But years of experience working with a variety of traders and investors has taught me that expertise development in markets is not so straightforward. The reason for this is that 'edges' in markets are ever-changing and thus ephemeral. What worked well at one period of time can fail to produce future results for a host of reasons. This ensures that even experienced and successful traders often have to return to the drawing board and develop new strategies as relative beginners.

When I began as a trading coach in Chicago in the early 2000s, I was privileged to work with unusually talented and successful intraday traders. In many cases, they were very short term in their holding periods, 'scalping' profits by monitoring moment-to-moment shifts in the order books of various futures products. They could see in real time when buyers were lifting offers and sellers were hitting bids, and they quickly processed how these activities were attracting supply and demand in the order book. Many times, they would place an order to buy contracts at the bid price and simply take a tick of profit when their market traded at the offer price. With low (exchange member) commissions/fees and the opportunity to trade meaningful size (hundreds of contracts if not more), such scalping was extremely profitable.

The talents and skills required by such rapid trading were impressive. Not only did traders need to process information unusually quickly; they needed to recognize patterns of supply and demand, and they needed to sustain unusually high levels of attention and intention through the day.

I found it interesting that the most successful traders were not necessarily the most intellectual and analytical, but rather were highly shrewd and keen observers of the marketplace. They reminded me of championship poker players who not only understand the odds of the cards they hold, but also cannily read the intentions of other players around the table. All in all, this kind of market making and scalping was an impressive blending of talent and skill.

Fast forward a bit and an increasing portion of market making was being conducted by trading algorithms. These could be much faster than human participants and could crunch far more data. To complicate matters, the algos could put multiple small orders into the market and see how the orders impacted the order book in real time. They could even enter bids and offers in the book to mimic demand and supply, only to pull these at strategic times. Such high-speed strategies greatly reduced the edge of traditional scalping, and the top traders needed to move to other markets and strategies to sustain their success. Even after having reached an elite level of performance, they needed to reinvent themselves and return to fresh learning curves.

> **The real edge in trading is the ability to discover and adapt to new trading edges.**

As described earlier, I've observed this dynamic at work in hedge funds as well. Winning strategies such as long/short equity investing and trend following across multiple assets have yielded more modest returns as these approaches have become increasingly crowded. A fixed-income trader I've known for years who specializes in emerging markets found initial success because these markets were less followed by macro participants. As this trader was successful, he was given much more capital to manage and could no longer participate in the less liquid markets that provided him with his initial edge. Like the scalpers, he had to reinvent himself, expanding his coverage and his range of strategies. This meant that he had to build a team and combine the diverse talents of its members. Over time, our discussions have been about leadership and team-building, not just the pursuit of opportunities in volatile markets. Like successful companies, such as Apple and Microsoft, what he does now is very different—and much more diverse—than what he did early in his development.

Success is not just about growing; it is about evolving.

In short, the evolving nature of financial markets means that a successful trading career requires not only the ability to make oneself, but unmake and remake ourselves. This is a particular psychological challenge. It is one thing to start on a learning curve, discover our calling, and grow our skills. It's quite another thing to go through all that and then have to put it aside and undergo the process once again, albeit from a more experienced base. When something has been your focus and passion for many years, putting it aside in favor of something new and unproven requires a unique capacity for flexibility, learning, and career-based risk-taking.

Many traders find success in one period or one set of market conditions, only to fail to adapt as the world changes. Adaptation is necessary for success; re-adaptation is necessary for ongoing success. Indeed, in my text *Trading Psychology 2.0*, I describe four 'best processes' of trading as ABCD: Adapting to change; Building on strengths; Cultivating creativity; and Developing and integrating best practices.[30] This is a continuous circular process, as ever-changing markets require ongoing adaptation.

Over the long term, I've found that the most successful market participants are those who continuously *engage in innovation.* In other words, they are able to evolve because adaptation is built into their work processes. They are always looking for new challenges and adapting to those. They are always evolving. Mark Minervini, in his book *Think and Trade Like a Champion*, emphasizes, "Those who choose to win seek successful role models, develop a road map for success, and accept setbacks as valuable teachers."[31] When we "accept setbacks as valuable teachers," we ensure that we continuously innovate and adapt.

At several of the trading firms and hedge funds where I've worked, I've been actively involved in recruiting talent. As a psychologist, I can pick up qualities of candidates that other interviewers might miss, just as those interviewers assess specific trading skills that are well outside my expertise. One question I have found helpful asks candidates to describe their 'pipelines' of new trading ideas and opportunities.

Think of it this way: if I were to invest in a pharmaceutical company, I would not only be interested in their current lineup of medications, but also their pipeline of drugs in various stages of research and development. A company with good current sales and little R&D would make for a questionable investment. Similarly, traders who lack a pipeline and have no processes for identifying new edges will be most vulnerable when market climates change.

Key to long-term trading success is the ability to sustain innovation and continually evolve as markets (and market participants) change. This, too, requires very specific talents and skills, as well as an entrepreneurial mindset.

> **Successful traders, like successful businesses, embrace the beginner's mindset: They love learning new things. Their true edge in markets is the ability to discover and pursue fresh edges.**

As referenced earlier, one way that traders are meeting the challenges of evolution is by building out teams. We're seeing this at proprietary trading firms and online trading communities as well as hedge funds, as the team dynamic facilitates mutual learning across a broad range of opportunity.

The combination of strategies pursued in a team helps ensure that, when the edge of one strategy begins to deteriorate, other sources of profitability can pick up the slack. On a few teams that I work with, some traders trade relative value strategies, selling one part of a market that might be priced too high (such as a point on the yield curve) and buying another part that might be priced low. The idea is that no matter what happens to rates overall, the spread on the curve should narrow. This is a strategy that works well in lower-volatility environments and in environments where central bank policies are stable. Other traders on the team focus on directional opportunities, which naturally benefit from momentum, trend, and environments in which central banks are 'in play' for rate cuts or hikes.

The combination of strategies helps the team make money in different kinds of markets—and also helps traders adjust their risk-taking to what their teammates are seeing. As each trader evolves their particular strategies, the team naturally evolves in its ability to exploit changing market conditions. Often, it's by adding to their teams that traders broaden and become more adaptable. A couple of teams that I work with have more than 10 members, covering quite different areas of specialization. As in medical schools, the ethos is 'each one, teach one.' Members continually work on their strategies and educate one other about the opportunities they're seeing.

It is difficult to become extinct when growth and adaptation are built into the DNA of your business.

Case study: adapting my trading

My bread-and-butter trading has always been short term (intraday), based upon patterns of shifting demand and supply within the stocks of the S&P 500 universe. My talent—as a psychologist and as a trader—is my ability to listen closely and detect subtle changes in the flow of information. (More on that later.) By tracking the S&P 500 Index and the strength/weakness of its component stocks (how many are making short-term highs and lows; how many are trading on upticks/downticks; how many are advancing/declining intraday; etc.), I can identify when there are meaningful shifts in the participation of stocks before the overall index moves significantly higher or lower. For instance, it is very common for a rising market to register fewer new highs and experience a decreasing lifting of offers vs. hitting of bids prior to actually reversing to the downside.

A while ago, the regime in the stock market shifted meaningfully. Large market participants were invested in equities, but were primarily placing bets that certain sectors of the market would outperform others. In the parlance of the investment world, institutions were high gross and low net. They were invested in the stock market, but particularly invested in relative bets within equities—not invested in overall bullish or bearish outcomes for the broad indexes.

Recognizing this shift, I began studying high-frequency data that could supplement my traditional research. For instance, I have always looked carefully at the NYSE TICK (a real-time measure of the number of stocks trading on upticks vs. downticks across the entire universe of NYSE stocks). Very often, we would see the market make lows on fewer downticks prior to bouncing higher on net positive upticks.

Thanks to my trading platform (Sierra Chart), I was able to track TICK measures for the NASDAQ 100 stocks, the Russell 2000 universe, the Dow 30 stocks, the S&P 500 shares, etc. I discovered that each of these TICK measures displayed their own patterns (which required observation and study), but what stood out were the patterns *across* the TICK measures. Thus, for instance, I would see net selling pressure in the NYSE and Russell TICK, but not in the NASDAQ 100. That often meant that selling was occurring in smaller-cap and value names and not in larger-cap growth shares.

Eventually, I became sufficiently familiar with these patterns to construct trades where I was, say, long the NASDAQ Index and short the Russell Index. Such relative trades provided multiple ways to win in an environment where institutions were not broadly buying or selling stocks, but rotating their investments from certain parts of the market to others. Thanks to the new data sets, I uncovered more ways to win: trading relative movement within the sector ETFs and not just the directionality of the broad market indexes.

Of particular note was how this evolution of my trading led to a meaningful boost in my trading psychology. Recognizing that I had more tools at my disposal and more ways to win gave me a fresh confidence that I could figure out what markets were doing each day and construct winning trades. *My mindset evolved once my trading evolved.* In becoming more adaptive, I also became more resilient and more decisive.

There is a subtle, but important point in all this. Tracking the new indicators and identifying patterns among them was a very time-consuming process. I had to immerse myself in market moves, tracking the behavior of the indicators and recording the patterns I observed—

again and again and again. Before I could get to the point of finding tradeable ideas, I had to identify meaningful patterns and, before I could recognize those patterns in real time, I had to study one example after another after another. I was like a naturalist in the wild, recording many observations before generating my ideas about the ecosystem. This searching and researching process occurred outside market hours and became a primary focus for my trading. In a very real sense, I went back to becoming a novice. Had I not done this, however, I would never have expanded my trading.

There's a very important lesson here: Creating a durable trading psychology sometimes means stepping back from trading and renewing our understanding of markets. Deep conviction and confidence come from deep learning and adaptation.

Again and again, we see that trading is a performance discipline. How we pursue our performance—and how we grow as performers—is what gives us the right performance psychology. No amount of positive thinking exercises or stress-management techniques could have provided me with the confidence I needed to adapt to the new market conditions. As I made my adaptations, my understanding grew and my psychology reflected a higher sense of mastery. I became a better version of my trading self.

The 'fractal' nature of evolution and adaptation

Just as market edges can change significantly over the course of months and years, those edges undergo smaller but significant shifts from day to day and even intraday. Volume and volatility can change from one period to another and the correlations among markets can shift meaningfully.

The successful quant traders I've known don't just rely on one or two back-tested strategies, but typically incorporate many systems that cover different time frames, market conditions, and markets. One team that I worked with developed systems that identified the kind of market environment we were in. Those regime signals then triggered the trading of those systems that had successful track records in the identified environment. Adaptation itself became a systematic process.

Experienced discretionary traders learn to adapt to different market environments, sizing positions differently according to recent patterns of volatility, and adjusting stop and take-profit levels in the face of breaking news. Even the decision to slow down trading during periods of low volume/volatility is a market adjustment. *It is true that successful traders develop and follow rigorous trading processes, but it is equally true that they adjust those processes for the market environments they face.* That is similar to a football team that adapts to changing defensive alignments by calling different plays, lining up differently, and bringing in different players. Small adjustments can make the difference between winning and losing. In a very important sense, peak performers are always adapting, always evolving.

This 'fractal' nature of adaptation illustrates a powerful idea: *Our day-to-day pursuit of profitability itself serves as a training ground for our trading psychology*. We often think of psychology as something appended to our trading—something we work on apart from our decisions to buy, sell, size up/down, hedge, and restructure risk. Each trading decision we make, however, exercises one or more psychological functions. Our decision to hedge a short-term position in the face of growing uncertainty is practice for the much larger adaptations we'll need to make when market patterns shift radically.

When we add to risk, we exercise our capacity for conviction and decisiveness. When we add an uncorrelated position to existing positions, we push the development of our open-mindedness and creativity. *Trading well* is *training in trading psychology*. The shifts we make from day to day and week to week train us in the capacity to make larger career shifts in the future. The self-restraint and perspective that we display during intraday periods of uncertainty train us to limit drawdowns when markets undergo radical shifts.

As we saw with Jeff at SMB, this means that the best mentoring in trading also serves as coaching in trading psychology. The psychological strengths modeled by mentors are internalized by students, building their character and preparing them for future challenges.

> Consistency in following our best trading practices creates consistency of mindset, keeping us grounded in our best trading psychology. Elite traders are consistent in their adaptive efforts.

A little while back, I wrote a post to the TraderFeed blog describing an insight I had during a workout at a local gym.[32] I discovered that *how* I do a single rep at the various exercise stations very much determines what I get out of the exercise. Specifically, when I lifted weights, either with my legs or my upper body, I found that if I performed each rep slowly, making sure I hit full extension of my limbs every time, each station in the gym gave me a far better workout. Indeed, it seemed to me that half of the value of each exercise came at those extremes of extension. The slow exertion taxed my muscles significantly, so I found myself engaging in mental strategies to sustain the effort. Focusing my mind, slowing my breathing, and talking myself through each rep enabled me to hang in there when fatigue started to take over.

When I'm in a position in the market and it's bouncing back and forth and neither clearly working out nor clearly stopping me out, I find myself engaging in those same mental strategies. I talk myself through what is happening bar by bar, tolerating the uncertainty just as I tolerate the stress of weight lifting. *All of this is real-time rehearsal of performance psychology.* The moment-to-moment strategies for handling risk and reward make it possible to manage those stresses through the day, and the daily practice contributes to our longer-term resilience.

The fractal nature of adaptation implies that daily efforts to maintain a performance mindset—even in areas outside of trading—contribute to our longer-term ability to adapt to fatigue and uncertainty. Our daily challenges prepare us for the inevitable upheavals in our trading careers when market ecosystems require more radical adaptation.

Case study: achieving trading success through adaptation

Gina is a Chicago-based trader of equity futures markets. She makes extensive use of relative volume in her trading decisions, identifying time periods when volume significantly varies from the average volume for that particular time of day. For instance, she might observe the market rally in the early morning and then consolidate for several five-minute periods with below average volume for those times of day. Seeing that higher prices are not attracting sellers, she will be open to adding to her position, expecting that the market will at least test its most recent high.

Drawing upon the seminal work of Jim Dalton and colleagues,[33] Gina makes use of graphic displays in Market Profile format. Market Profile charts total volume at each market price so that it becomes possible to visualize where demand is rising and falling. This enables her to identify specific prices that facilitate volume increases and use these as reference points for her trading. She also makes use of the anchored volume weighted average price (VWAP) concept taught by Brian Shannon to identify how we are trading relative to important reference points.[34] For instance, if we get a data release that is a potential game changer for the market, she'll track the relative VWAP from that point to assess unfolding supply and demand. When she is trading well, she feels in the flow of the market, responding to the ebbs and flows of demand and supply. Her trading has given her an unusual blend of intuition/market feel and analytic rigor.

As equity futures markets became increasingly popular and crowded, especially with the growing participation of systematic strategies, Gina turned her attention to options markets. She began tracking the real-time volume of put volume and call volume to determine the activity of sellers and buyers. She also separately tracked the activities of small options buyers and sellers to help differentiate less informed participants from more expert ones. By monitoring the skew of option pricing at various strikes (the differences in pricing among equivalent puts and calls), she was able to track sentiment extremes and shifts of sentiment. This information not only helped her with trading her products, but eventually led her to expand her trading to other futures contracts with active options markets, such as crude oil.

The ability to enter the flow of market information moment to moment in her core trading was essential to Gina's ability to read markets and, over time, created new trading opportunities. The incremental adaptation of adding derivatives to her analytics fueled her confidence as a trader. When I met with her months later, she was trading patterns of volatility in markets to supplement her directional trading. This expansion of strategies enabled her to manage larger and larger amounts of capital. In our conversation, she raised the idea of hiring an assistant to help her further expand the business to promising overseas markets.

Notice how, in this adaptation, Gina did not try to change who she is. Rather, she leveraged existing psychological and trading strengths to find fresh edges in markets. Indeed, it was her open-minded daily trading practice that cemented the skills and mindset needed for her career evolution.

Perhaps it's not surprising that, prior to taking up trading, Gina was an accomplished chess player. She could quickly identify the offensive and defensive styles of her opponent and adjust her playing accordingly to exploit weaknesses that unfolded on the board. When Gina was playing well, she could see the entire board and envision positions several moves ahead. In that flow of performance, decisions came naturally to her. She knew that she was on the right track in her development as a trader when she experienced that same flow.

How did she achieve that level of adaptation? It started with studying past games of chess masters and reviewing them move-by-move—and reviewing her own games with similar intensity. Each game for her was an exercise in adaptation. That eventually led to the much greater adaptation of pursuing financial markets. And how does she learn from her trading performance? Not surprisingly, she reviews each day's trading in detail the way she reviewed her chess games move-by-move. Her development as a trader followed the blueprint of her earlier success. In a very real sense, her best trading coach has been the mentoring she's received from her past successes.

Trading and talent

Because expert performance begins with talent, it is common to see the talents of exceptional traders manifest themselves long before they try their hands at trading. As we've seen with Gina, this is a fractal quality across our lifespans. What we do well and with passion in one arena typically shows up in other areas of life and in new areas of performance.

Gina's talents for processing large amounts of data in real time and reading patterns in the behavior of others were central to her success in chess and eventually became her greatest strength as a trader. Not surprisingly, Gina is happily married. She went on many dates where she could spend quality time with each person. She observed their responses to her and quickly noticed when there was a chemistry between her and her date. Gina figured out dating the way she figures out chess boards and markets. If you give yourself enough opportunities and can wait for—and go after—the right ones, the wins are inevitable.

During my training as a psychologist, I learned to pick up on the nuances of what clients told me. For example, a person might talk about conflicts with a boss at work and suddenly shift topics, describing an upcoming trip with his wife and children. The psychologist knows that, when a person switches topics, there is usually a psycho-logical connection between the topics if there is not an obvious logical one. Perhaps the person speaking with me is anticipating conflict in the family, or perhaps being at home feels much like being at the workplace. In any case, that connection is worth exploring. That same issue is likely to eventually show up in my relationship with him, which could pose a challenge for our work together but also an opportunity for insight and new learning. My talent as a therapist is the ability to empathically connect with people and identify the themes connecting their communications.

When I am trading markets, I find myself observing and reading patterns in the same way that I do when I'm in the therapy room. My most basic edge in the market is the ability to observe occasions of buying or selling pressure that can no longer move the market higher or lower. Those are the occasions in which traders are trapped and will most likely need to unload their positions.

When I'm very focused on the market, I can feel the pain points at which traders will need to bail out. Just as I track the conversation of a client, I follow the flow of market data to tell me what market participants are doing. As I described earlier, if I see persistent selling in the NYSE TICK and then notice: a) price for the index holding up and b) relative strength in a market sector that has very recently shown good breadth, I might buy the ETF for that sector, expecting that it will lead the market when sellers need to cover their positions. The talent that I draw upon as a therapist—the ability to detect and experience themes in flows of information—is precisely the one that underlies my best trading.

There is an important lesson here for developing traders. *Before you work on building your experience and skills, clearly identify your core strengths.* When you draw upon your greatest life successes, you're most likely to leverage the strengths that will anchor your best efforts in markets.

> **Whatever will make you successful in trading is something that, in some way, you've already done successfully in another arena of life.**

Of course, it is entirely possible that your greatest strengths are not ones that easily translate into the trading of financial markets. Ultimately, my greatest strength—and my greatest passion—is the ability to relate to others and become a meaningful part of their development. That shows up in my professional work, but also in my parenting and in providing a home for our family's rescue cats. Trading does not offer that ultimate fulfillment for me and, indeed, I felt quite empty when I attempted to trade full time for an extended period. I enjoy trading as one among many life activities, but I had to be careful to not make the mistake of trying to make myself into someone and something I am not.

My strengths anchor my trading, but they also ensured that trading could never be my full-time career. *Many, many traders fail, not because they're doing a poor job of climbing life's learning ladder, but because their ladder is leaning against the wrong building.* Trying to improve your game is not especially helpful if you're playing the wrong game. The pattern of your life's fulfillment to date is the best guide to your future fulfillment. That may or may not bring you to a full-time trading career. You will enjoy a happy and fulfilling life as long as you stay grounded in who you are.

In a TraderFeed blog post, I wrote about an insight that came to me during my morning jog.[35] I was contemplating how to take my trading to the next level and asked myself the question, "What has been your best performance to date?"

The answer that popped into my head was my success in controlling my blood sugar. Wearing a device that provides blood sugar readings in real time, I'm able to see how well I'm doing multiple times per day. This enables me to make small, but meaningful adjustments in what I eat, how much I eat, and how much insulin I take. Because I have Type II diabetes, those adjustments are important to me. They have resulted in a well-controlled overall level of blood sugar and an ability to stay in my proper blood sugar zone 100% of the time over the most recent three-month period.

What is interesting is that I achieved this control through very frequent deliberate practice and feedback. I feel in control of my health because

I'm immersed in controlling my health. The implications for trading are clear: No grand change of mindset will take me to the next level of performance. As James Clear has observed, what is needed is detailed and accurate feedback and very frequent, small efforts to improve results.[36] We grow by doing—and that evolution revolutionizes our psychology.

Trading must leverage our talents and passions. It must build upon our life successes. It cannot fill what is lacking within us. *In that sense, we develop a relationship with trading the way we develop personal relationships.* We can't expect someone else—or something else—to fill our voids. It's our talents and passions that ultimately bond us with what we do and with whom we share our lives. Find an area of life in which you're particularly successful, figure out how you achieve that success, and then explore how you can adapt those strengths to markets. That is the essential lesson of positive psychology.

Mentoring as coaching

As we've seen, talent is necessary for success in any performance field, but it is not sufficient. In so many sports, it's the influence of coaching that imbues raw talent with the skills needed for winning. In the trading world, the teaching of trading (mentoring) has often been separated from the psychology of trading (coaching). Indeed, it's not uncommon to find trading coaches who have very little knowledge of—or experience with—the actual trading of markets. If we look at how performance development occurs in sports and other performance fields, we can see that the teaching of the game and the work on mindset are often seamlessly integrated: *The psychology of the player is addressed directly in the course of teaching particular strategies or plays.*

During my time at Duke University, I had the opportunity to observe high-level coaching in real time while I served as a student manager of the basketball team. The coach was constantly instructing—in practice, from the sidelines, during timeouts—and the way he instructed almost always carried a psychological lesson and impact.

An important part of the coach's success was figuring out when a problem required skill rehearsal and when it required a psychological adjustment. There were many moment-to-moment shifts that players needed to make, depending on the defense they were playing and plays they were running. For example, a constant refrain to the players on man-to-man defense was "ball-you-man," which meant that you needed to position yourself between the ball and the player you were guarding. Of course, the ball was always moving and the player you defended was always moving, so there were constant shifts to be made in order to sustain the ball-you-man alignment. When you are defending in that fashion, the offensive guard might lob the ball over you to give the player you're guarding an open look at the basket. At that point, the player nearest to the one getting the ball needs to rotate over to defend. So not only did you have to be keyed in on ball-you-man; you also constantly needed to be alert to what was happening around you so that you could rotate when needed. And if one of the players on your team intercepted a pass? Then a completely different adjustment kicked in, as you were meant to sprint downcourt and participate in a fast break.

Players typically needed time and practice to make all these adjustments second nature. For instance, if you're positioning yourself between the ball and the player you're guarding and an opposing player takes an outside jump shot, you need to get around the player you are covering and position yourself for the potential rebound. Simply shifting from player coverage to rebound position requires skill and practice. When a player had trouble getting into position, the coach would stop the scrimmage and walk the player through the steps, making it a learning lesson for everyone on the team.

On other occasions, the player possessed the needed skills but might be distracted by an error on a previous play. At those times, the coach might bring the player to the sidelines and help the player work on focusing on the challenge at hand. The mentoring of skills related to defense and offense and the coaching of motivation, mindset, and teamwork were tightly interwoven.

This dynamic can be observed in the coaching of many sports and performance activities. An acting coach will help with vocal tone and movement, but will also address stage anxiety and perfectionism. A boxing coach teaches techniques of body punching and defensive positioning, but also helps with aggressiveness and maintaining the focus on strategy. *When learning processes are well structured, mentoring and coaching are interwoven so that psychology is developed in the context of performance.*

I recently observed the close integration of coaching and mentoring during a learning session Jeff Holden held with developing traders at SMB Capital. His direction to the students was that, when they learn a new pattern to trade, they trade it 20 times with small size to become familiar with both variations in the pattern and common mistakes in reading those variations. The correction of mistakes becomes an opportunity to build skills—and it's also an opportunity to maintain the positive mindset of a learner.

Trading a pattern 20 times in practice mode provides 20 opportunities to coach oneself. In a recent session during market hours, Jeff and I worked with traders to identify their emotions in real time by writing down what they were feeling. Once again, Jeff proposed doing the exercise 20 times in practice trading to develop the ability to observe our feelings rather than become wrapped up in them. As I emphasized in the TraderFeed blog, gaining real-time skill in identifying our emotions is also practice in building cognitive focus.[37] We're thus coaching ourselves in trading psychology while we are working on our trading.

Unfortunately, the integration of mentoring and coaching has become challenging in recent years. Coaching via the virtual medium (such as Zoom) became a staple during the Covid-19 pandemic and took hold after. It made sense from a monetary perspective. A hedge fund in London that employed me didn't need to pay for my airfare and hotel, and I could be more efficient in my work without the time needed for travel. Long after Covid became a dominant concern, Zoom-based coaching/psychology sessions remained the norm. *The problem was that the virtual format divorced the trading psychology side of development from the actual context of performance.* When I was on the trading floor of a hedge fund, I typically would hear from portfolio managers or team members who were struggling with that day's trading. Because I was readily available, they sought me out to sit in on their meetings, so that I could help with teamwork and idea generation in real time. Limited to the virtual medium, traders and I could only talk *about* trading, not necessarily address issues as they were occurring. In the past, for example, many of my most productive conversations with traders on the floor took place when they were doing very well. We could focus on what they were doing right, and we could ensure that confidence did not morph into overconfidence. Once we were limited to virtual appointments, those conversations were few and far between. Not many portfolio managers and traders thought to set up a Zoom call because they were doing well!

Here's why that is important:

A robust finding in the psychotherapy research literature is that people are most likely to make changes in their lives when they are in states of high emotional experiencing.[38] It is when we are feeling things most deeply that we're able to make and sustain deep changes. If I'm drinking alcohol frequently but comfortable with my intake and lifestyle, I'm unlikely to sustain the motivation to change. If I experience consequences to my drinking, I become upset and am more likely to 'hit bottom' and find the motivation to work on my sobriety.

When trading psychology is relegated to conversations *about* trading, away from the context of real-time experience, it loses much of its emotional power and thus its promise. A mentor who works side-by-side with the trader on the trading floor is most likely to catch issues arising in real time, when emotions are heightened. Similarly, we are best able to mentor ourselves and work on our own psychology in the real-time context of trading, not simply as part of watching videos and conducting end-of-week or end-of-month reviews. As we'll discover in Chapter Three, we can learn to coach ourselves and gain many of the advantages enjoyed by institutional traders.

> If you're not working on your trading psychology in real time, you're not really working on your trading psychology.

This is why the activities of elite military teams are always followed by after-action reviews (AAR). Waiting until the weekend to review how the team botched a rehearsed hostage rescue would strip the learning process of its immediacy and relevance. It's when the team leader is shouting at members and stressing to them the consequences of not following precise protocol that Army Rangers or Navy SEALs in training are most likely to take their lessons to heart. Mentoring is not just about filling the brain with information. It's designed to help learners literally 'take the lessons to heart': to *feel* the importance of what they're doing. The urgency of the training process is a vital part of what instills the right psychology.

If mentoring is a purely intellectual exercise, it is unlikely to yield peak performance. When the mentor also acts as a psychological coach, we're best able to internalize new ways of thinking, feeling, and acting. This is true whether we are experienced and mentoring ourselves in new ways of trading; whether we're team leaders growing our junior members; or whether we're beginners learning from someone who's been there and done that.

Case study: real-time trading psychology

Successful traders think outside the box. They innovate. Their ability to view markets in original ways helps them find unique trading edges. One savvy trader I worked with held many phone calls before the market open, talking with other traders he respected. He shared his views and listened to theirs. He had an uncanny ability to read other people and identify when they had genuine confidence in a particular view, when they were uncertain, and when they were simply going along with the crowd.

This individual took careful notes after each call and learned which traders in his network had the best batting average when they displayed confidence in their ideas. This became important to his sizing of trades, particularly when his own confidence aligned with theirs. What made this trader successful was that he wasn't only reading the market; he continuously read market participants and adjusted his trading accordingly. His great psychological strengths were teamwork, interpersonal sensitivity and communication, and open-mindedness.

A successful trading process always leverages our signature strengths. As Michael Lamothe notes in his book *The Trading Mindwheel*, our beliefs shape our performance.[39] When we ground our performance in our talents, we naturally bring positive and constructive belief patterns to our trading. He describes an extensive process of journaling, in which there is detailed analysis of the largest winning and losing trades.[40] Performed over time, this grounds us in what we do best and trains us to avoid the rest. Lamothe captures performance with the image of a wheel, where the axle represents our mindset—our beliefs, emotions, and habits—and the spokes represent the processes necessary for peak performance: journaling, analysis of trade results, risk management, trade management, portfolio management, post analysis of performance, and testing of our trade ideas. This is a powerful image, as it conveys that it is our performance psychology that brings together the activities that power our development as traders. "The market is a metaphor for life," he points out: our growth lies in how we handle inevitable setbacks.[41]

Anne-Marie Baiynd, in *The Trading Book*, observes how our habits—including our habitual patterns of thought—can sabotage our trading.[42] If we draw upon past successes in structuring our trading processes, we naturally import positive habit patterns to our trading and position ourselves to build upon success. She describes the evolution of her trade journaling, stressing how her writing became more focused as she emphasized the positive reasons for taking trades.[43]

That is true positive psychology: successes end up becoming our best teachers. Perhaps not surprisingly, Baiynd actively coaches developing traders in the Topstep community,[44] helping them learn from setbacks to become profitable and earn trading capital. She explains that, "The golden rule is this: the market is a living, breathing, and moving thing, and if you think you have arrived, it won't be long before you are watching it pass you by." In a positive psychology vein, she observes that "the traits that build good traders are the traits that build good people"[45]: the best trading psychology is an expression of our best positive psychology.

Jared Tendler, in *The Mental Game of Trading*, points out that "It's a myth that emotions such as anger, greed, and fear are the problem causing your trading errors. Rather, these emotions are actually *signals*."[46] This is a very important perspective, and it's one that fits well with our understanding of positive psychology. If I'm not focusing on what is most important in markets and I become frustrated, my frustration is a signal that something is wrong—and it can be a catalyst for a refocusing. I'm not frustrated because I'm broken; I'm frustrated because I'm wired effectively for alerts that cue me for opportunities to improve. Emotions, Tendler points out, "are like indicators you follow in the market"[47]: they are information that can be utilized positively. Of course, the implication is that positive emotions experienced during trading, such as confidence and pride, also serve as signals, pointing us to what goes into our peak performance. Indeed, he notes, a "stable confidence" is a key ingredient in our stable performance in markets[48] and a hallmark of our "A-game" as traders.[49]

A short time ago, I returned to trading after a considerable time away. It was fun getting back to markets, and I was pleasantly surprised by how quickly things came back to me. I also recognized, however, that markets had changed since I had last been active. There was much more activity taking out obvious support and resistance levels, only to be followed by significant reversals. It felt as though the market was hunting for stops and continuously trapping the weaker hands. This happened across multiple time frames. Needless to say, it created considerable frustration on those occasions when I was the weak hand!

One of my discoveries was that the prevalence of traps of the market (I was mostly trading stock index futures and sector ETFs) differed greatly as a function of: a) time of day and b) volume traded. In earlier hours of the trading session and during busier periods, we tended to take out levels with some follow through in momentum. In lower volume periods, markets were more likely to undergo frequent reversals. *I found myself viewing different times of day as different markets with different participants and different patterns of behavior.* Moreover, each time of day acted as a different market depending upon the nature of participation. Instead of simply viewing myself as trading one market, I approached each session as a collection of markets, defined by time of day, volume, and volatility.

After trading, I reviewed my performance the same way my first therapy sessions were reviewed by the teachers in my graduate school. Back then, we would go over audio or videotapes, discuss what was happening, what I was doing or not doing, and rehearse alternative ways of approaching the session. Similarly, in my trading reviews, I looked back bar by bar, advancing my screens slowly to recollect my thinking at the time and correct misperceptions. I often addressed my own mindset during the trade, particularly when—like many quarterbacks—I became so focused on a particular play that I didn't perceive the entire field and missed opportunities to add to or exit positions. This active replaying of my trading became my after-action review (AAR) process.

My performance improved when I began looking at each day and each time of day as a unique market. I focused on who was in the market and what they were doing. Over time, different market conditions took on familiar personalities and I was better able to recognize the particular traps and challenges of each market type. It was only after doing this for a while that I realized that I was reading markets like I read the people I work with as a psychologist. Just as each person has a unique personality and set of themes, so each day's market presents its own challenges.

By mentoring myself in adapting to each day's market, I was able to bring trading psychology into my work on trading performance. If there is an underlying theme uniting the excellent work of Lamothe, Baiynd, and Tendler, it is that psychology is the glue that holds together our talents and skills. By drawing on my optimal mindset in my work as a psychologist, I was able to bring that mindset to my real-time trading.

Your business plan as a plan for your positive psychology

If you are a trader, trading is your business. If trading is *your* business, you are an entrepreneur. Consider the questions of this book's prologue, but now specifically in the context of your trading: If you were to write a mission statement for your trading, how would it read? What is your business plan for achieving your mission? What is the team you're working with to achieve the goals of your trading enterprise?

Many traders have not thought through the big-picture performance context of trading. If you're truly an entrepreneur, you know your mission and business plan so well that, if you ran into a potential investor going to the same floor as you, you'd be ready to make your elevator pitch. Could you make an elevator pitch for your trading on the spot? If your trading is unique and well grounded, its differentiated strengths should stand out—and your plans for leveraging those strengths should be detailed and top-of-mind.

> Would you invest in the trading of another person who approached markets the way you do, with the same level of entrepreneurial planning, research and development, market edge, uniqueness of returns, and teamwork?

POSITIVE TRADING PSYCHOLOGY

If you are the entrepreneur of your own trading business, then you should be readily able to capture your approach to performance in a business plan. That plan should be visionary: it should spell out what makes your business distinctive and why you are positioned to achieve unique and distinctive success. Approaching trading as a performance activity is not just about skill building and maintaining a positive mindset. It begins with the recognition that you are entering a competitive arena of thousands of other investors and traders and that you will only succeed if you are doing something that sets you apart from them. Successful traders invest: *As a trader, your success comes from investing in the distinctive strengths that make you special.*

This is why positive psychology is so important for trading performance. Coaching, from the perspective of positive psychology, begins with a simple question: What is special about your trading? How is your trading an expression of your unique talents? How have you built the skills that will enable you to succeed across a range of market environments? What special qualities define the team you've (formally or informally) assembled to assist with your trading business? How do their strengths complement your own? *When you have a true startup venture with a vital mission—a business that captures the best you have to offer—you sustain the drive and optimism to weather even significant setbacks.*

Consider every successful business out there, from Apple to Walmart. Their business plans today are far different from the ones they began with. As their markets evolved along with consumer needs, they evolved. It is that way with every successful enterprise. Business planning is never a one-and-done activity. It is continuous, as some areas of opportunity fade away and others become clear. Every trader with a long career of success has found fresh ways to leverage their strengths in ever-changing markets.

Such ongoing adaptation is impossible without a deep sense of mission and purpose. If you're an entrepreneur, your work is not a job or even a career. It's a calling. One of the activities outlined by Zelenski in his review of positive psychology is visualizing or writing about "an ideal future self."[50] Yes, it's important to follow markets and stay in touch with what is going on in the world, but without a vision of our ideals, will we truly be able to invest energy, optimism, and inspiration in our trading activities?

At one hedge fund where I worked, the mission statement was posted prominently at the front entrance of the building. Everyone who entered saw it, most especially the people who worked there. It was a valuable way to start each day: a reminder of the meaning and significance of our efforts. I recently asked traders to take 30 minutes and write out their mission statements, then spell out in detail the business plans that bring those missions to life. I then asked them to return to their statement and plan after a few days and see if they were actually inspiring and informative. Success in trading is not to be found in chart patterns, indicator readings, news reports, or platitudes about mindset. Nor can you pursue trading in order to become successful in life. *Your success in trading will be an expression of what has already made you successful in your previous endeavors.* The challenge highlighted by positive psychology is figuring who you are at your best and leveraging that as a market entrepreneur. You know you have found your true mission and best business plans when these capture the best within you and inspire you to greater and greater efforts. Positive psychology implores us: *Do more of what inspires us and gives us energy.*

Case study: figuring out markets by figuring out yourself

As I described in *The Psychology of Trading*, I enjoyed playing pinball machines when I was in college.[51] My friends and I would go out to eat and drink and I would try my hand at winning free games on the different machines. Once in a while, I'd get lucky and win. Most of the time, I'd lose a fair amount of change. Still, I enjoyed the challenges of different machines and had a good time while playing.

My pinball career took an unexpected turn when I was playing a machine and the ball came hurtling toward my left flipper. Normally, I would try to catch the ball on my flipper or I would flip it back up to the area where I could score points. On this occasion, however, I did something I had never done before: I didn't move my left flipper. I just let the ball hit it. To my amazement, the ball did not simply drain down the middle, but instead bounced to my right flipper. Once the ball was captured on my right flipper, I could send it through the chute, where it would score points and come back to my left flipper. Again, I would let it hit the left flipper and it would go to the right. And I would send it through the chute again, score more points, and collect the ball yet again. Before long, I was so good at getting the ball to my right flipper that I was routinely winning free games.

Was I a good pinball player? I certainly won a lot more free games than my friends. But I won because I figured out a quirk in the machine that allowed me to score almost at will. If I didn't take advantage of that quirk—or if I played machines that didn't seem to have a quirk—I lost my money just like everyone else. What made me successful was that I was willing to spend a good amount of time and effort (and change!) to learn the idiosyncrasies of the machines I played. And, almost always, the idiosyncrasies involved doing something that no one else would consider doing, like not hitting the ball with the flipper. (Another quirk for a different machine was aiming the ball for a specific target and hitting it many times. The point value of hitting the target rose dramatically if you hit it many times, so the entire game was devoted to hitting the ball in that direction.)

Years later, it's not so surprising that I trade the way I played pinball as a college student. There's a particular quirk in the stock market where buyers or sellers will accumulate but fail to move price meaningfully. When this occurs, a number of participants become trapped in their positions when the market moves the other way. For me, the whole game is figuring out when there is a historical tendency from recent price action and breadth; then identifying who's trapped and when; and then entering a trade to take advantage of their 'puking' when the market action lines up with the historical tendencies. That's it. That's how I trade. No grand understanding of macroeconomic fundamentals. Just a quirk that occurs across different time frames and different stocks and indexes that allows me to enter trades when the historical odds are in my favor. The market is my pinball machine. And when the bigger picture and the shorter-term quirk don't line up? I don't trade. It's like not using the left flipper. A big part of the edge lies in not playing the game unless there's a clear advantage.

What I do with people as a psychologist is not so different from what I did with the pinball machines. The positive psychology perspective tells us that there are always occasions where people act in ways that work for them: that bring them closer to their ideals. It's in the exceptions to our problem patterns, the solution-focused view tells us, that we find the key to successful change. *Those exceptions are our 'quirks.'* If you can figure those out, you can help people be more and more of who they want to be. My talent is my ability to hang in there; listen, listen, listen; stay patient; try different things; and eventually figure out the quirks that catalyze a person's successes. What has helped me as a trader is also what has helped me as a psychologist and what helped me as a pinball player. Once again, we see that so much of winning in any domain is leveraging the processes that have contributed to our past success.

Of course, markets are different from pinball machines. Markets change how their quirks play out from one time frame to another. If you do the same winning thing again and again on a particular pinball machine, you'll rack up free games. If you do that in markets, you'll suddenly find that what had worked no longer makes money.

The challenge of running a successful business enterprise, trading or otherwise, is similar to the challenge of sustaining a successful romantic relationship. From the excitement of getting off the ground and falling in love with what you're doing come the challenges of changing conditions and the need to keep things ever-fresh, ever-exciting, and ever-promising.

Falling into mindless routine is a sure formula for mediocrity. At each phase of life, a marriage finds new forms of expression. The ideal marriage when children are small is not the ideal marriage once they've left home or once both partners have retired. The marriage always draws upon the best of the partners, but in different ways across life circumstances. Similarly, the successful trading business is founded on core talents and skills, but must adapt to radically different trading conditions and the introduction of new products and markets. *Business plans are meant to evolve.* That ensures that business planning becomes an ongoing priority of successful traders.

Trading is a performance activity. We are always in training, we are always learning, we are always evolving. We are always playing different pinball machines. The creative challenge is to continually find fresh ways to apply our strengths to emerging opportunities in the markets. We do not succeed simply because we have a positive psychology. Rather, we grow our psychology as we leverage the best of our talents and skills. *One of the most valuable exercises you can perform is to review your best trades of the day or week and identify clearly what you did well.* This is a positive psychology approach to a trading journal. Literally decompose each successful trade, process step by process step, and track what you did right in terms of generating the trade idea, sizing and structuring the position, managing the risk, and timing your entry and exit. Do that again and again and you will see patterns emerge. You will see where your talents and skills lie; you will see the trading psychology that accompanied your success. You are most likely to be a peak performer if you intensively study and learn from your performance at its peak.

Practical takeaways from Chapter One

1. Because trading is a performance discipline, success depends upon the right combinations of talents, skills, and mindset. This means that, if you're new to trading, it's important to give yourself the

time and space to explore different markets and different trading strategies. Only that first-hand experience will truly show you where your talents and interests lie. During that time, you'll make plenty of mistakes and hit a number of dead ends. That makes it extra important that you explore trading with little or no risk at the start. It also suggests that you can greatly benefit from joining a trading community or trading firm where there is ongoing mentoring, once you've settled on the kind of trading that is right for you. The ideal trading community will offer multiple mentors and teach a variety of trading skills, from recognizing opportunity to order execution and position sizing. Learning from multiple mentors will allow you to take away the best from each of them, helping you synthesize the learning into your own trading style. Note: The best trading firms and communities only make money if you do. You want to be with people who are invested in your success, not who look to sell you hopes and dreams. Performance in any field is built upon real-time training.

2. Many disruptions in trading psychology result from short circuiting the learning/development process and trying to make money before accumulating the necessary experience and expertise. Emotional trading, such as trading on tilt, occurs when we take more risk that we're ready for and when we encounter challenges that we haven't yet experienced and mastered. The right trading psychology develops from a sound process of expertise development. Proper training builds focus; focus keeps us in the flow of mastery. Positive psychology suggests that the key to trading psychology is not overcoming negative emotion; it's learning to sustain the cognitive, physical, and emotional states that accompany our best performance.

3. If you're not new to trading, you've probably learned that markets and market opportunity change over time. This means that, to some degree, we're always learning and going through the process of finding new edges in markets. The ability to reduce risk when

markets change and give ourselves time and space to adapt to new market patterns is essential to long-term success. This, too, can be a tremendous advantage of working with trading partners and teams. Learning from the experiences of others speeds our learning curves and our adaptation to ever-changing markets. Positive teamwork is a gateway to sustained positive psychology.

4. Every trader needs a regular process of preview and review. In preview, we observe markets, see how things are trading, how markets are responding to news, and where there might be unique opportunity. In review, we go over in detail the trading decisions we made and highlight what we did right and what we could have done better. It is from the set of things we did well and not well that we set goals for the next trading session and seek to make improvements. This regular, ongoing process of deliberate practice is essential for skill development and a mindset of mastery. It is also what makes traders true performance professionals. By studying, studying, studying our successes, we can clearly identify the ingredients of our success and anchor our processes in those. Talent is essential to trading success; what we have done well in other performance fields will offer important clues as to what we will need to incorporate in our trading. Positive psychology tells us that it is when we draw upon our talents and interests that we are most likely to sustain a flourishing mindset that keeps us motivated and performing at our best. It is because trading is a performance discipline that we acquire a winning psychology in the course of learning how to win. The most positive trading psychology is one that is developed and rehearsed in real time.

This first chapter showed us how successful trading is similar to success in other performance fields, drawing upon our interests, talents, and skills. The second chapter will look at some of the performance challenges unique to trading and how we can master those.

CHAPTER TWO

THE UNIQUE PERFORMANCE CHALLENGES OF TRADING

Payton is a senior member a hedge fund team that largely focuses on interest rate and currency movements around the world. He experienced initial success in his trading, benefiting from the mentorship of his team leader. He successfully researched global economic trends and statistics and built a dashboard for his team that highlighted areas of opportunity and aided his idea generation. His trading was 'quantimental,' which means that it was based upon mathematical relationships among the economic variables that he followed. For example, Payton broke down the GDP (gross domestic product) releases of various countries to identify the segments of economies that were relatively hot and those that were not. These patterns of strength and weakness provided Payton and the team with valuable clues for trading rates, stocks, and currencies.

For instance, strong growth stats for several oil-consuming countries in Asia led Payton to recommend a long position in crude oil as well as long positions in the equity markets of those countries versus the markets of countries displaying slower growth. By digging into economic releases and talking with analysts in each of the countries, Payton gained a nuanced appreciation for shifts in strength and weakness before those became consensus market views.

When the Covid crisis hit in 2020, markets went into freefall and central banks were forced to add liquidity to economies so that they could weather the shock of suddenly reduced consumer and economic activity. These developments overwhelmed the variables that Payton was studying. He had no way to make sense of the huge jump in volatility across markets and no way to trade it.

This shook his confidence and made it difficult to resume his trading once markets normalized. Only with time, coaching, and considerable research was he able to build screening tools that could tell him when to pursue his strategies, when to reduce his risk-taking, and how to benefit from high market volatility.

So far, we've seen that trading is a performance field. What we will learn when we analyze Payton's experience is that trading poses a set of challenges that are unlike those encountered by most performance professionals. A big part of developing our trading psychology is learning to anticipate the distinctive demands of managing money and normalize our responses to the non-normal behavior of financial markets. Let's take a look at several ways in which trading is distinctive as a performance discipline and how these impact our quest for a positive trading psychology.

Adapting to shifting market conditions

Payton's example shows us that what works in one set of market conditions can blow us up when trends, correlations, and volatility change. As noted earlier, these market shifts are fractal, occurring across all time frames. Intraday, for example, a market may be trading in a relatively consistent manner and then suddenly change when a news event breaks, when there is a surprise economic data release or earnings print, or when there is a report of a likely shift in the policy stances of central banks. The need to rapidly adjust to real-time changes in performance conditions is not something that most of us have had to deal with.

In my research for the book *Enhancing Trader Performance*, I specifically sought out training and performance lessons from elite military units and police teams.⁵² For such teams, surprise attacks and sudden changes in tactical situations must be expected. I wanted to know how Special Forces and SWAT teams learned how to deal with sudden life-threatening developments. The answer, I found, was that they rehearsed these scenarios in lifelike simulations. By encountering a variety of risks in many practice scenarios, the soldiers and police units gained familiarity with the unfamiliar. This helped ensure that, when actual crises occurred, they would have the experience needed to handle it constructively. The repeated training, making crisis situations almost routine, greatly reduced the fight-or-flight extremes of emotionality, allowing teams to focus on evolving circumstances and adapt in the moment.

An important reason that developing traders wrestle with their fight/flight states of stress is that they are not prepared for abnormal developments. Very often, newer traders seek help in dealing with emotional reactions to markets when their focus should be on the market conditions that triggered those reactions. When a piece of unexpected market-moving news hits the tape and we get a jump in price and volume, newer traders are taken by surprise and, like Payton, cannot adjust to the development. They react on impulse, rather than on training, which is often the worst possible response. They have a sound trading process, but not a sound process for adapting their processes to changing market conditions. *Simply working on dampening emotionality cannot substitute for the intensive rehearsal needed to cope with the unexpected.*

It was during my work in Chicago that I first observed traders making use of market replay at the end of each trading session. Their goal was to re-experience the day's action and figure out how they could have better handled unexpected developments. I recall one talented trader staying long after the market close, playing and replaying the leadup to a Federal

Reserve announcement, the price action following the release of the Fed action, and then the responses to the ensuing press conference. He had gone into the day with a fixed opinion of how the market would digest the central bank news. That prevented him from being flexible, as his market traded in volatile gyrations following the announcement and during the subsequent press conference.

Only after he had replayed the entire market action bar by bar, noting volume and the behavior of correlated markets, was the trader able to go away from the difficult trading day with any sense of understanding and mastery. Indeed, whenever a challenging market period occurred, he made sure to replay it and understand what was going on. Over time, he increasingly responded to market shifts with a sense of 'been there, done that,' allowing him to place trades calmly and deliberately even in frantic market conditions. He did not master his trading psychology by performing any psychological exercises. His mastery came from what psychologists have termed 'corrective emotional experiences.' In making change familiar, he eliminated much of its threat.

> **Practice makes perfect when it comes to our trading psychology, but only if it's the right kind of practice, conducted intensively, in detail, and close to real time.**

At one hedge fund, the traders approached the practice issue differently. They conducted research studies of how markets have behaved in given situations and used these historical scenarios to plan their trading should the situations occur in the present. To take the previous example, the portfolio manager and team would study how various markets tended to behave when the Federal Reserve announced an unexpected rate hike. They examined which asset classes moved first, which moved most, and how those movements carried over to other markets. Studying multiple historical examples, the team was able to assemble a road map of possibilities and then investigate how to best profit from the movement, how to best manage risk, how to size positions, etc. Once again, the impact of the exercises was to take the surprise out of the market as much as possible. By creating decision trees of what to do in various scenarios, they helped ensure that trading would be active and proactive, not reactive.

So what was my role as a trading coach? Once the traders had examined market behavior closely, I became the Socratic questioner, asking what they would think and do in various scenarios. I've often referred to my role as one of "comforting the afflicted and afflicting the comfortable." If we've been in a relatively quiet, trending market period where performance has been good, I want to do as much afflicting as possible—before market shifts inflict their damage. Recently, I spoke with a portfolio manager who had been quite successful in tracking and trading trends in the stock market. He understood that, in a period of stable growth and inflation, growth stocks would outperform value stocks across different market sectors and subsectors. Given his recent success, his goal was to increase the size of his positions, take more risk, and make more money.

During our meeting, I showed him a research study from a service that I subscribe to that identified a tendency for extended downtrends in volatility to mean revert within a matter of weeks to months. That led us to a conversation about how to identify if and when we were seeing a rise in realized and implied volatility and how sectors of the market might respond to the shift. We playacted scenarios that would likely lead to a spike in volatility and how he would shift his portfolio to adapt to the circumstances using hedges, changes in position sizing, etc. My role was not simply to exhort him to trade with discipline and follow his processes. Rather, my job was to help him anticipate when he might need a new discipline and a modification of his processes.

> **When we repeatedly rehearse challenging trading scenarios and practice our responses, we build emotional resilience and foster a mindset of mastery.**

A few portfolio managers make it a habit to contact me for a meeting only after they've gone on a winning streak. Realizing through hard experience that 'this, too, shall pass,' they use our meeting to ensure that confidence does not become overconfidence. And how do they do that? By doubling and tripling down in preparing for scenarios that could make them vulnerable.

One savvy trader recently sent me information that suggested that the exposure to stocks among institutional investors was quite high, favoring growth shares over value ones. In other words, these large participants were counting on growth in the economy and thus expected sectors of the equity market such as consumer discretionary and technology to outperform more defensive sectors, such as consumer staples and utilities. Immediately the trader and I mentally rehearsed scenarios that could reverse the recent patterns of strength and weakness. For instance, a meaningful decline in interest rates (and rising recession concerns) could stimulate the high-yielding defensive sectors that, up to that point, had been underperforming growth shares. As elite military and police teams have found, it's difficult to be thrown by a surprise attack if you've thoroughly rehearsed such surprises in advance. As it happened, rates did decline and sectors experienced significant reallocations in the face of weakening economic statistics. Because the trader was prepared for this possibility, he responded with planned action rather than reactive emotion.

Notice that the average trading journal is inadequate as a substitute for this intensive, scenario-based deliberate practice. A journal is very helpful in terms of tracking performance, identifying areas for improvement, and setting goals, but—in and of itself—it cannot train us how to respond in unfamiliar market periods. Imagine that a military force needs to occupy a town and prepare for sniper attacks, booby traps, and armed resistance from enemy forces. No amount of writing in a journal would substitute for drills that train the soldiers how to move from building to building, how to avoid sniper fire, how to recognize traps, and how to make the element of surprise work in their favor. Similarly, my journal entries might alert me to the possibility of a spike in volume and volatility in my market when energy prices break out of a range, but they don't *train* me to respond to the heightened risk and reward of such a scenario. What enables us to master our psychology is facing adversity under simulated and real-time conditions. Direct experience fosters adaptation and a sense of mastery.

The need to adapt to radical shifts in market conditions makes trading unlike many performance activities. Yes, in basketball or football we face different opponents, but the rules of the game and the dimensions of the playing areas remain the same. Trading is more like mountain climbing, in that abrupt changes in weather conditions can change the entire activity and pose wholly new challenges and threats. The climber who practices in a variety of weather conditions is prepared to deal with uncertainty. The best practice in such cases is proactive: simulating conditions of danger in our practice prepares us for the actual dangers of performance.

Case study: mentoring ourselves by talking aloud

How can we bring deliberate practice into our real-time trading to train ourselves to adapt to ever-changing market conditions? One way that I stumbled upon in my own trading has been to narrate aloud what is happening from bar to bar, almost as if I were a sports announcer covering the action of a game. My talk is purely descriptive, focusing on what is changing in volume, what is changing in terms of the sentiment of market participants (shifts in patterns of lifting offers vs. hitting bids from transaction to transaction), what various sectors of the stock market are doing in relative and absolute terms, what is breaking out and what is rangebound, etc. There is no talking about putting on risk, and there is no talking about P/L. I am purely absorbing myself in the real-time activity of the market.

As I've indicated earlier, this is similar to what I do as a psychologist when I meet with someone for the first time. I focus my attention and listen intently. I'm looking for patterns in what my client is telling me. Before

I attempt to come up with any suggestions, I bond with the other person and listen to them. As a trader, I establish a similar bond. If I care about the market and truly listen to what the market is saying, it will speak to me. If I'm properly focused from moment to moment, I'll pick up on subtle cues of shifts in tone and cadence. I don't need to anticipate what is going to happen if I can quickly pick up on what *is* happening. That comes from repeated experience, reflection, learning, and adjustment. Sometimes I'll say something to a client in therapy and it will fall flat. The person isn't ready to hear what I have to say, or I'm saying the wrong thing. That, too, is information that I need to process in the helping relationship.

Talking aloud in real time during trading is powerful, because it engages us in real-time mentoring. At times, I'll put an order into the market and notice that volume is slowing down as we approach the edge of a range. I'll also notice that various sector indexes are pulling back from their range extremes. I'll say out loud, "This isn't right" and quickly pull my order. *In talking to myself, I'm training myself.*

During a recent trading session, I noticed significant selling pressure across the broad range of NYSE stocks. Specifically, the NYSE TICK was staying in negative territory longer than usual. At the same time, the NASDAQ TICK was oscillating around zero, with little or no net selling. I told myself aloud that, when selling pressure in the broad market abated, it would be worth seeing if the lack of weakness in the NASDAQ shares would translate into outright strength. This is a pattern I've seen repeatedly: directional moves are preceded by shifts in relative strength and weakness. When I saw the NASDAQ TICK rise to a new high on a bump higher in the overall market, I quickly jumped aboard the emerging uptrend in the NASDAQ shares. I had talked myself through the trade as if I were mentoring a developing trader.

An important benefit of talking aloud is that it keeps traders highly focused and engaged. If I'm absorbed in what the market is telling me, I can't concern myself with how much money I need to make or whether my next trade will be a winner. Imagine the moment-to-moment mindset of a rock climber who is ascending a steep, dangerous mountain. The focus is on the next step and the immediate path ahead. Similarly, a surgeon moves forward with a procedure one step at a time focusing on established protocols. *The successful performer is process-focused, not outcome-focused.* Talking aloud during performance ensures an ongoing process focus. The stream of talk is our rational mind speaking to us, serving as our mentor. Many times, we know what to do in tricky market situations, but our reason becomes clouded by our emotional processing. Talking aloud bypasses this emotional processing, allowing us to gain from the understanding that's been there all along.

Recently, Jeff Holden and I, working with developing traders at SMB Capital,[53] have encouraged the traders to notice what they are feeling during a trade and talk those feelings out loud. For example, I might notice that a leading market sector is breaking out of a range on nice volume and I will say out loud, "This could be it. I'm feeling good about a broad market breakout." Of course, this might be something I'd say if I were on the trading desk next to my teammates. I know that, if I say something aloud to people I care about, I must really believe it. I would never want to mislead them. By talking my conviction aloud, I become an observer of my emotional state—and that helps me use the emotional information as information. An important implication of positive psychology is that we can learn as much from our positive emotional states as our negative ones.

Markets are ever-changing. Therein lies their threat—and their opportunity. Simple self-help techniques to help us think positively or to help us stay calm with a few breaths cannot possibly train us to perform under rapidly shifting conditions of risk and reward. Our trading psychology emerges from our preparation and adaptation. When we actively make sense of markets, we're most likely to respond to them sensibly. Mark Douglas, in his classic book *The Disciplined Trader*, points out that, to adapt to changes in the outside environment, we must undergo our own internal changes.⁵⁴ When we are most flexible and open to change, we're most likely to profit from changes in markets.

Handling inevitable losses

None of us are perfect. Sometimes we fail to execute on our plans, and sometimes our plans fail to address market contingencies. I've worked with portfolio managers and traders who have sustained years of success in markets. Quite often, their trades are not profitable much more than 50% of the time. Their profitability comes from the ability to maximize their gains and minimize the size of their losses.

The best traders quickly recognize when they're wrong and exit trades. "It's not that they're always right," as Tom Hougaard explains in *Best Loser Wins*, "it's that they do a great job of being wrong." *This requires an uncommon cognitive flexibility: the ability to generate and sustain the confidence and conviction in one's ideas at the same time one is ready to pull back from trades based on those ideas when circumstances change.* Only an open mind can achieve such flexibility. As I emphasize in my ebook *Radical Renewal*, if our egos become attached to the ideas we're trading, we're unlikely to achieve and sustain this open-mindedness.⁵⁵ While athletes and performing artists are primarily focused on success (even as they learn from mistakes), traders have to be focused on the inherent uncertainty of financial markets and the very real possibility that doing the right things can end in losing money.

The flexibility of mindset needed to handle failure must be hard wired into our trading plans. The plans I encounter with successful traders include detailed steps for what to do if the trade begins to work out. In a higher- and/or rising-volatility environment, the plans might include adding to the positions as they move the trader's way. In choppier, non-trending, lower-volatility markets, the plans might include aggressive methods for quickly taking profits. The plans also cover contingencies if positions move against the trader: stop-loss levels for exit and pullback levels where the trader might add to positions. By planning each trade and reviewing multiple contingencies, the trader exercises cognitive flexibility and normalizes the experience of making and losing money.

This proactive planning is especially important for traders who enter positions based upon market catalysts, such as earnings prints, economic data releases, and central bank meetings. Much of the professional trader's time and attention is given to understanding expectations for the catalyst by speaking with analysts and experienced peers. Still, there is always the potential for a massive surprise. Earnings may blow out to the upside and create immediate buying. A central bank may surprise by failing to deliver an expected rate cut, sending bonds lower.

Depending upon positioning going into the catalyst, the responses to such surprises can be extreme. What do you do if you are long the U.S. dollar against the Euro and Yen and the Federal Reserve unexpectedly reveals a dot plot of significant rate cuts going forward? Do you take immediate profits? Do you add to your position at much better levels? It is very difficult to make such decisions in the heat of battle.

> A good trade is planned, not reactive. Detailed planning reinforces sound trading processes.

This is yet another example of how our trading processes build our trading psychology. Simply exhorting ourselves to be 'disciplined' and 'process driven' does not substitute for the actual, detailed work of anticipating different paths of price movement and adjusting to those. *Our planning programs our minds; our lack of planning sets us up for reactivity*. We learn to deal with the inevitability of loss one trade at a time, by how we plan for—and normalize—all possible outcomes.

An excellent book that tackles the challenge of managing P/L is *Best Loser Wins* by Tom Hougaard. He begins his text with an enlightening observation: "How you feel about failure will to a very large degree define your growth and your life trajectory, in virtually every aspect of your life." If we pursue growth, we necessarily push the envelope: in our work, our relationships, our physical exercise, and our trading. In pushing that envelope, we will inevitably fall short at times.

During a recent exercise routine at the gym, I tried bumping up the weight for one of the exercise stations. I strained and soon realized I would not get through an initial set of ten repetitions. Can you imagine if I internalized that experience as a failure and then either avoided that station or made sure I never 'failed' at my lifting again?! Moving from one challenge to another means testing our limits—and that means that we have to become very good at falling short.

Hougaard encourages traders to 'flip the switch' in their development, and that starts with assuming that one's trade is wrong until proven right and expecting to be uncomfortable during the trade.[56] When the switch is flipped, the trader adds when shown to be right and never when wrong. This mindset places risk management at the heart of the trading process, allowing the trader to achieve wins that are more sizable than losses. The key to his trading success, Hougaard explains, is that fear "no longer acts as a debilitating force in my life. I have trained the fear out of my decision making."

Carefully note the wording of Hougaard's observation. He has not reduced or eliminated fear through acts of will or through self-help methods directed to positive thinking. Rather, he has 'trained' the fear out of decision making. Repeated trade planning and rehearsal of trade plans is the training that moves us from fear and greed to rational decision-making. If we expect to be uncomfortable, discomfort no longer becomes a threat or disruption.

Steven Goldstein, in *Mastering the Mental Game of Trading* explains that trading mastery is grounded in self-mastery. In defining that mastery, he distinguishes between the 'self' and the 'ego.'[57] He notes that the ego is necessary for trading success—and indeed for success in any endeavor—but can also hijack sound trading processes. This "occurs when traders interfere with a planned trade," he notes, "because they fear losing gains or making losses. The ego wants the praise, and thus overrides the trader's process." Goldstein defines 'letting go' as a necessary phase of trading, where "the trader mentally disengages from the outcome of the trade." He explains that "the ability to let go is the greatest and most under-appreciated skill a trader can possess," and goes on to describe trading as a series of "performance process cycles" that lead us to produce ideas and act on them, track their outcome in real time, let go of our attachment to those outcomes, and then reset for the next opportunities.[58] What makes trading distinctive among performance activities is the ongoing need to intensively engage and thoroughly 'let go.' Again, this requires a flexibility that can only be achieved through repeated experience; it is not something that comes naturally to us.

Linda Raschke, in her insightful book *Trading Sardines*, points out that "Experience counts not just in knowing the markets, but in understanding your own personal trading patterns."[59] She found that her personal trainer, 'Mr. Bill,' provided her with some of the best lessons for trading: "Stick with the basics, follow a methodology, be consistent, use rituals to achieve consistency, concentrate on your form, keep records of your progress, and above all, practice positive thinking!" This is a great example of how optimal trading psychology is a psychology of peak performance. How Linda worked out in the gym—and how Mr. Bill mentored her physical development—offers a template for our development as traders. It is not coincidence that Linda was able to get to the point of winning a bodybuilding competition, and it isn't coincidence that she has long been viewed as a 'market wizard.'[60] She points out that, "If you substitute the word 'trading' for 'training,' Mr. Bill's lessons are the perfect recipe for success in the markets."

Bodybuilding is but one activity that can help us make sense of our participation in markets. In a text that was fundamental to my development as a trader and trading psychologist, Victor Niederhoffer finds market insight in games that we play, horse racing, music, and ecology.[61] Surprisingly, Niederhoffer was criticized when he spoke in

England "to tell an audience that music and speculation were similar languages for expressing rhythm and emotion." He explains that "the guiding principle of music and markets starts with a central tone and a gravitation back after departing in various tension-provoking dissonant intervals. Lowly speculators and great composers are compensated if they are skillful in resolving the tensions." Undaunted by the criticism, Niederhoffer shared, "Whenever I am severely criticized, whenever I am in turmoil... I have a patented method of resolution. I take out my pencil and quantify. And then, based on the outcome, I go out and trade." Sure enough, he performed his research and found evidence that market themes early in a period tend to repeat late in that same period. In the face of negativity, Niederhoffer created a positive resolution.

In *Radical Renewal,* I emphasize that we cannot succeed at trading if we don't have proper outlets for our needs and strengths. Whether it's bodybuilding or music, we can find inspiration for our trading in what most inspires us in life. If we hijack trading to meet our ego needs—needs for success and recognition—then it will be impossible to let go, accept discomfort, and benefit from it. *From a positive psychology perspective, sound trading can only proceed from a fulfilled life; it cannot bear the entire burden of our fulfillment.* What enables us to weather the emotional impact of inevitable periods of being wrong and losing money is the resilience that comes from a full life portfolio, where we are always 'winning' in our other life's efforts. Once trading no longer has to meet our ego needs, we can trade from the soul: from our deepest levels of understanding. We're free to take losses in our trades when we're buffered by wins in other spheres of life.

> **A great reflection is: What is the emotional P/L of your life outside trading? We are free to succeed in trading once trading no longer bears the burden of our emotional P/L.**

My experience is that a positive psychology perspective goes even further in helping us deal with trading's inevitable drawdowns. *If we have a sound, well-sourced trade idea and we execute the trade well, adverse price movement is important information.* Many times, I have been able to reverse my position after stopping out of a trade, turning the loss into a greater gain. This recently happened when my research suggested that a strong stock market could go still higher, but could be vulnerable to a pullback in the near term.

I entered a short position for a near-term trade, but was surprised to see weakness in the overnight futures market quickly erased by buying during European trading hours. Talking aloud during the trade, I recognized that money managers who had missed the initial thrust higher were using any pullbacks to get into the market. That led me to cover my short position at a modest loss and enter a larger long position to go with the medium-term trend.

The market continued higher the next day, more than erasing my loss. In this case, a scenario grounded in historical analysis did not play out—*and that was useful information.* Instead of lamenting the loss or viewing it as a threat or failure, I was able to embrace it and use it as input for the next, winning trade. A sound trade idea that doesn't work out can provide a useful trading cue. Perhaps this time truly *is* different. *Our mindset can't always be positive, but it can always stay constructive.* Trading is distinctive as a performance field in challenging us to embrace failure as a catalyst for learning and success.

An insightful text regarding the distinctive challenges of trading is *Think and Trade Like a Champion* by Mark Minervini. He emphasizes 'contingency planning' at the heart of his trading process, to ensure that—in advance—we know how we will handle any foreseeable outcome.[62] He notes that such planning "enables you to make good decisions when you're under fire," which is when we most need to be calm and collected. Note that Minervini does not start from the perspective of how to handle emotional, reactive trading. Rather, he outlines proactive processes that prevent us from becoming reactive in the first place. Losing money due to our fallibility is not a choice, he points out, but how much we lose is very much in our control.

In his *Stock Market Wizards* interview, Minervini quotes Jesse Livermore that the "fruits of your success" come from the willingness to "take 100 percent responsibility for your results."[63] *Contingency planning—and constructive response—can only occur when we own our outcomes.* Many performance activities train us to perform well. Trading, as Tom Hougaard points out, rewards us for how well we lose.

Case study: recovering from loss the right way

A while back, I met with a junior portfolio manager, Gil, who was managing capital for a successful macro team. He was relatively new in the risk-taking role, having graduated from his previous position as an analyst. Now he had the opportunity to manage a sleeve of capital and actually profit from his ideas. Understandably, he was quite motivated and wanted to prove himself.

Gil got off to a good start, focusing his efforts on trading only his best ideas and doing so with modest size to avoid starting out with a large drawdown. That's when the problem began. Encouraged by this early success, Gil's portfolio manager—as well as members of the firm's risk department—told him to significantly increase his trading size. Gil was excited by the vote of confidence, bumped up his risk-taking, and promptly saw a meaningful increase in the volatility of his day-to-day P/L. When one of his ideas did not work out, that single loss wiped out much of his previous profits. Undeterred, Gil continued trading with more moderate risk and made his loss back. Once again, buoyed by his success, he sized up his trades and then went through an even deeper drawdown. That was when he reached out to me. He was exhausted, and he was discouraged.

Right away we can see the first problem that Gil made. Instead of seeking coaching proactively, at the time he began taking more risk, he enthusiastically went about business as usual. In a very important sense, his trading psychology shifted: from careful building of a track record to aggressive pursuit of profits. To no small degree, the management of his team and hedge fund unwittingly fueled this shift. They no longer perceived Gil as a developing portfolio manager. Instead, they viewed him as a profit center—and they pushed him for profits. In this new risk-taking regime, he was not emotionally prepared for his P/L gyrations and he could no longer be that 'best loser' described by Hougaard. Losing became too threatening and, as we've seen from Goldstein's work, he could no longer 'let go' when his well-researched ideas did not yield winning trades.

I encouraged Gil to return to his initial, more modest level of trade sizing and return to doing the things that had worked well for him. To their credit, the portfolio manager and risk department supported this move. After initial success, we then set a schedule for gradually bumping up his trade sizing, so that his new level of risk was quantitatively different, but not qualitatively so. This was the equivalent of gradually increasing how much he sought to lift on the weight machine at a gym or gradually increasing the distance he tackled in his jogging. The goal was not just growth, but *sustainable* growth. This created a stairstep pattern of progress: increase risk moderately, achieve consistency and success, then bump the risk by another moderate notch, etc.

Not only did this stairstep pattern build Gil's confidence, it also built his resilience. By the time several months had gone by, he was responding to larger losses the same way he had dealt with smaller ones when he was responsible for less capital. A 20 basis-point loss felt like a 20 basis-point loss, whether it was on $15 million of notional capital, $30 million, or (eventually) $100 million.

Gil did not build his trading psychology because of any grand insight that I imparted. Nor did he achieve his breakthrough via a dramatic psychological change. Rather, coaching helped him utilize his trading strengths to build his emotional resilience and consistency. As Gil progressed, he was able to bump up his risk-taking on his own and do so in a sustainable fashion. At that point, he became his own trading coach. This is the ultimate goal of work on trading psychology: to teach the skills and provide the experiences that enable market participants to manage and coach themselves. Gil became able to weather losses when he made those losses a natural, expected part of his stairstep path to trading success.

Gil's development as a money manager illustrates an important principle outlined by Mark Minervini in *Trade Like a Stock Market Wizard*. Minervini advises that "Your goal is not risk avoidance but risk management: to mitigate risk and have a significant degree of control over the possibility and amount of loss… To win in an environment where everyone has the same objective," he explains, "you must do the things that most investors are consciously unwilling or subconsciously unable to do." Again and again, when we read the wisdom of successful traders and successful trading coaches, we encounter the idea that what comes naturally is what gets us in trouble. It is human nature to avoid loss, and it is human nature to be drawn to big profits. *In a very real sense, successful trading requires that we rewire our emotional responses—and it is the function of training, practice, and planning to achieve and cement that new wiring.*

As we read books from successful traders, we consistently find that they achieve their positive trading psychology by implementing a rigorous trading process. Mark Fisher, in *The Logical Trader*, describes an ACD system that uses trading ranges early in the market day to help us define the type of market we're in, where we're meant to find opportunity, and where we're meant to preserve our capital.[64] Linda Raschke, in *Trading Sardines*, stresses that it is the time spent in preparation outside trading hours that leads to success. She advises, "Focus on the process and it leads to profits in the long run."[65] This is because "You can't predict in advance where the big wins are going to come from—just keep taking every system signal." Mike Bellafiore, who, with Steve Spencer, has mentored many consistently profitable traders at SMB Capital, emphasizes that developing our 'playbooks' of success—the templates that capture our best trading—is "a personal journey of trader rehearsal."[66] Planning for success and preparing for loss makes trading different from many competitive arenas in which losses are truly setbacks to be avoided. It is the process focus that keeps traders in a constructive mindset even during periods of setback.

> If we don't have very concrete plans for losing and drawing down, we cannot prepare ourselves for the levels of risk-taking that could make us truly successful.

Independence requires depending upon others

On Independence Day 2024, I recorded a podcast with trading coach Agnieszka Wood. The theme was traders' desire for independence. Many individual traders and members of trading teams dream of the day when they can achieve financial independence. For them, trading success implies the freedom of a significant income where they can determine their working hours and choose their working conditions. One point I made in the podcast was that freedom can only be achieved through freedom of will. If we find ourselves reacting and overreacting to market events, we cannot truly be free. As we've just observed, freedom means that we're free to take losses and can exercise the choice to contain those and indeed learn from them.

There is, however, another context of freedom and independence. Many traders are attracted to trading as an entrepreneurial activity. They want to achieve success, but they want to do it on their own. For them, freedom means freedom from relying on others. Indeed, for them, having to depend upon others to get work done might feel more like a bureaucracy than an entrepreneurial endeavor. As we noted earlier, however, trading has moved dramatically toward being a team sport. Even in the day trading world, there are too many markets and stocks to track, too much information to follow, for any single individual to possibly process it all. The team structure allows traders to divide and conquer, increasing their bandwidth. *Ironically, relying upon others becomes the surest path to independence.*

This is a reality for which few traders are prepared. It suggests that one can work diligently and do all the right things and still not win if the advantages of teamwork are missing. I recently met with a group of very motivated independent day traders over lunch. We discussed the morning trade in the stock market and focused on how they traded a sharp move higher that began at 8:30 am ET. Some of the traders explained that they faded the move; others seemed confused by the price action. I shared with the group that an economic report had been released at the 8:30 am time, indicating that growth in the economy was solid. I pointed out the significant action in the bond market following the data release, as traders reduced their bets on recession (and their expectations of rate cuts from the Fed).

My point to the traders was that this was a game changer for large, institutional investors. *It was important that day traders not only understand what is happening from minute to minute in their market, but also what was happening among the larger participants who move the markets.* Without team resources to count upon in their preparation, the day traders focusing on the 'text' of short-term market action could not step back and process the 'context' in which the price movement was occurring.

To broaden their vision, teams at hedge funds have moved toward specialization among their members. A new team member might be brought on because of an expertise in applications of AI or because of unique experience in a given market or region of the world. During team meetings, everyone brings fresh insights and information to the group. In addition, each member builds their own professional networks that further aid the team's search for tools and information. On top of all that, the hedge fund may hire its own research staff, providing even more specialized expertise to teams. One fund where I work sends money managers to specialized conferences and sets them up with conference calls with world experts in different fields. The only requirement that the fund makes is that the person attending the conferences share the unique information within the fund's community of traders. This greatly enriches the process of idea generation, providing more and different inputs for creative brainstorming.

> If we don't achieve differentiated views, we become part of the herd. Distinctive returns require distinctive ideas and methods—and a variety of perspectives on markets.

This need for breadth of perspective has led day trading firms such as SMB Capital to adopt a team structure. Traders work in 'pods,' where they share trading styles and benefit from the mentoring of a team leader. In turn, the team members contribute to the search for trade ideas, greatly expanding the vision of the senior traders. The firm subscribes to research and news services and invests in technology that enables traders to easily track multiple markets in real time. More than once, I have observed a trader struggling with P/L reach out to team members to see what is working for them. Team membership greatly expands the scope of learning via role modeling.

What does this mean for trading psychology? In a nutshell, *the psychology of the team is absorbed by the team members.* We naturally internalize our surroundings. Working within an opportunity-focused team becomes a reliable path for enhancing one's trading mindset. As noted earlier, the research I've conducted on the success of traders has consistently identified intellectual curiosity as the number one predictor of solid, risk-adjusted career returns. When curiosity is a signature strength, we naturally seek out new and different information and play with ideas based upon those inputs. That is intrinsically rewarding. *A team that consists of intellectually curious members who focus on different areas of market opportunity becomes more than a team: it's a think tank.* In such an enriched environment, we're much more likely to learn and grow. We're more likely to see promising opportunities if we process more possibilities. There is no way that can be replicated by an individual, isolated trader. The risk to our psychology is not just negativity and loss of discipline. Stagnation is an equal threat, robbing us of the energy needed to be on top of our game.

Not surprisingly, successful traders operating in solo mode make special efforts to communicate with valued peers, creating virtual teams. My own trading is very much an individual affair, grounded in tracking shifts in high-frequency data that reveal fresh buying and selling. Any conversation during the trading process would be painfully distracting for me. Where teamwork assists my trading is in brainstorming the ideas that lie behind the trades I place. For instance, many of the colleagues I've maintained relationships with value the historical testing of market patterns. Those might be patterns in fundamental data, patterns in recent price action, or patterns among market indicators. My colleagues and I also benefit from a wealth of research resources from such sources as sentimentrader.com;[67] barchart.com; marketcharts.com; quantifiableedges.com, and stockcharts.com. These offer data that allow traders to benefit from back-tested ideas and test their own trading edges.

For example, one breadth measure I have found particularly helpful is the number of stocks in the NYSE universe that generate buy and sell signals on technical trading systems each day. Each day, for instance, I will track the number of stocks closing above their upper Bollinger Bands and the number closing below their lower bands. These bands represent two standard deviations of movement above and below the market's 20-period moving averages. Such data capture tendencies for momentum and mean reversion, especially when combined with price action on various time frames. I share this kind of information with my colleagues and they share information that they may have gained from research reports, their own studies, and from market commentaries. Such interactions provide more puzzle pieces to play with, helping all of us see if a bigger market picture is setting up. If so, I know I can find good risk/reward points to buy or sell by focusing on high-frequency data that track shifts in buying/selling pressure. The collegial interactions also ensure that I am not socially isolated in my trading. The friendly banter and support are as important as the sharing of ideas in that context.

> When we participate in stimulating teamwork, we don't need to be stimulated by P/L. There is nothing as inspiring and energizing as working with others on shared dreams.

What we're seeing is that the dream of achieving independence via trading is best achieved by achieving *interdependence.* Teams at hedge funds have senior traders in different markets; junior traders who assist with execution and trade structuring; quantitative analysts who perform and track empirical research; and developers who build tools for the traders and analysts to use. The sheer amount of data shared within such teams is mind blowing.

Of course, not all data are information and drowning in too much data can be as destructive to trading as the lack of information. *Where team structure enhances trading psychology is through the processes by which the team makes sense of the information.* It is not uncommon that teams I meet with use morning meetings to review new findings, breaking news, and latest data releases to brainstorm their significance. For those teams, creativity is a shared process, with everyone feeding each other's heads. Such teamwork fuels trading psychology when it produces new insights and ideas and stimulates meaningful discussion.

Unfortunately, this perspective is not often encountered in the writings (and practice) of trading coaches. They largely work with individual traders (often developing ones) and rarely if ever sit in on the meetings where ideas are actually discussed, debated, and generated. Without that experience, it's natural to assume that trading psychology is purely a function of individual mindset. The best trading is a team sport and the quality of our teamwork is an important determinant of whether we're focused or distracted; inspired or discouraged; actively engaged in markets or passively observing them.

Case study: helping a portfolio manager build her business

A hedge fund referred a portfolio manager, Naomi, to work with me, asking me to help with her development. The person making the referral indicated that they felt Naomi was a future star and they wanted to do everything to facilitate her growth. Naomi and I scheduled an initial Zoom call, and I asked her to outline what she trades (markets and instruments); strategies she trades within those; and the goals she wants to pursue. It turned out that she wanted to grow her trading and eventually build a team. In the recent past, she had attempted to trade larger only to go through frustrating drawdowns. It seemed to her that she had hit a ceiling in her development.

My first step was to ask Naomi for a chart of her historical P/L and then to break this down by markets and strategies. I specifically wanted to know the degree to which her different trades were correlated. Obviously, growing unique trades/ideas is very different from growing correlated ones. Many times, traders think they're trading unique ideas, but those ideas are merely variations of a single strategy. For example, a trader may trade trends in rates markets and could have different ways of defining and entering those. The returns from the different trades are often correlated, because they're ultimately dependent upon a single underlying factor (momentum).

Of course, what I'm also doing with my homework exercise is assessing Naomi's motivation and readiness for change. If she is willing to assemble her historical data and undergo analyses of these, that shows that she's actively engaged. At a more contemplative phase of the change process, she will not want to dig into data and instead will need to sort out the pros and cons of taking on more risk. As it turns out, Naomi was very much in the action mode and sent me the information quickly. What the data revealed was that her returns were quite positive with modest drawdowns. It was clear from her high Sharpe ratio (the Sharpe ratio tracks the average size of winning trades relative to the average size of losing trades) that she managed risk tightly and benefited from trading different markets and time frames.

In my research with portfolio managers, a distinctive finding has been that the personality traits of high-Sharpe traders are quite different from those of high-absolute-return traders. The traders with smooth equity curves (positive returns, small drawdowns) are usually quite conscientious and emotionally balanced. They avoid drama in their P/L, just as they avoid drama in their lives. What Naomi had attempted to do was turn herself from a good risk-adjusted trader to a high-absolute-return one. That brought drama to her day-to-day P/L, disrupting her mindset and trading processes.

Such traders find that they are best able to get bigger by getting broader. By finding opportunities in new markets and/or different time frames, they can deploy more capital without creating disruptive P/L volatility. For the intellectually curious portfolio manager, this engages a strength rather than risk a potential threat.

Psychologists call this 'reframing a problem.' Instead of working on the anxiety around large size and P/L swings, we work on generating new research, new information networks, and new ways of managing positions. *From a positive psychology perspective, we get a lot further by building on strengths than by focusing on vulnerabilities.*

Broadening as a way of getting bigger posed an exciting challenge for Naomi and fueled her efforts to build a team. She hired a quantitative analyst to research new markets and quickly benefited from the unique perspectives of this research. She also found that bouncing ideas off her analyst and using meetings with the analyst to talk aloud trade plans helped with just about every aspect of the trading process.

Many, many times, when we focus on the building of strengths, problems go away. There's little problem getting bigger if we're also getting broader. We find our freedom when we exercise our free will, and that is often best accomplished through strengths-based teamwork. Naomi became a better version of herself not by changing herself, but by extending herself. Thanks to the input of her quant analyst, Naomi was able to exploit market opportunities on longer time frames and also able to exploit opportunities in new markets. She retained her smooth equity curve, even as she grew her capital.

To no small degree, our trading psychology is built on the foundation of our interactions with colleagues. What fuels our development is what challenges us, and it is difficult to sustain challenge and intellectual curiosity in a vacuum. The independence and autonomy of a trading career are alluring, but they are best achieved by teaming up with the right people.

There was a time when I valued my independence and wondered if I would ever get married. After 40+ years of marriage, I can attest that I am far more independent—and have grown far more—than if I had lived my life in solo mode. Becoming a successful trader means building a successful business. Finding the right people to assist in that effort increases the likelihood of success—and it makes the journey far more fulfilling. In our trading, as in our relationships, we are most likely to grow when we can absorb the strengths of others. In interdependence, we find our independence.

Great trading requires distinctive cognitive development: idea generation

We've seen that trading success requires an emotional rewiring in which we embrace the possibility of losses and remain emotionally detached from P/L. Less well recognized is that successful trading requires a *cognitive rewiring*. Our routine ways of processing information—and our routine states of consciousness—do not enable us to sustain trading success. Yes, we hear that trading requires the right mindset. What is less appreciated is that our mindset crucially depends upon the depth and flexibility of our cognitive functioning. *Trading is distinct among performance fields in that it requires continual growth in how we think and what we think about.*

Observe your stream of consciousness in real time. You'll see that your mind naturally flits from topic to topic, only occasionally focusing on something specific for deeper consideration. On a walk, I'll notice birds and trees; I'll turn my attention to rabbits and squirrels; I'll see something interesting about the lighting of the sky; and I'll note the landscaping of the houses I pass. Interspersed with these observations are thoughts about the day ahead, items to do, and goals for the next few days. If you were to write down all of my thoughts and feelings in real time, you'd quickly conclude that I have an attention deficit disorder! Rarely do I spend more than a matter of seconds on any particular observation or topic. My experience is that I'm not unique in that regard. In a very real sense, all of us operate with attention deficits relative to the focused concentration demanded by work in financial markets.

There are two parts to trading as a cognitive process. The first is the analysis and synthesis of information that underlie our trading ideas. The second is the tracking of real-time price action to identify specific times and prices to act on our ideas with superior risk/reward. *These are quite different processes, requiring different strengths.*

When we are first searching for trade ideas, we might read news reports, review price action across different instruments and markets, talk with team members and personal contacts, perform our own research, and consult written research reports. What we're looking for is a lining up of information to indicate when there is a unique, promising opportunity in the market. *This process requires depth and breadth of processing and most crucially involves sustained focus across information-processing modes.* The successful trader holds multiple information flows in their head at any time, just as a football coach needs to focus on the team's strengths and weaknesses as well as those of the opponent and then balance all that with ever-changing real-time game conditions. The strategy for the football coach, just like the trader's strategy, evolves with the assimilation of fresh information. Imagine a coach whose attention during the game flits from the quality of the refereeing to frustration over the last play to concerns about not making the cutoff for tournament play. The decisions of such a coach would be reactive rather than proactive and would almost certainly lack coherence.

The trader's initial task in markets is to identify opportunity. We've seen that this phase of trading, referred to as 'idea generation' by hedge fund managers, is fundamentally a creative process. We assemble a variety of observations and ideas across time frames and markets in order to determine if the asset(s) we're trading are mispriced. Recently, we experienced an unusual day in the stock market in which the stocks that had been strong (technology shares) sold off sharply and the market segments that had been relatively weak (small- and medium-cap stocks) soared. To the casual observer, this looked like a mixed market, but careful observation suggested otherwise. The shift in patterns of strength mirrored a rally in the bond market, as investors—on the heels of moderate inflation news—bought bonds in anticipation of Federal Reserve easing. This was relatively easy to see by comparing price action within short-term Treasuries (three-month to two-year maturities) and also between the shorter- and longer-dated ends of the curve. At the same time that fixed-income investors were buying Treasuries, the breadth statistics for the stock market blew out to the upside. By the end of the trading session, we had over 800 stocks on the NYSE close above their upper Bollinger Bands and only 16 that finished below their lower bands. In short, there was a breadth thrust in stocks corresponding to anticipation of moderating inflation and lower rates. Investors clearly expected strength in the economy to follow from the shift in rates.

After noting all this, I spent a focused block of time consulting my historical data and studying what has happened in stocks following similar breadth thrusts. Sure enough, there were consistent, above-average returns over a multiday period. The breadth strength very often represented the start of a momentum move to the upside.

However, after the breadth thrust, we had a situation in which over 1,500 stocks on the NYSE were making fresh monthly highs and less than 150 making new monthly lows. Historical returns following such skewed new highs and lows tended to be subnormal over the next several-day period. Putting those historical analyses together, I developed the thesis that we were going to see continued market strength, but perhaps only after a short-term correction.

The idea generation process did not end here. I examined trends in breadth sector by sector for the past couple of weeks and indeed found that—even before the release of the inflation data—rates had begun moving lower and breadth in rate-sensitive sectors (such as real estate and utilities) had improved meaningfully. Relative breadth strength in smaller-cap stocks was particularly evident. This alerted me to specific areas of opportunity to focus on going forward. In other words, I was not only generating ideas about market strength, but relative sector strength.

> Unique data fuel the generation of unique ideas and the achievement of unique returns. To achieve a special trading psychology, we need to be doing something special.

Of course, none of these analyses would have been possible had I not scraped data on market and sector breadth every day for years and assembled them in a database that allowed for rapid analysis. With the broad array of data available, I was able to absorb myself in analyses that made eminent sense out of an otherwise confusing market session. By the time I completed my idea generation, I felt a quiet confidence in my understanding of the market. *The intensive period of analysis and synthesis transformed my trading psychology.* I was not confident because of any tricks that I had played to improve my mindset. Rather, my mindset improved as the result of a fulfilling creative process. This is a phenomenon familiar to scientists, artists, and performing artists. Our cognitive absorption leads to clarity of perception and that leads to confidence.

Routine consciousness is poorly suited to idea generation. Lacking the ability to sustain intensive focus and lacking the conscientiousness to examine large amounts of unique data, we find that our minds gravitate toward easy short cuts. Idea generation becomes little more than trading off pieces of news ("Oil should go higher because there is conflict in the Middle East") and trading off of simple chart patterns ("We are forming a double top"). Most of us have not trained ourselves to sustain highly focused effort for hours at a time. We thus never generate a distinctively positive trading psychology because we're not doing anything of distinctive value. "We're overbought and due for a pullback" is shallow and superficial idea generation; it certainly is not a trading edge. *Much of trading psychology is built during the hours when we're not active in markets: when we're generating ideas to pursue in markets.* When traders take the time to assemble ideas from unique information, they achieve the confidence that comes from clarity. They no longer merely have an idea; the idea has grabbed them.

Case study: expanding a trading process

The breakdown of trading into idea generation and execution is common among hedge fund managers, but not so much among prop/day traders. Many short-term traders simply assume that their mission is to find 'setups' to trade. A setup is often a technical pattern on a chart, such as buying an upside break from a range following a declining market. In such trading, there is not necessarily a distinction between the setup and the execution of the trade. The trader simply places his or her trade when the technical/chart criteria are met.

Of course, if the chart-based setup by itself actually did possess a positive expected return, it would be easy enough to demonstrate this by coding the conditions for the arrangement of the bars on the chart and then conducting a back test of the results. This is rarely done. When I've performed such back tests myself, results have been inconsistent and mediocre. That makes sense: if market edges were as simple as looking at well-known technical indicators or chart patterns, those would have been exploited by experienced traders and quant algorithms long ago.

I was looking forward to my first meeting with Molly. She was an active day trader with a multiyear track record of success. At her prop firm, she was rightly viewed as a rising star. A manager explained that her talent consisted of finding great setups in actively traded stocks. It seemed to me that there must be more to her success than that.

Fortunately, I was spending the day on the trading floor and had the opportunity to observe Molly in action. Her goal in working with me was to expand her trading by participating in longer-timeframe trades, including ones that she would hold overnight. She recognized that this wasn't her bread and butter and wanted help in developing that part of her business.

My first observation with Molly was that she was very good at running multiple scanners simultaneously. She had several programs open at the same time that scanned for trading conditions across a broad range of stocks. What grabbed her attention were stocks that showed up on several different scans. Some of the scans were very short term (minutes in length) and some scanned patterns played out over hours.

Molly did not focus on earnings or other fundamentals; nor did she spend much time on macroeconomic conditions. When she said that a trade was "setting up," she was referring to far more than a chart pattern or a shift in a technical indicator. Her idea generation was based upon focusing her scans on unusually strong or weak sectors and stocks, often those for which volume and volatility were higher than normal, and then identifying occasions when shorter-term price action was nested within similar longer-term price action. Indeed, she often used the term "lining up" to describe trades she would take based upon the multiple scans.

Once she identified a stock that lined up in terms of longer- and shorter-term price and volume/volatility patterns, she then drilled down to very short-term market action to buy on weakness or sell on strength. Her process was as differentiated as that of any hedge fund manager I had ever worked with, but she looked at completely different variables on very different time frames.

> Generating profitable ideas and actually
> trading those ideas are independent processes
> that draw upon different strengths.

In attempting to extend her holding periods, Molly recognized that she risked 'style drift': getting away from her trading strengths. When we explored the parts of her trading process that most excited and engaged her, we found that she was really drawn to the pattern recognition of putting multiple scans and charts together and generating a view on a stock. In that sense, she was like someone who loves assembling puzzles. This was her genuine talent and, as positive psychology research indicates, exercising such a talent is intrinsically rewarding.

From this perspective, the style drift to avoid would be any move to a style of trading that no longer engaged her pattern recognition. Rather than try to add a new style of trading, Molly needed to figure out how to extend her current trading approach to longer-timeframe data. This meant *reconfiguring* charts and scans, not changing them altogether.

Sure enough, by focusing on daily and weekly data after the market close and during the weekends, Molly was able to identify stocks setting up for medium-term trends and breakouts. She used her meetings with me to brainstorm longer-term scanning criteria for stocks, including the stocks at the end of each day that met particular technical criteria (closing x% above or below various moving averages; trading significantly above-average volume; etc.). She added these to her traditional scans, improving her identification of opportunity. I found it fascinating that she was able to use her traditional short-term scans to help with the entry and exit execution on the longer-term positions. In expanding her time frame, she broadened—and also sharpened—her trading edge.

Her growth came from building upon who she already was, not changing herself in any fundamental way.

A very important takeaway from Molly's development is that successful idea generation leverages very specific cognitive talents and skills. It is an intimate expression of who we are and how we process information.

In any aspect of life, when we follow our strengths and develop a process that speaks to us, discipline and consistency cease to be problems. Do I have to struggle to achieve the discipline to feed my four rescue cats first thing each morning? Has it been 'discipline' that has kept me lovingly connected to my wife of 40 years?

A little while ago, a trader asked me how to be more consistent in taking the trades from their best setups. Sure enough, the trader had learned the setups from others; there was no unique idea generation that drew upon the best the trader had to offer. *It is difficult to give voice to our trade ideas if those ideas don't speak to us.*

The best discipline comes from the deepest conviction; we are most likely to commit ourselves to ideas if we have made committed efforts to generate those ideas.

Great trading requires distinctive cognitive development: implementation

Idea generation is only the first part of our cognitive process as traders. Once we've generated a view of a particular asset, we still have to convert the idea into a trade. That means that we have to figure out how to best express the idea (trade structuring) and then find inflection points that would give us highly favorable risk/reward over our anticipated holding period (execution). Moreover, we need to size the trade so that positive returns will be meaningful but also so that losses won't be debilitating. As the trade moves for or against us, the bet that we initially made changes and we can adjust our sizing based upon our fresh assessment of risk and reward (trade management).

For the successful trader, the implementation and management of a trade is every bit as cognitively rigorous as the generation of the idea underlying the trade. It is a different rigor, however.

In esteemed psychologist Daniel Kahneman's terms, trading requires both 'fast' and 'slow' thinking: quick integration of information to manage risk and deep analysis to figure our opportunities worthy of our risk-taking.[68] Where much of idea generation is grounded in the analysis and synthesis of multiple information flows (slower, deeper thinking), the management of our positions requires constant adjustment to fresh price action and news (quicker, broader thinking). As Kahneman's work suggests, our quick and deep modes of processing information make use of very different talents and brain functions.

> **Trading is unusual among performance disciplines in that it requires rapid, continuous shifting between thinking fast and thinking deep and slow.**

I recently came across a situation in the market in which defensive stocks (utilities, consumer staples, value stocks) were significantly outperforming more growth-oriented shares. This occurred at a time of declining market breadth. While the overall market index was hovering at recent highs, the dynamics of the price movement suggested caution. Indeed, that is what my historical back test suggested, and it also fit with slowing economic data.

Having identified a potential bearish opportunity, I now faced a different task of defining my best bet. Did I want to simply sell a stock index, or might I sell a couple of sector ETFs to place my bet on the parts of the economy—and the companies—most likely to be negatively impacted by slower growth? Did I want a directional bet or a relative one? For instance, I could go long the sector ETFs most likely to benefit from lower growth and short the sector ETFs that would likely see outflows in a slowing economy. Structured properly (making sure there was equivalent volatility for the longs and shorts), such a trade could have taken the broad market out of the equation entirely, providing positive returns as long as the stronger sectors outperformed the weaker ones, regardless of market direction.

Still another trade structure might have been possible: If volatility were relatively low but rising, could it make sense to buy options to express the slowing growth views and achieve aggressive profit potential relative to downside? Or to combine a stock position with an option position and hedge the directional bet?

As noted previously and illustrated with this example, trade structuring/expression is every bit as rigorous as idea generation, but it is rigorous in a different way. When we generate ideas, we're synthesizing different information flows in a creative fashion to perceive opportunity that others might miss. When we structure trades, we are defining possible scenarios and the P/L implications of each. For that reason, trade structuring can never be a one-and-done process. As markets move for and against us, the bets we initially placed may no longer reflect the current risk/reward. *Skilled traders are as good at trade restructuring as they are at trade structuring.* In other words, they are constantly adapting because their positions are constantly moving. This is a unique facet of trading as a performance discipline. Just at the time we arrive at high confidence and the conviction to put our capital at risk, we need an ongoing open mindset to recalibrate this confidence in real time. Such a dynamic is just as relevant for the longer-term investor as the day trader.

Our bets—the odds of our success and our getting stopped out—are ever-changing. The ideal mindset of the trader is not so much positive or negative as focused and flexible, open to adapting to fresh risk/reward as markets move and information flows change.

Many of the best traders I've worked with spend as much time and effort in the structuring/restructuring process as in the idea generation process. Not surprisingly, a sizable portion of their returns come, not just from the ideas they trade, but from how they structure the bets they place.

It's not unusual to find traders who trade similar views in the same asset classes but who have very different P/L numbers. How they express their ideas and how they manage their positions are just as important to their success as the ideas themselves. *One reason this is the case is that the ability to structure ideas in multiple ways can provide meaningful diversification.* If I identify a market breaking out to the downside and have well-grounded reasons for anticipating lower prices, I might sell the asset in question, but I might also purchase straddles to bet on rising volatility and structure relative bets on the instruments that are most and least vulnerable in the breakdown scenario. The multiple structures provide multiple ways to win, broadening risk-taking and potentially reducing the P/L volatility of allocating large size to highest-confidence views.

Unfortunately, many traders spend time finding trades but spend little or no time figuring out how to structure and manage those trades. They may not be lazy in generating their ideas, but they make no special efforts to figure out how to best express their views and manage their positions while their trades are on. Structuring and managing positions require in-depth inquiry, often in time-limited conditions. Once we've generated a sound idea, we don't necessarily have all day to determine best ways to trade the idea, as the market may move without us on board. *For that reason, we need efficient processes of trade expression and position management, just as we need efficient processes of research.*

When every facet of trading is process-driven and well defined, a focus on best practices replaces the focus on moving P/L. We respond to moves in our positions with focus and clarity, not emotion.

Even relatively simple efforts in becoming more process-driven can generate meaningful improvements in returns. Let's say, for instance, that breadth data within the technology universe suggest a short-term upside edge in the related XLK ETF. Taking the time to identify the highest-relative-strength members of the XLK universe and trading those rather than the ETF itself can add to performance significantly.

> The effort we put into the sizing and structuring of trade ideas is like the effort an artist puts into a canvas or sculpture. The value and beauty of our work can be found in the details of what we craft. We are most likely to stick with trades if we have committed effort to them.

From the standpoint of cognitive development, the most important element of performance success is the ability to sustain focused effort. Many, many times, it is mental fatigue that makes us vulnerable to impulsive, emotional trading. As we shall see in our review of positive psychology research and practices, techniques that build our capacity for prolonged, intensive concentration can be tremendously valuable for our trading performance. Of course, we're most likely to draw upon our cognitive resources when our ideas excite us, drawing upon our distinctive interests and strengths. It's the combination of emotional/personality and cognitive talents and skills that provides our true edge in financial markets.

Case study: taking trade execution to the next level

Gene was one of the most successful traders at his hedge fund. He was very open with his trade ideas and we engaged in many discussions about markets. I was initially puzzled during these discussions, because his ideas didn't sound all that different from the ideas of others I spoke with at the firm. Still, Gene's returns greatly exceeded those of the other portfolio managers.

What did strike me as distinctive was the way in which Gene thought about trade execution. *His execution was not a single process, but rather a collection of connected processes.* For example, let's say that Gene was following news regarding Middle East conflict and fundamental data on oil production and concluded that energy prices were headed higher. He might buy crude oil, and he might go long the assets of crude oil producers such as Norway. All of these initial positions were sized modestly. They would have stop levels, but they were intended as core positions that he could hold through ups and downs. In short, Gene's core positions were his investments.

What Gene was looking for, however, were 'inflection points' where he could see the energy trade playing out in real time. Sometimes, these inflection points reflected a specific catalyst in the markets that could generate a momentum move. Other times, the inflection occurred at points of enhanced volume at a key price level. At those inflection points, Gene was quick to get quite large in the trade, placing a stop for the added portion of the position at the point where the inflection began. So if news of an escalation of the Middle East conflict led to a pop in oil prices, Gene might treat this as a breakout move, buy the first short-term pullback, and place his stop for the new (large) portion of the trade at the lows immediately prior to the breakout.

As a result, Gene always had more than one position for a given idea: a smaller, core position with a relatively wide stop to allow a move to develop (his investment) and a larger position with a tight stop to take advantage of short-term momentum (his trade).

Similarly, Gene was quick to take profits on portions of his inflection point trades, actively scaling out to harvest profits. *Gene's process ensured that he was always acting as an investor* and *as a trader.* The reason he was making more money than others in the same space was that he was very good at recognizing short-term patterns of momentum and quickly capitalizing on them.

Particularly important was that Gene's trading process <u>was</u> his way of managing his trading psychology. I cannot emphasize this point strongly enough. In creating a differentiated execution process, Gene allowed himself to be smallest in his sizing when his idea was least proven and then largest when it was actually playing out. *His approach to execution enabled him to blend risk management and profit maximization, so that he could take meaningful risk and not stress himself out.*

Other traders at Gene's firm, without the differentiated execution process, battled an either-or mindset of either being too small in an idea or too large. It wasn't that their psychology interfered with their trading. Rather, their less differentiated trading processes exposed them to P/L swings and hence psychological swings. For Gene, execution was not just about entering and exiting trades; it was also a process of knowing when to get bigger and smaller based upon catalysts and price action.

In sum, we've seen that trading is unique as a performance discipline in its cognitive complexity. Successful trading requires the deep processing of multiple streams of information to generate ideas, and it also requires the quick processing of multiple streams of information to express those ideas and manage them as trades. As Gene's trading illustrates, trading requires both quick integration of information to manage risk and deep analysis to figure out opportunities worthy of our risk-taking.

The ability to coordinate many information streams over many time frames reflects both talent and skill. When we create trading processes that exploit our faster and deeper cognitive talents and enable us to build skills specific to our time frames and markets, the result is a growing sense of mastery and confidence: a positive mindset grounded in our ongoing development. *The implication of all this is that successful traders are continually switched on—and are unusually able to sustain the switched-on state.* In my trading office in Chicago, I hung a signed photo of a military sniper in the weeds. That was my metaphor for the short-term trading I was observing. Wait, wait, wait, and then act decisively before returning to the weeds. Not all traders are snipers; some participate in large scale campaigns. *Common to all successful traders, however, is the blending of focused waiting and bold action.* Both require switched-on processing, but across very different cognitive modes. The sniper analyzes wind and terrain patterns in focusing for the shot; the sniper also develops an intuitive feel for when the target is setting up for a high-probability shot.

Focus on opportunity, focus on timing; focus on strategy, focus on tactics.

> **Trading is distinctive among performance activities in that it requires both continuous cognitive effort and flexible cognitive effort.**

Just as the sniper is wholly engaged in making one good shot, the trader focuses entirely on placing one good trade.[69] Different kinds of trading require different blends of fast/intuitive and slow/analytical thinking, but it's difficult to identify an area of trading that does not demand talents in both spheres. As we've seen, it's the role of training to hone these talents into the unique skills that lead to success in various strategies and markets.

To recapitulate, a durable positive trading psychology emerges:

a. when trading draws upon our unique talents and interests; and
b. when trading is process-driven, grounded in practices that take advantage of our distinctive skills.

The rigor with which we learn trading—and the rigor with which we make trading decisions—define the resilience of our trading psychology. Examine the developmental process in any major performance field, from athletics to the performing arts, and you'll see that it takes years to achieve expertise. That means that it takes years to earn the right to risk money with a positive mindset. How we structure our learning, how we structure our review processes, and how we structure our trading practices represent our investments in trading mastery. There can be no stable, positive performance psychology without ongoing efforts to extend our mastery. The combination of talents and skills demanded by successful trading is unique, specific to the challenges posed by ever-changing markets.

THE UNIQUE PERFORMANCE CHALLENGES OF TRADING

Practical takeaways from Chapter Two

1. Trading is a performance discipline that poses distinctive challenges and demands, both emotionally and cognitively. Our normal states of mind and our usual levels of cognitive functioning cannot sustain trading success. For that reason, developing the depth and breadth of our processing and sustaining the intensity of our focus are essential to our development as traders. We want to break down every element of the trading process, from the generation of ideas to the management of risk, and rehearse them to build our capacity for quicker, deeper, and more sustained information processing. In developing ourselves across the range of trading processes, we develop the focused mindsets of mastery that characterize our positive trading psychology.
2. We expand our trading—and our trading success—by leveraging strengths and skills we already possess. No style of trading works in all markets under all market conditions. When we understand how we best process information and manage risk, we can bring those processes to new time frames, new markets, and new strategies. Every successful trader is actively growing a business based upon his or her unique strengths, combining rule-based discipline and ongoing innovation.
3. Success in trading requires concerted work on our processes for developing trade ideas, and also our processes for implementing those ideas. An effective review practice requires reflection on how we generated our trade ideas and also how well we managed them as market positions. The best reviewing of performance involves a true 're-viewing,' with clear feedback regarding what we did well and what we need to do to improve going forward. This deliberate practice must include all facets of trading processes. We develop our positive trading mindset by continually honing the ways in which we identify and exploit opportunities provided by markets, growing our ability to sustain intensive slow/deep and fast/broad information processing.

Thus far, we've mainly focused on how our development as traders can shape our psychology and fuel our trading performance. Now let's examine the reverse: how work on our psychology can further our trading.

CHAPTER THREE

THE ROLE OF PSYCHOLOGY IN TRADING SUCCESS

IF THERE IS one theme that dominates the work of trading psychologists and coaches, it's that improving our psychology—our frames of mind—can improve our trading performance. Indeed, without an opportunity mindset, it's difficult to take risk and weather drawdowns. As we shall see, however, there is more to sustaining a positive psychology than optimistic thinking and buoyant mood.

These are complementary perspectives: Developing the right way nurtures a sound psychology, but maintaining the right psychology also helps us best make use of our talents and skills. Psychology and performance are intimately connected, each building upon the other.

How psychology impacts performance: lessons from medical school

During my full-time tenure at SUNY Upstate Medical University, I directed the student counseling program. My role was to help medical students and residents progress academically and professionally. A frequent presenting concern among students seeking counseling was preparation for final exams. Grades on these tests determined grades for the courses which, in turn, impacted overall GPA and the students' odds of entering competitive specialties and residency programs. Performance stress and anxiety were common experiences and real threats to the aspirations of the students. They were all too aware that one bad grade could literally alter their entire professional future.

I was not entirely unfamiliar with exam stress. During my undergraduate studies at Duke University, I had known that I needed to maintain a minimum 3.5 GPA (out of 4) to have a shot at entering competitive graduate school programs in clinical psychology. That placed tangible emphasis on each and every final exam. I recall pulling all-nighters on a regular basis, knowing that every grade in every course was important. Upon joining the medical school faculty, however, I quickly sensed that the pressure of medical school was different. For that reason, when I assumed the student counseling role, I made special efforts to sit in on classes and attend students' study sessions. It quickly hit me that there was more material in the books and lectures than students could ever hope to learn thoroughly.

The performance anxiety experienced by the students was grounded in reality. They recognized that they could never hope to master everything and ace their tests. Yet they felt the need to ace their tests to advance in their field. I only later appreciated how this situation was not so different from our trading of financial markets, where there are more data and more interrelationships of asset classes and time frames than a person could ever thoroughly process.

Over the course of the academic year, I closely examined the study practices of the most successful medical students. I learned that they were very good at identifying the most important information from their lectures and readings. For example, anything that appeared in both the texts and the lectures was emphasized. Anything that was repeated by the lecturers was sure to find its way into the students' notes. The best students did not spend more time studying than their classmates; *rather, they were laser-focused on the highest-yield information—and they were savvy at identifying what was most important.*

I was struck by the realization that a majority of the best students studied in groups. This helped keep all of them motivated (and awake!) during late study sessions, but it also had a second function: *It allowed them to fill in each other's gaps.* If a student's three study partners thought that a topic from a lecture was important and it wasn't in the student's notes, that helped the student fill in the gap. Similarly, the student's notes helped the study partners augment their study sheets. Sitting in on these group study sessions brought me to an important additional insight. *The groups studied their material in more varied ways than did the students who studied solo.* They exchanged notes and diagrams; they talked aloud; they quizzed each other. Information was much more likely to stick if it was encountered in different ways at different times. Theirs was a more varied processing and thus became a deeper processing.

What struck me most, however, was that the students who studied in groups entered their exams with the best mindsets. It was rare to find a student who studied in a good group who suffered from performance anxiety. Students who studied solo, on the other hand, were most likely to be overwhelmed by the sheer amount of information in front of them. Partly this was because the study groups served as a support mechanism; partly it was because the groups were an efficient mechanism for sifting through large amounts of information and picking out what was most important. How the students approached test preparation very much determined their mindset in studying and test-taking and that, in turn, made a meaningful difference in their performance.

This is precisely what I've observed among traders who work in virtual and actual teams. As noted earlier, there is simply too much information in different markets across different time frames for any one person to process fully in breadth and depth. In team environments, information bandwidths are expanded and creative processes of idea generation are enhanced. Like the medical students, successful traders review the mass of information in front of them and compare notes. They figure out what to focus on in markets by understanding what their teammates are focusing on. If everyone on the team thinks that an unemployment report is a game changer for a central bank, that means that I cannot afford to treat it lightly. I am far more likely to feel prepared for the day's trading if I have processed market information in multiple ways with different peers. Looking at charts, reading research reports, tracking data and original research, and consulting with experts in related fields provides a well-rounded preparation that, as in medical school, is more likely to stick in our minds when we're tested.

Trading teams, like study teams, also serve a vital support function. Members keep each other focused and productive, but they also have fun together, ensuring that trading never becomes too stressful. Indeed, that was one of the more fascinating findings from my medical school observations: study teams took breaks together; they didn't just study together. Keeping each other fresh was a huge part of their productivity during long study sessions. As a result, those working in teams tended to have a much more positive—and constructive—mindset than those working solo, who were more likely to be overwhelmed. Because of my experience at the medical school, I quickly appreciated that *the very structure of the workplace meaningfully impacts the psychology of traders.* Encountering more market information and processing it in different modalities led to a noticeable sense of mastery and self-confidence that made it easier to weather inevitable drawdowns.

Later in my career, when I worked full time as a trading coach for hedge funds based in Connecticut, I held many meetings with teams after trading hours over craft beer and bites to eat. The day's review became a social occasion and an opportunity to celebrate successes. This built the morale of team members—which in turn led to improved trading performance. The energized teams with the best outlooks simply put more quality time into preparation and were the most likely to be on the front foot in terms of acting on their ideas.

> How we pursue our work shapes our mindsets. Our trading psychology is a reflection of the trading business we create—and it contributes to the growth of that business.

Think of a basketball coach's work with a team; think of my work with the medical school study groups and the trading teams. The most effective coaching is embedded in the performance environment, helping define the culture of a team and an organization. It was when I left the comfortable confines of my faculty office and actually joined students' classes and study sessions that I was able to truly understand what goes into performance success. My role was not to tell medical students what to do. My role was to understand what the most successful students do and help the others replicate that success. As we shall see in our investigation of solution-focused psychology, some of the best help comes from reverse-engineering success and doing more and more of what works.

Trading psychology isn't something we have; it's something we do

At any given time, we may or may not pay attention to our trading psychology. When things are going well in markets, we may not focus on our frame of mind at all. When we lose money and start to actually feel our loss, suddenly we can become concerned with our mindset. This is not how true performance professionals operate. The winning boxer, Olympic sprinter, or Broadway actress always works to maintain a peak frame of mind. Indeed, practice sessions are not just for skill rehearsal. They are opportunities to sustain the positive, achievement-oriented mindset needed to operate at peak levels during actual competition.

In that sense, performance psychology is something successful performers are always doing. *They continually hone their focus and enthusiasm, so that every step of preparation and every phase of performance becomes a psychological workout.*

Consider the professional weightlifter. Every workout is an opportunity to push limits and build mastery and confidence. Every meal is an opportunity to build the body the right way. *All of us, all the time, are shaping our performance psychology, whether we're aware of it or not.* If we prepare for trading and review performance in poorly planned, random ways, can we really expect to achieve the focused mindset needed for consistent success?

Case study: the power of the calendar

When I began work at a large hedge fund, one of my first steps was to set up an appointment with one of the firm's most successful portfolio managers. I went to his online calendar to identify possible meeting days and times. I noticed that the times were only at certain periods of the day—never right before the market open, for example, or during the first hour of equities trading in NY—and the times were quoted in 15-minute increments. I later inquired about this practice, and the portfolio manager explained to me that his calendar was one of his ways of organizing his trading process. Every period of the day was accounted for and used purposefully, from the time spent eating breakfast and doing morning exercise to meetings and calls with valued analysts and colleagues.

His advice stuck with me over the years: "If it's not in your calendar, it's not part of your process." By breaking his day into 15-minute periods and making each period count, he ensured that he operated at peak productivity. *What most struck me was that this way of organizing his time was also his way of sustaining a productive, positive mindset.* Every day was a kind of workout, pushing him to operate at peak productivity. For that same reason, each day was an exercise in positive psychology, placing him in control of the activities most important to his business.

THE ROLE OF PSYCHOLOGY IN TRADING SUCCESS

One of the most common complaints I hear among traders is that they spend too much time staring at screens. That is their way of saying that their time is not organized and efficient. Because they don't have a prioritized schedule that structures their search for opportunity, they don't experience the same level of control and mastery as the portfolio manager—and that impacts their subsequent trading.

What we do and how we do it helps define how we feel about our performance and how much energy we will bring to generating ideas and managing positions. How we *do* what we do has a tremendous impact on how we *feel* about what we do. *The best way to work on our trading psychology is to work on how we work.* The message of positive psychology is that we will feel our best when we draw upon our best.

Sadly, much of the focus on trading psychology is reactive, not proactive. We work on ourselves only when things have gone wrong and our state of mind has interfered with our best decision making. A proactive approach, grounded in positive psychology, is that everything we do in markets—and indeed in life—is an opportunity to build a focused, energized mindset.

During my sessions with traders, we will sometimes intensively review their best trades (or best periods of trading) and identify what they did at those times to maintain their optimal trading psychology. This typically consists of recounting the leadup to the trades, including what they did in their personal lives, as a way of uncovering their best mindset practices.

For example, my normal wake-up time is 4:15 am. If I sleep in, even just until 5 am, I feel rushed in my day's preparation. That rushed feeling starts my day in the reactive mode and that carries over to my trading. Conversely, waking up early gives me time for family, exercise, and reviewing markets and market data in a leisurely way.

Some of my best ideas germinate while I'm in that leisurely mode. I rarely generate good ideas and plans when I feel pressed for time. Mark

Douglas, in *The Disciplined Trader*, identifies an "energy loop" that connects our inner and outer environments.[70] He explains that a great deal of what we experience in our world is "shaped from the inside."[71] When our inner environment is in turmoil, there is no way we can be sensitive to the nuances of what is happening around us. In his text *Mindset Secrets for Winning*, Mark Minervini challenges us to look at our lives—our relationships, our health, our happiness, our success—and identify what that tells us about our beliefs.[72] Like Douglas, he is pointing out that what occurs in our lives is a reflection of what goes on within us.

How we trade inevitably reflects what is going on in our lives. In their unique book *The Lifecycle Trade*, Eve Boboch, Kathy Donnelly, Eric Krull, and Kurt Daill emphasize that unusual trading success comes from trading 'super growth' stocks. In the afterword to that text, I note that "successful money management pushes us to refine ourselves: to maximize our strengths, minimize weaknesses, and find the motivations beyond the push and pull of ego that can sustain a happy and fulfilling career."[73] Without a life grounded in 'super growth,' we're unlikely to achieve super returns.

When I work with traders, I sometimes have them track their daily routines in detail, along with their energy level, alertness, and emotional well-being. It's a great way to identify the things we do that keep us psychologically fit. In that context, even the breaks we take during the trading day can be valuable in keeping us energized and forward-looking, contributing to our performance.

Everything we do has psychological implications. For better or for worse, we're always shaping our performance mindset when we make choices with our time. Consider the traders who tell me that they're spending too much time in front of screens watching price action. They aren't actively scanning for opportunity, and they're not in a problem-solving mode of figuring out how markets are moving and why. Rather, they passively watch their trades and the moment-to-moment ups and downs of their P/L. They recognize that they're not utilizing their time well, but they're not always aware that they are actively reinforcing a passive trading psychology. In the ideal world, every element of our trading process contributes to our best frame of mind for performance.

> How we start our day creates a mindset that resonates throughout the day. If we are active, purpose-full, and productive, we internalize a psychology of competence and achievement. What we do, we internalize.

In their book *Complete Guide to Trading Psychology*, Steve and Holly Burns emphasize that our focus is a trading edge and that it is essential that traders create filters that tune out the noise of markets and life.[74] Indeed, they point out that it is just as important to filter out noise as to detect market signals.[75] This is because "Calmness comes from trading inside your current comfort zone," even as we gradually extend that comfort zone with adaptations to new market edges.[76] Steven Goldstein, in *Mastering the Mental Game of Trading*, stresses "the power of purpose" in shaping how we trade and how well we trade.[77] Purpose is our life's filter, either focusing our efforts or diluting them. When we are focused, we are most open to the intuitions that underlie great trade ideas. Goldstein points out that long before we know something, we *kind of* know it.[78] That signal is only apparent if we can tune out noise—and if we are fully committed to a lifestyle that is relatively noise-free.

As Mark Minervini points out, there is an important difference between interest and commitment.[79] A genuine commitment summons the will to persist; mere interest can be diverted by anything that seems more interesting at the time. Lamothe illustrates how checklists—before and after trading—can structure our commitments to success.[80] All traders are interested in succeeding in markets; how many are living lives of purposeful commitment? How many of us can truly say that we follow *life checklists*?

How traders coach themselves

The majority of traders, of course, don't have a coach onsite to help them learn from successes and setbacks and reinforce best practices. Indeed, many traders are not part of teams and don't have ready access to the psychological benefits of teamwork. *That means that most traders need to serve as their own trading coaches and create processes that sustain peak performance mindsets.* Each day, traders must fulfill multiple roles if they are to achieve consistent profitability.

An analogy might be the entrepreneurial chef who opens his own restaurant. Preparing the daily menu and the meals is only one part of the restaurant's success. The chef also has to supervise others in the kitchen as well as the wait staff; has to greet customers and maintain positive relations; has to order the right ingredients at the right times; has to maintain the books and stay on top of income and expenses; has to develop and implement effective advertising campaigns; and much more. *By necessity, startup businesses require multitasking.* For many traders, trading *is* their entrepreneurial startup. They not only have to stay focused on markets and trading processes; they also must be immersed in researching and developing new trading edges, as well as reviewing performance and adapting to new market conditions. Every entrepreneurial startup is intimately involved in performance *and* requires standing back from performance to engage in self-coaching and the development of the business.

Trading psychology is shaped by this self-coaching function. *Every successful independent trader must be a successful trading coach.* It is *how* we review markets, *how* we generate ideas, *how* we review our trading, and *how* we pursue improvements in our work that shape our mindsets. In that sense, we are always doing trading psychology: sometimes in planned, intentional ways; sometimes reactively and impulsively.

A simple question we might ask is, "If an Olympic athlete pursued their sport with the rigor that I bring to my trading, would they be likely to win a medal?" Rarely can traders answer this question in the affirmative. We focus on our psychology when it turns negative. We do not consistently work to internalize an ongoing winning mindset. In a very real sense, trading is our garden. If we're not regularly watering and fertilizing, it cannot flourish. Many, many individual traders fail, not because they don't put attention into their trading, but because that attention isn't conducted in a way that fertilizes their psychology. To reemphasize: For better or for worse, *every trader is ultimately their own coach.*

In his interview in the first *Market Wizards* book, Dr. Van Tharp points to five psychological factors that account for trading success: a well-rounded life, a positive attitude, the motivation to succeed, a lack of conflict, and taking personal responsibility for trading outcomes.[81] Notice that one cannot sustain these elements of success without active self-management. Aziz and Baehr observe that trading is a "nightmare for perfectionists," as losses are inevitable in an uncertain environment.[82] This is why Yvan Byeagee points to the acceptance of uncertainty as the hallmark of successful trading. He emphasizes, "To do well as a trader, one needs not just a surface-level acceptance of uncertainty but a profound, soul-deep embrace of it."[83] The term "soul-deep embrace" is important: If we are not actively coaching ourselves and preparing ourselves for the ups and downs of performance, it is all too easy to lapse into distraction and frustration. And how do we ensure that our embrace is soul-deep? Aziz and Baehr emphasize that it is vital to "define yourself as a trader," so that losses can help us learn and grow and not become the baggage of self-betrayal.[84]

A useful exercise is to assign yourself a trading psychology P/L each day, grading yourself on how well you've proactively built and sustained a peak performance state of mind and body. Yes, we review our trading daily. How often do we truly review how well we're coaching ourselves?

Case study: the life of a successful trader

Ed was a successful portfolio manager at a large macro hedge fund. He led a relatively small team, but his trading was anything but small. At any time, he deployed hundreds of millions of dollars to ideas across global currency, rates, and equity markets. His team largely stayed in touch virtually through regular chats, video meetings, and phone calls. This meant that Ed could often work from home. As we became comfortable with one another, he invited me to his home office to work with him in real time. It was a rare opportunity to see a master at work.

What immediately struck me was the modesty of Ed's home office. I had expected to see dozens of open screens, a massive phone bank, and large piles of research reports and charts. All of that, Ed explained, created distraction. His goal was focus.

The early morning started with a quick overview of markets, but quickly transitioned to a vigorous exercise routine (alternating between running and strength training on weight machines) and a healthy breakfast. The breakfast, which provided quality time with Laurie, his wife, was high in protein, low fat, and included one of his favorite juices and a small amount of coffee. During the breakfast, he set aside the phone and there was no checking of prices. Laurie, a market maker at an investment bank, talked about the workday ahead following an evening of volatile price action overseas. Ed agreed it would be a busy day and suggested that they make reservations for dinner at one of their favorite restaurants. I was struck by how focused they were on one another.

After breakfast, I asked Ed about his diet. He explained to me that he was preparing for a distance race in a few weeks and had to keep himself in shape. Quite literally, he was always in training, making sure he got the right amount of sleep, ate the right foods, and engaged in the right balance of challenging exercises. Indeed, it seemed to me that, in his morning routine, Ed was more concerned with this training (and his marriage) than with his trading. Yes, he kept an eye on his positions, but he was particularly focused on optimizing his time apart from markets.

Only after Ed finished breakfast did he truly immerse himself in the business of trading. His prep time followed a routine similar to his morning workout. He began by speaking with each of his team members and catching up on information they had gathered in the past day. When something struck him, he jotted it down in a notetaking app shared with the team members. After that, he selectively went through his many emails, downloading information from valued sources, including respected sell-side researchers he had met through Laurie. He scanned these reports for nuggets of information that piqued his interest and added notes about these to the team app. Finally, he reached out to his closest colleagues and updated views on economic developments, global markets, and ideas in progress. Again, notes from these interactions were added to the team app.

What particularly impressed me during this process was the efficiency and intensity of Ed's conversations and his detail orientation in asking questions and taking notes. He came across more as a researcher than a trader. He was assembling a complex puzzle, and he was working as intensely on the idea generation process as on his early morning workouts.

When this work was completed, Ed jumped to a team meeting before markets became active. During the meeting, I realized that each team member had been going through their own version of Ed's morning process. Each of them had spoken with colleagues, gathered and collected research, and tracked the movement of assets across markets and regions. Each of them also had added notes to the team app, so that everyone's input was readily available to everyone else. The resulting team meeting was truly a brainstorming across all the notes from all the team members. The constant focus was, "What does this mean?" Ideas to take positions, add to or reduce existing positions, increase or decrease risk-taking, and adjust the portfolio were freely shared, with the goal of reaching a consensus.

From my front row seat, I could see that everyone was highly engaged, everyone had a voice, and everyone pushed themselves to bring as much value to the meetings as possible. The meeting concluded with concrete action items that team members felt strongly about. All in all, it was an impressive display of creativity in action: the team emerged from its deliberations with ideas and action items it did not start with.

Midday, the team circled back for a short meeting to review market action and update ideas and observations. Once again, these had been added to the app and were readily available during the morning trade. For instance, one of the team members noted an apparent unwinding of positions in a crowded commodities trade and suggested the possibility that this was overdone, creating potential value. The theme of the midday session was, "Has anything changed?" Everyone's head was on a swivel, scanning for both threats and opportunities.

The team's final meeting at the end of the day began with, "What did we learn today?" There was a detailed review of actions that had been taken, what had been done well, and what needed attention for improvement. Ed made a particular effort to single out each team member's valuable contributions for the day. This meeting had a very different tone from the previous ones. Everyone brought their favorite beverage to the session and the trading review was interspersed with anecdotes and lighthearted chat about the evening's plans. It was clear that this was a bonding period as well as a time to work on performance. Ed explained to me that it was important that the teamwork always conclude the day with team building.

After that, there was very little focus on markets as Ed and Laurie went out to meet friends and enjoy dinner. Ed explained that the lifestyle of a money manager does not always allow for quantity of time together, so he and Laurie needed to make extra efforts to create *quality* time. This was especially important because they were planning to have children and needed to make sure their personal and professional lives were in order before taking on this new commitment.

THE ROLE OF PSYCHOLOGY IN TRADING SUCCESS

I left the day of observation feeling exhausted. It felt to me as though the entire day had been a continuous period of being switched on. There was no time-wasting; every activity had a purpose. I recognized that, for Ed and the team, trading psychology was much more than an attitude about risk or a level of confidence about trades. The usual bromides about emotional control and discipline didn't seem to apply. *The trading psychology of a very successful market participant was truly a performance psychology—and every part of the day was designed to optimize outcomes.* From the early morning workouts to prepare for the distance race to the quality time at home and the enhanced intellectual environment created by sharing information in real time, Ed was living the psychology he needed for peak trading performance. He truly was *doing* his trading psychology, even when he was not trading.

Postscript: Shortly after spending time with the team, I received a call from Ed. He had heard about a meteorologist with an interest in financial markets who might want to join a macro team. For a while Ed had been wanting to expand his involvement in commodities and this seemed like an intriguing possibility. He asked if I could interview the meteorologist, share my impressions regarding the team, and see if a fit might be there. This, I realized, is what excited me about working in the financial world. It wasn't an endless series of conversations about FOMO and blowing through one's stops. It was part of a high-performance lifestyle, in which everyone shared in the quest to be the best they could be. In that sense, it was no different from being part of a championship basketball team or an elite military unit. Positive psychology was woven into daily performance. When not engaged in the day's business, there was engagement in building the business.

While the trader entering the field solo can (and must) coach themselves, in truth the psychology of trading is so much more than the psychology of beginning retail traders. Just as with winning basketball teams and crack military units, the optimal performance psychology is developed and maintained by surrounding oneself with peers who are dedicated to successful performance and who are living that focus. It is when we are part of high-performing teams that we internalize the attitudes and skills of peak performance. *If performance is not embedded in our lifestyle, it never truly becomes part of us.* Everything we do can be an opportunity to make ourselves better. When we collaborate with peers who are devoted to great achievements, we nurture greatness within us. Even if we are trading solo, we can participate in networks of colleagues who push each other to continually learn, improve, and reach their ideals.

Ayn Rand once observed that the most heroic form of devotion occurs when our actions draw upon our capacity for independent thought. Positive psychology blossoms in environments of dynamic creativity. Ari Kiev, in *The Mental Strategies of Top Traders*, points out that the strategic trader is a creative thinker, capable of thinking outside the box.[85] Tom Hougaard refers to the ideal trading mindset as being one that is "flexible in the extreme."[86] "When markets change, rigid discipline keeps you doing the wrong things," I stressed in *Trading Psychology 2.0*.[87] "We can only master the future," I pointed out, "if we embrace the fact that the present is temporary."[88] It is precisely because edges come and go in markets that we need to sustain lifestyles that keep us at our peak, always ready to learn and adapt. In describing "the ten tasks of top trading," Van Tharp, Ph.D. and Hank Pruden, Ph.D. start with "daily self-analysis."[89] If we don't begin our trading with flexible thought and an open mind, we set ourselves up for reactive decision making.

When coaching embraces individual psychology

To this point, we've examined psychology and performance in team contexts. Interestingly, the great majority of medical students at my school in Syracuse—like the great majority of traders at firms where I've worked—chose to meet with me for individual sessions. *They were progressing in their development and they were benefiting from teamwork, but they still experienced significant emotional challenges.* That is because each of us comes to life's challenges with our own histories, our own past conflicts, and our own habit patterns. Recall Tom Hougaard's insight that doing what comes naturally in markets is what loses us money.[90] If we come to markets with patterns of thought, emotion, and behavior that are natural for us, but not suited to peak performance, only concerted work on ourselves can position us for success, as markets are otherwise guaranteed to push our buttons.

It is the role of individual coaching—and sometimes ongoing counseling and therapy—to help us identify the patterns that interfere with our success and make changes to those in real time. An analogy would be marriage, where divorce rates are highest in the first year following the wedding. Living together in a committed relationship is very different from life as a single person. Inevitably, members of a couple push each other's buttons and the result can be conflict and eventual alienation. When we enter an entirely new performance arena, such as trading, we experience similar frictions. New challenges and demands have an uncanny way of triggering our unmet needs, opening the door to the all-too-familiar fear and greed.

As we've seen, because markets are ever-changing, the challenges they pose can shift greatly. The demands of a low-volatility environment are quite different from those of high-volatility markets. The demands of risk management and the pursuit of opportunity are not the same if we're operating in drawdown or with a solid P/L cushion.

The role of coaching is to help traders adapt to ever-shifting circumstances in constructive ways and not react out of mindless habit. Because markets can change quickly and profoundly, Steve and Holly Burns note that there are two kinds of traders: those who are humble and "those who will be humbled."[91] An important part of our development as traders is learning to be fallible.[92] This is why Hougaard emphasizes that "the best loser wins" in financial markets, explaining that "It is not what you know that kills you. It is what you think you know, but which just isn't so, that kills you."[93] He cites a newspaper article describing London hedge fund trader Greg Coffey as "humble and arrogant in equal measure—the perfect trader."[94]

We need the self-confidence to believe that we are capable of distinctive success, and we need the humility that allows us to lose well. Dr. Ari Kiev notes that winning traders don't display a single, common trading style, but all have "a capacity for conviction... without letting their ego get in the way."[95] As Gary Dayton, Psy.D. explains, our problem is not our emotions, but our tendency to become "fused" with our emotions.[96] Do losing trades stimulate and challenge us to learn and adapt, or do we 'fuse' with them and unwittingly invite anger, frustration, and a sense of defeat? This is the challenge posed by Denise Shull in her insightful text *Market Mind Games*: sometimes what we feel is mere impulse and sometimes it represents the "implicit knowledge" of intuition.[97] She teaches that if a feeling appears with urgency, we can suspect that it represents an impulse, but if it comes "out of nowhere" in a state of calm, it may very well represent what we know deep down inside.[98] Our positive psychology is one that operates in that state of calm knowing, which means that our trading has to be mindful, not impulsive.[99]

> **Our learning curves in trading are shaped in part by the life issues we bring to our trading.**

Successful trading coaches have developed a wealth of methods to help us operate at our best in situations that otherwise can bring out our worst. Markets have an uncanny way of triggering unresolved issues we may have over success, failure, safety, threat, and so much more. In a recent TraderFeed blog post, I proposed that each one of us is Superman.[100] Underneath our average, Clark Kent appearance are superpowers that enable us to do good, but also super vulnerabilities that are our kryptonite. Key to our trading success is understanding, accepting, and leveraging who we are beneath our average exterior: the greatness and the weakness. So much of peak performance is learning to access our superpowers while avoiding our kryptonite.

Case study: coaching traders to grow their size

Proprietary trading firms are unique environments that pose distinct challenges. At a hedge fund, a portfolio manager's compensation is typically based upon a salary plus a guaranteed bonus. The salary is enough to cover living expenses in areas like New York and London, but that's about it. The bonus is a fixed percentage of money earned during the year, and that is what provides the bulk of a successful trader's income. So, for instance, if the portfolio manager (PM) is paid 15% of annual trading income and achieves an 8% return on a $100 million portfolio, the performance bonus (before expenses) would be $1,200,000. As a result, managers at hedge funds are incentivized to make as much money as they can, but they also know they cannot lose significant money.

In our example, the manager's stop level might be 7%, which means that they stop trading for the year (and risk being let go from the firm) if they lose $7,000,000. *The psychological challenge is that the PM needs to aggressively pursue opportunity at the same time that they proactively manage risk.* The appeal of a million dollar-plus income is balanced by the threat of being fired. The successful manager is one who makes consistent money and thus merits higher and higher allocations of capital to manage. Those allocations, in turn, provide the funds for hiring and expanding a team, growing the business significantly.

At a proprietary trading firm, there often is no fixed salary. Instead, one might be given a monthly draw against future income, much as in certain sales positions. If there are losses, the trader risks losing their position, but there is a real press to make money because you only eat what you kill. The portfolio manager can afford to have a flat period of performance and run small size in an uncertain environment, because they always have the salary to cushion them. Flat performance at a prop firm can mean no income at all, especially since prop firms typically deduct overhead from earnings. A flat month thus becomes a losing month after expenses. This dynamic results in extra pressure for the prop trader to grow their size and increase their earnings.

These business realities mean that coaching portfolio managers to grow their risk-taking can be a different challenge from coaching short-term prop traders to bump up their sizing. Built into the DNA of hedge funds is an emphasis upon diversification. Taking more risk often means broadening out one's trading and finding uncorrelated streams of returns.

I recently met with a portfolio manager in Singapore who achieved success in his core trading and now was ready to manage more capital and take more risk. Most of our conversation focused on finding new areas of opportunity by emphasizing markets and strategies that were overlooked by the largest institutions. For that manager, *taking more risk meant taking new risk*: growing trading size was a function of expanding idea generation and trade structuring/execution.

The prop trader, often working solo and trading shorter time frames, tends to define growing size in terms of sizing up his or her existing trading. Instead of trading 1,000 shares of a stock, they will now trade 1,500 or 2,000. *This creates higher volatility of P/L, which can be destabilizing for the trader's mindset.* The hedge fund manager, finding uncorrelated opportunities, can actually dampen volatility by managing more capital. This is not typically the case for individual, independent traders and proprietary traders. Portfolio managers can also manage the volatility of sizing up by creating hedges (sometimes in the options space). Individual traders, focused on directional trading with a stop, often lack experience with hedging and portfolio construction. As a result of these dynamics, my coaching conversations with portfolio managers and teams are much less about the emotional repercussions of growing size and much more about creatively deploying additional capital to improve risk-adjusted returns. My discussions with solo traders often focus on creating sustainable frameworks for bumping up size so that the increased volatility of P/L will not result in increased emotional volatility.

As I explained in *Trading Psychology 2.0*, "Making sure losses are planned and known ensures that we can live with drawdown and have plenty of dry ammunition for coming back."[101] At the same time, the individual trader needs to properly manage opportunity as well as risk: failing to take proper advantage of a favorable odds situation can be as much of a threat to success as failing to manage risk during drawdown.[102]

> Proper bet sizing allows for winning the game,
> and it allows for staying in the game.

As it happens, the money manager in Singapore wanted to deploy his additional risk in markets that were known to be less liquid and less efficient. He knew that money managers in Asia have to focus on the largest countries because of the amounts of capital they manage. Thus, they would trade China and Japan, and spend much less time with smaller countries, such as those in Southeast Asia. Our discussions became a blend of work on process to identify when uncorrelated currency markets were mispriced and work on sizing and hedging in the event of outsized adverse moves during periods of thin trading. The portfolio manager found that he needed to cultivate information networks in each of the countries where he traded to better understand economic data, central bank developments, and overall market sentiment. Hearing distinct themes from his networks gave him the confidence to expand his risk-taking. Much of our meetings focused on how he assembled this information to achieve true conviction in an idea.

Successful coaching requires an understanding of the challenges facing the trader and how these are likely to impact emotions and teamwork. When it comes to building trading psychology, one size cannot fit all. The individual trader needing to size up his or her trading must find a way of ensuring that increased P/L volatility does not bring undue emotional volatility. *That means we must habituate to one level of sizing before bumping up in sustainable increments.* The emotional need to trade big can undercut the developmental need to get bigger. A useful rule is to not bump up trade sizing until one is consistently profitable at the existing level of risk. Growing our trading gradually, steadily, and organically is the best self-coaching of all, because it is preventive: avoiding disruptions of trading before they can occur.

> Psychological consistency is the
> underpinning of trading consistency.

In a recent mentoring session run by Jeff Holden at SMB Capital, Jeff walked traders through price and volume patterns that occur when oversold markets can't go lower and overbought ones can't sustain their strength. He illustrated how the ability to enter reversal trades quickly and decisively dramatically improves the risk/reward of the trade, transforming an average setup into an 'A' trade. With this superior risk/reward, the trader has more room to size up the position, getting bigger without risking debilitating losses. It was a powerful reminder that trading success is often found in the nuances of execution and position management. *We get bigger, not just by having better ideas, but by implementing them better, transforming good trades into great ones.* If we are not in the right frame of mind to pounce on promising trades when they show up, we will miss our most promising opportunities.

Now imagine that the trader wanting to increase their risk-taking and size up their positions is also dealing with their own psychological issues: a failing romantic relationship; a history of struggling with authority figures in a dysfunctional home; a tendency to become distracted and negatively self-focused when under stress. In such cases, the coaching of traders becomes similar to the counseling of students that I performed at the medical school. The pressures of performance meld with the pressures we bring to our work to create unique challenges. It is for this reason that our pursuit of optimal trading psychology must blend an understanding of our distinctive personal issues as well as the general challenges posed by particular market conditions and trading strategies.

In *The Psychology of Trading*, I pointed out that our trading patterns typically reflect our emotional patterns and are anchored to particular states of mind and body.[103] Although it may feel as though we have many problems, typically we just have one or two core issues that repeat themselves across life circumstances. Our goal is to trade mindfully and purposefully, not reactively once those core issues are triggered. Dr. Gary Dayton, in *Trade Mindfully*, explains that successful trading requires "a different kind of thinking," in which the goal is not to eliminate emotions but to expand our awareness of them.[104] All of us bring our baggage and biases to markets. The goal is to become a keen observer of these, standing apart from our impulses, so that we can make the best-planned decisions possible.

Coaching ourselves to success: assessment

The interplay of performance challenges and personal issues that can impact performance means that the very first step in working on ourselves is a thorough assessment. We need to understand the degree to which our challenges are ones that we bring to trading vs. ones that are unique to our development as traders. The single most important assessment question you must address before working on yourself is: "Is the issue I'm facing something that has impacted my life before trading and that interferes with my current life outside of trading?" Recall the Superman analogy from the TraderFeed blog post. Each of us brings to trading superpowers and super vulnerabilities. The question you want to pose if you run into challenges with your trading psychology is whether the problems you are experiencing are normal, expectable ones that occur for all developing traders or whether those problems are part of the super vulnerabilities that many of us bring to markets. *In other words, is this a situation in which you can work on your psychology by improving your trading, or is it a situation where psychological work is needed to help with trading?* This is the first question traders must ask as they begin their efforts at performance improvement.

For instance, imagine that I was plagued by self-doubts as a young adult and then later in life when I was dating. Those doubts now lead me to be unusually harsh on myself, criticizing myself whenever something goes wrong. This occurred when I was a student in college and has occurred in work settings. Now, as a developing trader, I find myself wrestling with the same self-doubts and acting as my own worst critic. This leads me to shut down after losing money, preventing me from acting on the opportunity that could turn my trading around. Clearly, simply addressing trading issues (accept losses, stick with trading processes) won't be sufficient to change my performance. I need to tackle the much larger issue of how I process adverse events in my life. Conversely, if I've been relatively confident and constructive in dealing with setbacks in my life prior to trading, it will be much easier to leverage coaching by applying the resilience of my daily life to my learning curve as a trader. We cannot properly address and improve our performance psychology unless we diagnose where our performance problems are coming from.

> As traders, we are like high-performance cars. At times, warning lights go off on our dashboards. Those are not problems. They are opportunities to diagnose a vulnerability and prevent it from becoming a serious problem.

In *Enhancing Trader Performance*, I emphasize that "What we do not envision, we cannot prepare for."[105] Our emotions are our dashboards, alerting us to the potential for disruption to our trading. By rehearsing these emotions and our best responses in advance, we prepare ourselves to act on our warning lights and engage in preventive maintenance rather than high-priced repairs. The goal, as Ari Kiev points out, is to live outside our "limiting constraints," creating a visionary goal that is an effective counterweight to our past programming.[106] We are much less likely to fall victim to our constraints if we're able to stand apart from them and respond as observers. Every potential disruption of our trading is an opportunity to activate our visionary goals and trade with mindful awareness.[107]

Case study: overcoming our psychological baggage

Lee was a promising trader who came from a difficult upbringing. He left home at an early age, entered the military, and met and married someone who helped him establish a stable life. Along the way, he ran into problems in his work, usually as the result of conflicts with his superiors. Lee had grown up with a harsh, distant father who had an alcohol problem. All too frequently, Lee was punished for not meeting his father's expectations. Even after he left his childhood home, he found it difficult to deal with corrective feedback from those he worked with. His stint in the military was extremely helpful to his development, as it pushed him to accept criticism constructively. When Lee began trading, however, he experienced unusual frustration during losing trades. His frustration often boiled over, putting him on tilt in his trading. To his credit, he was able to identify that the feelings he was having when losing money were similar to the ones he experienced as a child growing up. Only now, it was the market pushing his buttons, not his father. I realized quickly that solely focusing on improving Lee's trading process would not eliminate the disruptions caused by what he was bringing to markets.

To return to our Superman analogy, positive psychology teaches us that we have superpowers as well as super weaknesses. Indeed, one of the most powerful ways of overcoming our vulnerabilities is to ground ourselves in our strengths. This is a hallmark of an approach to psychological change that we will explore shortly: solution-focused work. *In the solution-focused mode, we look for occasions when problems are not occurring, because those are often ones in which we are tapping into our superpowers—often without realizing it.*

When I heard about Lee's problems in trading, I immediately asked him why he didn't melt down in basic training and get himself discharged from the military. He explained that he had often considered dropping out, but he liked his fellow trainees and felt a responsibility to help them get through. This made sense to me, as Lee had previously mentioned how important it was to him to protect his younger sister from his father when he was growing up. *Lee could be undone by his frustrations, but his loyalty and commitment to those he cared about were his strongest motivations.* His problems with frustrated, tilt trading melted away when he joined a virtual group of developing traders. His commitment to helping them brought out the best in him and their support buffered the normal frustrations of his learning curve.

Strikingly, what was best for Lee's psychology was best for his trading. No amount of advice regarding discipline and accepting loss could have substituted for tapping into his greatest strength and finding inner reserves of resilience.

Positive psychology teaches us that the best way to tackle our super vulnerabilities is to tap into our superpowers. In a sense, Lee's problem was not his frustration, but his lack of awareness of his relationship strengths. If our superpowers are as clear as our problems, we can often find our way out. *The purpose of assessment is to understand not only our shortcomings, but also the strengths that can balance them.*

> **Positive psychology is an affirmation that we are bigger than our problems.**

When we review our periods of best performance and greatest success, we discover the best within us—and, so often, that turns out to be the most promising path for navigating our challenges. Mike Bellafiore, in *One Good Trade*, identifies an important reason why traders fail: "they don't love trading."[108] The key word here is "love." We love something because it speaks to us; it resonates with us; it brings out the best in us. Loving to make money is different from loving trading.

As we saw with Lee, our best trading is grounded in the best of who we are. That means that it is not enough to cope with and adapt to market changes and uncertainties. We actually have to *love* those changes and uncertainties, and love the ever-changing processes of finding opportunity.

Yes, we need to assess our vulnerabilities and be aware of them. Equally so, we need to assess our greatest strengths and passions and draw upon them daily in our trading processes. It is necessary, but not sufficient, to contain our losses. Success requires "having the guts to be your best trader": to know when and how to press our advantages.[109] That is impossible if we haven't thoroughly assessed our superpowers as well as our vulnerabilities. *Self-assessment precedes self-awareness: we cannot know our strengths if we have not taken a detailed inventory of our successes.*

Practical takeaways from Chapter Three

1. Successful trading requires the ability to sustain a constructive mindset and process large amounts of information under conditions of pressure and time constraint. Collaboration with dedicated peers allows us to process more information in a greater variety of ways, and it also helps us stay constructively focused. Often, we can best work on our trading psychology by working closely with others.
2. Positive trading psychology is something we actively do, not just something we possess. How we structure our time can place us in greater control during periods of uncertainty and ensure that we stay focused upon priorities. A well-defined trading process builds a sense of mastery, freeing us to focus on markets and their challenges.
3. Successful traders coach themselves. Through regular performance review, they identify what they do well and what needs improvement. Their continual efforts at honing their craft, making small changes regularly, allow them to evolve meaningfully over time. When we look at the daily activities of successful traders, we find that self-improvement is a common theme, even during non-trading time: it is a lifestyle.
4. The emotional challenges we've experienced earlier in our lives can intrude on our trading and trading psychology, leading us to trade

in unwanted ways and repeat our mistakes. Positive psychology shows us that we can overcome these negative patterns by playing to our strengths and tapping into motivations stronger than our past patterns.

CHAPTER FOUR

CHANGING OUR TRADING PSYCHOLOGY

Thus far, we've seen that our psychology is an important determinant of our trading performance. In this chapter, we will explore strategies for improving our trading psychology and coaching ourselves to ever greater levels of success.

How we change our trading psychology: immediacy

There are many psychological approaches to making life changes. How do we know which methods might be of help to us in breaking negative patterns of thought and behavior and building new, positive ones? Interestingly, when my colleagues and I at SUNY Upstate Medical University reviewed the research literature detailing the methods and outcomes of counseling and psychotherapy, one particular finding stood out: *At an underlying process level, all forms of psychological helping are doing the same thing.*[110]

That sounds implausible on the surface. After all, the behavioral therapist who teaches breathing techniques to assist a patient in handling anxiety is different from the cognitive therapist who helps people with their anxiety-producing thought processes, and both differ from the analytic therapist who helps clients rework the anxieties from unresolved childhood experience.

What we discovered was that successful therapy consists of three common processes:

1. building a relationship through empathic connection;
2. heightening emotional experience through recollections of powerful events and/or structured exercises; and
3. introducing new understandings, experiences, and skills during the heightened state that enable the person to view their situation—and deal with it—differently and constructively.

In the textbook we wrote summarizing our findings, we used the term "translation" to describe what good therapists do: They take a person's definition of their problem, which typically leaves them stuck, and translate the problem into new terms that open the door to fresh paths forward.[iii] So, for instance, I may come to therapy feeling guilty because I'm a bad parent. During the sessions, my solution-focused therapist might ask me to relive occasions when I wasn't a bad parent and might have actually done a good job as a father. In the new emotional state of reliving my successes, I begin to appreciate my parenting strengths and become open to exercises that push me to expand my best efforts.

> **Successful change occurs when we are in heightened states of emotional experience, often because of the pain created by our habitual patterns of thinking, feeling, and acting. If our self-coaching is merely an intellectual process of performance review, it's unlikely to shake up our old patterns and open us to new ones.**

This integrative view of helping—the perspective that there are common core processes underlying all effective forms of psychological intervention—has led to innovations in training therapists, and it has led to new approaches to helping that maximize the common effective ingredients of therapies.

This perspective applies equally to coaching and to our efforts at self-improvement. It is when we *feel* our trading challenges—when we truly experience our best and worst trading—that we best process new information and skills. *For that reason, immediacy is essential to the success of our change efforts.*

The best time for coaching is when problems are fresh and we are most open to corrective feedback. That is why some of the most effective coaching occurs during halftime of basketball and football contests. As I note in *The Daily Trading Coach*, "feelings contain information."[112] The idea "is to transform feeling, not ignore it and not revel in it."[113] It is in our states of emotional experience that we can make our greatest trading mistakes and implement our greatest trading improvements.

From a positive psychology perspective, we can be as aroused by joy and success as by setbacks and frustrations. At those halftime talks, coaches don't just focus on things that have gone wrong. They emphasize what has been working and help players figure out how to build on that. If our efforts at improvement only focus on problems, we'll wind up internalizing the sense of being deficient, setting in motion a downward spiral. Ironically, it's when we're high-fiving and celebrating a win that we most want to step back and view that, too, as a teachable moment. *Our work on ourselves has the greatest impact when it is closest to performance.* Emotionless reviews of performance, conducted via journal entries on weekends and far removed from trading performance, will not be internalized deeply. The research in Syracuse taught us: *Emotion is an essential gateway to change.*

Interestingly, however, outcome research in psychology clearly identifies an even more important predictor of success in psychological change: *the quality of the relationship between therapist and client*. If there isn't a positive bond, we're unlikely to internalize what we learn from a mentor or coach. Emotion opens us to change largely because it opens us to relationship experiences. This is how children learn from parents and teachers. It's also how team members learn from mentors in work settings.

This reality poses special challenges to solo traders attempting to guide the development of their trading psychology. In one study that my colleagues at SUNY Upstate Medical University in Syracuse and I reviewed, people interested in making changes were given detailed self-help manuals that told them what to do according to evidence-based therapies. The results were mediocre at best. Without the bond of the helping relationship, even effective change methods were relatively ineffective.

When there is a good relationship, we are motivated to engage in change efforts because that is what our therapist—our 'teammate'—expects. *A good working relationship adds a degree of accountability to our work on ourselves.* This is an important reason for seeking trading buddies and mentors in communities. It is difficult to sustain a sense of urgency when we work in isolation. Recall how Lee overcame his emotionally abusive upbringing and his tilt trading: Relationships are a powerful source of motivation, creating a fresh source of emotional immediacy. Aziz and Baehr emphasize the relationship between lifestyle and trading, reflected in a community (Bear Bull Traders) that features sharing and learning among members.[114] At SMB Capital, there is a culture of calling out trades, as traders assume responsibility for fueling the success of their teammates.[115] Kiev emphasizes that the best portfolio managers exemplify leadership and teamwork and an ability to put their egos aside and empower those around them.[116]

There is yet another way in which relationships are gateways to positive change. Through our connections with others, we can see markets through their eyes, alerting us to opportunities and contributing to our positive psychology. In *Market Mind Games*, Denise Shull stresses that, for traders, it's more important to figure out what others are about to know than what they don't know. Trading success is not about eradicating feelings from our decisions, but is fueled by connecting with the thoughts and feelings of others.[117] When we see the world through the eyes of others, we broaden our awareness, stimulate new connections, and replace the negative emotions of uncertainty with the positive experience of insight. The immediacy of our connections to others prompts the shifts in state that enable us to process new information deeply. As Shull observes, this fuels our psychological capital.[118]

How we change our trading psychology: repetition

It is romantic to think of change as happening all at once as the result of a single powerful experience and insight. The reality of change processes, however, is that they are far messier. Relapse is an inevitable part of making changes. In that sense, every negative habit pattern that we have can be considered an addiction. We oscillate between denial and commitment to change, at times hitting bottom and feeling a need to change and at times operating in total denial. Motivation only gets us so far in the change process. It does spark the shifts of emotional state that can open us to new possibilities, but it's habit and repetition that cement new, positive patterns of thinking, feeling, and acting. *Once we learn a new skill or a fresh perspective, we typically need to rehearse this again and again in various life situations before it becomes a natural part of us.*

A big part of coaching our own trading psychology is setting up the conditions to practice new ways of approaching ourselves and markets. Most of us would not think of beginning the trading day without having first examined markets and scouted for opportunity. We know that performance—in any field—demands preparation. Athletic teams always warm up before a contest in order to get hot on the field. Similarly, we warm up when we get a feel for markets and mentally prepare for potential opportunities.

What traders rarely do is warm up their trading psychology. They prepare to trade, not to make themselves ready for trading. As a result, they miss the opportunities for rehearsal and repetition that would enable them to consistently trade at their best.

> We internalize what we repeatedly do; what we repeat, we become. When we practice a calm, focused mindset every day, we set the stage for calm, focused trading sessions.

Following the lead of Gary Dayton[119] and Yvan Byeagee,[120] imagine making a meditation routine a standard part of your preparation for trading. Before you look at charts, read research, and speak with colleagues, you warm up your concentration by focusing your mind on an image or a verbal mantra, sitting totally still, and making your breathing deep and regular. This is not simply a relaxation exercise. Rather, as we saw with biofeedback work, you are pursuing the 'zone' of heightened processing. How do you know if you are in that zone? What you'll find is that, when you have sustained a quiet mind for a sufficient period of time, your self-talk shuts down. You truly have a still mind. In that state, it often feels as though the world has slowed down. In reality, of course, it's you who have slowed down. You're now in a mindset where ideas can come to you. You've not only shut down the inner chatter of unmet needs and negative self-talk; *you've opened yourself to enhanced intuitive insight*. Patterns that we miss when we're fretting about missing opportunities or counting our P/L suddenly jump out at us. Markets that seem confusing can make sense if we're in the proper receptive state.

Of course, no one masters the quieting of the mind—especially in competitive circumstances—without sufficient practice. That is the role of rehearsal. If we make work on our mind state a standard part of our preparation for the trading day, that practice makes us better and better at entering the zone. We can actually measure our progress in that regard. Initially, it might take us 20 minutes or even more to get to the point of shutting down our self-talk. With practice, we can enter our zone quicker and quicker, eventually getting to the point at which we can center ourselves with a few deep breaths. That is tremendously helpful during the heat of trading.

Case study: turning peak mindset into a positive habit pattern

The ideal mindset for optimal trading is not just less emotional, but more intensely focused. When we sustain high levels of concentration, we deepen and broaden our perception. We become more sensitive to the nuances of market movements that signal those occasions when average trade opportunities show up as 'A' trades. Through practice, we can become better and better at entering and remaining in our zone. Imagine that you have a job where your role is to defuse bombs that have been placed in public places. The key to your success will be your degree of focus, as you carefully, carefully figure out how the bomb is constructed and how you can defuse it. Each action that you take will be planned; your enemy is not the bomb, but anything that would distract you and lead you to take a wrong action. It is the acute awareness of consequences that creates the intensive level of focus. The professional who has seen and worked with many different kinds of simulated bombs in their training and practice is most likely to approach an actual terrorist situation with calm mastery. Familiarity masters fear.

As mentioned in *Trading Psychology 2.0*, I create my own simulated challenges during biofeedback sessions.[121] Just as I have morning routines of working out physically (weight lifting, jogging, stretching), I engage in cognitive workouts using the Muse device, which is a wearable biofeedback unit for measuring brain waves and providing us with real-time information about our level of focus. The Muse app keeps score for me, so I know that I'm becoming more focused. I then will use imagery or absorbing music to deepen my focus and get further and further into the zone. The algorithm providing the Muse feedback indicates that there are levels of being 'in the zone.' Without the real-time feedback, it's tempting to stop our efforts once we've relaxed and turned off our worries and frustrations. *There's a considerable difference, however, between quieting negative self-talk and sustaining a highly focused state.* Indeed, active, constructive, and focused self-talk can be helpful in maintaining peak performance, as in the case of a bomb expert who talks themselves through each step of defusing a dangerous device.

This is one reason I like the rainforest exercise in the Muse app. Through headphones, we can hear rain falling in the forest. As we become distracted and our brain waves are in active mode, the rain sounds increase. When we focus and enter the zone, the rainfall slows down. Eventually, in a very quiet, focused zone, we shut down the rain altogether and begin to hear birds chirping. At the end of the exercise, the app keeps track of how much rain has fallen and how many chirps have occurred. We can set the length of our rainforest session as a way of challenging ourselves to sustain the chirps for longer and longer periods. *Quite simply, we turn the development of cognitive focus into a deliberate practice routine, working out day after day to become better and better at maintaining a state of alertness and concentration.*

My very distinct experience is that I am quicker to notice trading opportunities when I'm highly focused, and I'm quicker to pounce on those. That creates superior reward relative to risk. The subjective sense is one of seeing the market more clearly, with a greater openness to patterns that arise in real time. In the state of sustained concentration, ideas come to me as I scan relevant information and screens.

Repetition creates mastery.

In the Muse exercise, I find that it's pretty easy to slow down the sound of the rain by clearing my mind and paying close attention to my body and my breath. It's harder to sustain deep focus and bring out the sounds of the chirping birds. With consistent practice, it gradually becomes easier to access the birds and keep them chirping. The concrete feedback of the exercise makes it easy to incorporate in my trading preparation. Quite simply, I don't begin preparing for the market day—and I certainly don't begin trading—if I haven't sustained my chirps!

In the final chapter of this book, we will examine brain wave training in greater detail and learn about how feedback about blood flow to our brain's frontal cortex can help us avoid flight and fight reactions during trading. Training the brain is perhaps the most exciting—and least appreciated—frontier in sustaining a positive trading psychology.

I've found that active day traders benefit from repetition when they take breaks during the trading day and re-establish their focus. For example, as markets slow down around midday or during a period of uncertainty and distraction, traders will step away from the desk and put themselves through their meditation or biofeedback routines. The idea is to use the 'time out' from the trading day to return to an even emotional keel and a deepened state of focus and prepare for the remainder of the day. *This extension of practice to the trading day itself means that we get more and more reps and become better and better at maintaining our ideal mindset.*

Because trading breaks can take place during challenging, frustrating periods of trading, the repetition of focus skills at those times can very much assist our training in mastering our psychology. As a rule, it's helpful to not return to trading after a break until you've re-entered the zone and truly re-centered yourself. With sufficient practice, even a short break can very much shift us from distracted to focused mind frames.

On a related note, a useful practice for active traders is one that I've written about in the past: *formally dividing the trading day into two sessions.* There is a morning trading session with its own P/L and loss limit and then there is an afternoon trading session with a fresh P/L and loss limit. Between morning and afternoon sessions, there is a formal break that gives time to review morning performance, examine how markets have been trading, and develop new ideas for the afternoon. As recently mentioned, the break between morning and afternoon is also an ideal time to renew our focus by doing the meditation/biofeedback exercises. *Note how this structuring of the day creates two trading days out of one, doubling our experience and learning*. It is a great example of how we can make use of repetition to speed our learning curves. Quite literally, the developing trader who breaks the day in two gets twice as much experience in markets and in the mastery of their performance psychology.

> If we are not actively practicing optimal trading psychology, we are unlikely to achieve optimal trading performance. Repetition prevents relapse.

Much of our development as traders occurs not through motivation, but through the creation of routines that build positive habit patterns. We say that "practice makes perfect," but as James Clear describes, the reality is that practice makes habit and habit makes perfect.[122] If we can figure out the cues that trigger our worst habits, we can utilize them to interrupt our 'tilt' and establish new, constructive routines. Mindset is something we actively cultivate through repetition, sustaining our competitive focus.

What positive psychology teaches us is that there is an intimate connection between our cognitive fitness and our ability to effectively and efficiently navigate complex situations in life and markets. *When our routines include cognitive workouts, we expand our perception, but also our capacity for fulfillment*: in seeing more, we discover more and generate more fulfillment and joy. Diener and Biswas-Diener, in their research review, find that happiness contributes to our work success[123] and the quality of our relationships contributes to our happiness.[124] The challenge for our trading processes is to create happiness habits that keep us energized, inspired, and fulfilled, so that the power of repetition can not only help us undo our negative patterns, but instill new, positive ones. For the peak performer, every day should be practice in building happiness habits.

How we change our trading psychology: self-awareness

The major approaches to psychological change recognize that we cannot change a pattern of behavior if we're not aware of that pattern. When problem patterns have been with us for a while, they have become overlearned and entrenched as habits. This means that, if we do what comes naturally, we will likely fall back into our routine ways and repeat the thoughts and actions that have brought us problems. Situations can trigger our habitual negative thought patterns, our conflicted emotions, and our worst patterns of behavior and we often don't recognize what is happening until adverse consequences wake us up. The term 'wake up' is particularly appropriate in this context. The mystic philosopher G. I. Gurdjieff taught that we exist in various states of sleep, automatically moving from thought to thought, action to action.[125] The goal of self-development, he believed, was to wake from our sleep—our habit patterns—so that we can truly exercise our free will.

If we are to awaken, a first step in psychological change must be the ability to recognize our triggers as they occur. We need to become so familiar with the triggers for the patterns that interfere with our trading that we can stop ourselves from following old, destructive habits. This takes considerable practice. When we're focused on markets, we naturally tend not to focus on ourselves. That gives our habit patterns plenty of opportunity to play out and interfere with sound decision making.

From this perspective, our most basic problem is not that we make impulsive decisions to buy or sell or that we go on tilt. *Rather, the problem is that we are in the autopilot mode in which our triggers can easily fire.* If we are fully self-aware—truly mind-full—we become observers to our triggers, not their victims. Self-observation distances us from our problem patterns.

A practice that I have written about, first used in my work with active day traders in Chicago, is that of taking our 'emotional temperature' during hourly breaks in the trading day. Are we running cool or hot in our emotions? Is our mind calm and focused or racing and distracted? Are we feeling jittery and unsettled, or are we operating in our zone?

In this exercise, traders have sheets in front of them with pictures of thermometers. During their short hourly break, they reflect on their state and mark on the thermometers how hot or cool they are feeling; how distracted or focused; how uncertain or confident; etc. *The act of taking the short break and reflecting on the thermometers takes the trader out of 'mindless' mode and reinforces their efforts at becoming good self-observers.*

The breaks also train traders to become increasingly sensitive to the feelings that accompany distraction, so that they can eventually intercept negative patterns as they occur. With practice and repetition, traders gain skills in self-observation and increasingly learn to operate in a self-aware mode. *Self-awareness—our ability to observe ourselves in real time—is itself a skill that we can cultivate through deliberate practice.* Over time, traders internalize their thermometers, recognizing in real time when they are running hot, so that they can quickly shift gears and return to markets in a cool, calm, collected mode.

Case study: anger as a catalyst for change

Jai Li was a successful commodity trader at a hedge fund, where he worked with a portfolio manager and two analysts. He was remarkably consistent in his trading results, religiously following a process that he had written out. Indeed, he maintained a checklist that he kept by his monitors to make sure he was doing the right things at the right time. The checklist was a powerful tool for sustaining self-awareness, ensuring that he didn't get so caught up in the market that he could forget to be patient in his execution or fail to size and hedge positions properly. I was surprised that the issue Jai Li wanted to work on with me was keeping his emotions in check. From all appearances, he was quite cool and organized.

What happened every so often, Jai Li reported, was that his markets—power and natural gas—would become highly volatile. This volatility could be the result of a data release, or it could come as the result of actions taken by producers. At such times, Jai Li had plenty of contacts he could reach out to, many of whom worked at firms involved in physical production. Indeed, these contacts often helped him anticipate periods of volatility before they could create undue P/L swings in his portfolio. Other times, the spikes in volatility came unexpectedly. For example, a sudden shift in weather patterns (and forecasts) created turmoil in his markets during a period of limited liquidity.

Jai Li felt trapped at such times and found himself bailing out of positions, often at the worst time. At those times, the organized checklist went out the window. In a quarterly review, Jai Li estimated that the majority of his drawdowns occurred when he unwound his trades in the face of thin markets and volatile price action.

It wasn't the unwinding of his positions that upset Jai Li. Rather, it was the impulsivity of his decision making. In the heat of the moment, he didn't make a quick assessment and explore his alternatives. He simply acted out of panic. Once he (and his market) had settled down, he realized there were other steps he could have taken, including hedges that could benefit from the uncertainty of the environment. He was truly disgusted with himself for acting without proper discipline.

This disgust became the focus of our work together. During preparation time, Jai Li mentally rehearsed possible volatility triggers for his markets and—during his visualizations of these—he vividly reminded himself of the literal cost that fear caused his trading. He imagined the disgust he would feel if he acted on impulse and, indeed, summoned anger toward his own impulsivity. He hated this aspect of his behavior, and staying in touch with that hatred enabled him to avoid acting upon his triggers. Basically, through repetition he programmed himself with the idea of, "I'm not going there." Eventually, he created a separate checklist for volatile periods, complete with questions he needed to ask himself to quickly adapt to the market conditions. His anger toward his old patterns created a positive motivation to expand upon his strengths: his ability to make planned, organized decisions.

> If we truly hate a pattern of behavior that has hurt us and stay in touch with that anger, it is very difficult to find ourselves triggered and caught in that pattern. Our anger keeps us away from our weaknesses and gives us an opportunity to act upon our strengths.

Perhaps the most interesting part of Jai Li's work on himself was that, as the result of anticipating his emotional reactions, he became better at anticipating and identifying volatility in his markets and making quick adjustments. His ability to rehearse his disgust and anger over his trading mistakes allowed him to build his self-awareness, so that he was making decisions mindfully, not on autopilot.

When we are aware of the triggers for our trading mistakes, we gain an important layer of control over our trading. *Less well recognized, however, are the triggers for our positive trading.* In other words, there are situations that facilitate our best trading and set us up for success. We don't typically think about positive triggers, so we fail to notice them. Awareness of these positive triggers can help us make the right decisions in real time.

A great example of a positive trigger that occurs in my trading is the feeling of being in sync with the market and having an insight come to me spontaneously while in that flow state. Recently, I noticed the S&P futures start the morning session with some selling. The selling was orderly and I noticed that it didn't pick up as we neared the lows of the overnight session. I knew that we had data coming out at 10 am ET, with the potential for a meaningful move if employment numbers looked good. The thought suddenly struck me that market participants—overnight and at the open—were selling ahead of the release, but could not move the market meaningfully lower. I realized that they would have to re-enter the market if the numbers were favorable. "We're not going to take out the overnight low" was the thought that went through my head. I bought ahead of the release with a stop below the overnight lows and told myself that we would take out yesterday's highs. That ended up being a nicely profitable trade.

The positive trigger in my case was being in a calm, focused mindset and having an insight come to me. I've learned that such spontaneous intuitions have positive expected value. If I can sustain my focus, I can best benefit when patterns of market action trigger the intuitive sense. *Self-awareness keeps us from our worst habits, but can also keep us grounded in what we do best.* We build our positive psychology when we identify our positive triggers and sustain the states in which they can keep firing.

> Our worst—and best—trading is state-dependent. Our states energize our triggers—for better and for worse.

How we change our trading psychology: well-being

Let's return to one of the themes of Chapters One and Two. Trading is a performance activity and peak performance requires that we keep ourselves at our physical, cognitive, and emotional peaks. The term well-being includes our happiness, but also our sense of purpose, our levels of physical energy, and the quality of our relationships. One of the common pitfalls of trading psychology is that we lead lives that lack well-rounded well-being and then seek to make up for what is missing in our lives by pursuing profits in our trading. At that point, our desire to succeed in markets becomes a *need* for P/L.

Instead of tracking markets in open-minded ways and acting only when what we see lines up with our trading strengths, we actively *look* for trades. Our need to make money—which really is a reflection of our (partially unmet) need for self-esteem and well-being—now controls us. That leads us to take trades that are out of our wheelhouses, setting us up for losses, frustrations, and emotional trading. Recall the day in the life of Ed, the trader whose home I visited and whose work so impressed me. From the start of his day with physical exercise to his quality time with Laurie to the stimulation of his team processes, Ed was living a life that fired on all the cylinders of well-being. How he ate, how he slept, how he alternated between intensive work and rejuvenation: each day was organized to keep him at peak well-being.

What we can learn from Ed's example is that sometimes we can best work on our trading psychology by working on our lives outside of market hours. Ideally, you want to have a full life outside of trading so that you have plenty of emotional and physical energy in the tank when you hit those inevitable periods of drawdown and confusion. When you have people in your life who you love, regular activities that give energy, and the stimulation of personal interests, drawdowns become a challenge but not a personal threat. We can best weather our negative triggers when we are living lives of well-being. We can always have a positive life P/L even when the trading P/L is struggling.

> Our lives are our portfolios. When we have diversified holdings—valued activities that are independent of one another—we create many paths to well-being. It is difficult for negative emotions to dominate our trading if we consistently experience joy, meaning, energy, and closeness in our lives.

We've seen that the best path to change creates positive habit patterns. It's romantic to think about coming to every trading session and every review totally pumped up. That isn't realistic, and it's not ideal. The best mindset is a highly focused one, not one spewing adrenaline. Imagine being on military patrol in an area littered with land mines. To be effective, you need to be quiet and intensely focused, like the sniper. A pumped-up soldier on patrol is too likely to miss one of those land mines. Markets offer their opportunities, but also their land mines. If we turn our focused mindset into a positive habit pattern, we're most likely to recognize when it's time to attack and when it's time to stop moving forward. *Our trading psychology grows from consistent change, not necessarily dramatic change.*

I've found that my productivity is directly related to the organization of my time. It is when I create and follow a daily routine that I get the most done. Today, for example, I woke up at 4:15 am, engaged in prayer and brief stretching, greeted our four cats and brought them food and water, treated Margie with a favorite coffee, prepared breakfast in bed for her, went for a jog, performed a workout routine at our neighborhood gym (standard series of stretching, lower and upper body exercises), took my shower, and then proceeded to a session of book writing. The day then transitioned to reading mail and messages, preparing for trading, following markets and trading, holding meetings with traders, more cat feeding, and going out with Margie and family members before getting to sleep early.

That is the rhythm of a typical day, as I move from family time to physical time, to work time, to errand time, to hang out time, to wind down time. I've been able to sustain the writing of many books, long work hours, and an active family life not because I'm so motivated, but because I'm organized and save my energy for the most important life priorities. During free time, there's plenty of opportunity for fun and spontaneity. What there isn't time for is wasted time. There can be no well-being in time spent aimlessly.

> How we spend our time shapes our mindset.
> A positive trading psychology requires a
> positive life that maximizes well-being.

The framework of positive psychology teaches us that it is not enough to avoid or even resolve personal problems. We must maximize activities that are deeply, personally fulfilling. Spending time with my wife of 40+ years is always special; for me, it has the feeling of coming home and being where I'm supposed to be. Spending time with our rescue cats and giving them a loving home is deeply satisfying. Being a part of the growth of our children and grandchildren feels amazingly rewarding. I devote time to prayer and religious study and feel a fulfillment I can't get through career and market activities. As I note in the online book *Radical Renewal*, an important part of well-being is grounding ourselves spiritually, even as we passionately pursue life's practical challenges.[126] Every trader will find their own way of maximizing positive experience in day-to-day life. As Dr. Jason Williams points out in his book *The Mental Edge in Trading*, our ultimate challenge is understanding what makes our personalities tick and grounding our trading—and our lives—in what speaks to us. Successful traders, he explains, are ones who best draw upon their unique personal strengths.[127] In *The Daily Trading Coach*, I point out that "Emotional well-being fuels cognitive efficiency. We think best when we feel good."[128]

I seriously doubt that we can sustain quality trading if we're not living lives of quality. It is the positive psychology of life that gives us the positive energy and mindset to perform at our best: in markets, as well as in relationships and in personal endeavors. As I write this, I've recently celebrated my 70th birthday. I know that I'll soon throttle back the busy coaching schedule, but I also recognize that a life of retirement and free time is not for me. I've prepared my market research, as well as the lessons I've learned from working with talented traders over the years, and will devote mornings to active trading. My commitment will be to devote a significant portion of profits to causes I believe in and organizations that are doing good work. At that point, I'll be trading, not to validate myself, but to engage in just a bit of repair of the world. I suspect I won't be going on tilt and trading impulsively if I'm trading for noble causes.

Our positive psychology is grounded in the best of who we are.

The surest path to change is to trade from a motivation that is greater than our need for P/L. That motivation might be making a team better; it might be intellectual curiosity and learning; it might be donating profits to worthy causes. More powerful than fighting negativity is recruiting our greatest positivity. That is the key insight behind Traders4ACause, an organization that provides education for traders and donates proceeds to worthy causes. *We trade most purposefully when we trade for a purpose.*

How we change our trading psychology: behavioral methods

Let's now turn to specific psychological approaches that can make a meaningful, positive difference in our trading. There are numerous frameworks for psychological change that produce lasting change in relatively brief periods of time.[129] Among the most straightforward for traders to implement are behavioral, cognitive, and solution-focused methods.

Behavioral approaches to psychological change involve learning patterns of action that interrupt, disrupt, and ultimately change our problem patterns. In the context of trading, behavioral methods typically use the body to shift our states, placing us in modes that are incompatible with the negative emotions triggered during trading. The utility of behavioral methods is that their techniques can be actively practiced outside of trading hours, so that it becomes possible to quickly gain mastery. Once we learn the skills, they become part of us and we are able to work on our mindset in real time. With frequent practice, these skills are developed over period of weeks, not months or years. *The key to success is the frequency and duration of practice.* We need to work on behavioral skills often enough to make them part of us. We need each 'session' of behavioral work to last long enough to truly place us in a new physical and mental state. Taking a few breaths and calling it meditation, for example, won't create meaningful or lasting change.

Because many of the problems that disrupt trading involve activation of our fight/flight responses, some of the most effective behavioral methods are those that teach us how to quiet ourselves in real time. Everything speeds up when the adrenaline flows due to fear or frustration. If we can slow our thoughts, slow our heart rates, and slow our breathing, we can counteract fight/flight. *Slowing the body ultimately quiets the mind and enables us to make decisions calmly and deliberately, not reactively.*

The first step in behavioral change is learning the skills needed to take us out of fight/flight mode. The most basic skill is sitting in a comfortable, quiet setting and staying completely physically still while breathing slowly and deeply from the diaphragm. While sitting still and deeply breathing in and out, we can listen to relaxing, absorbing music or we can fix our attention on a particular image. Whatever best holds our attention is ideal for the exercise. As I've shared in previous writing, I like to listen to repetitive, hypnotic music from Philip Glass during my sessions of focusing and quieting. I also like to focus on favorite images or scenes and hold these in my awareness. The key to the success of the breathing work is truly slowing ourselves down while maintaining our attention and then holding this quiet, focused state long enough to shut down our self-talk.

> **The goal of behavioral work is to become observers of our minds, not victims of their frantic activity.**

My experience is that it takes weeks of daily practice to become really good at turning our minds off. At first, we might have to listen to the music, slow our thoughts and breathing, and bring ourselves back to focus again and again when random thoughts and feelings intrude. It can take 20 minutes or more before we truly enter the zone. With frequent practice, perhaps as part of preparation in the morning, as part of a midday trading break, and as part of a nighttime wind down routine, we can enter the zone faster and faster. For someone who is experienced, it takes less than a minute to shift gears, quickly focusing the mind, holding the body still, and maintaining the quiet mode. This becomes extremely helpful during busy trading periods.

Earlier I mentioned the use of biofeedback to accelerate the process of learning stress-management skills. The biofeedback gives us real-time information of our body's level of arousal, so that we know we are being truly successful in shifting gears. Biofeedback apps can also put us through exercises that train us to control our heart rate variability (a useful stress measure) and brain wave patterns. In my use of the Muse neurofeedback (brain wave) device, I found that using the app to keep score of the success of my exercises turns the behavioral work into a competitive game. That actively engages my drive for mastery.

The other valuable use of biofeedback is the immediate information that tells us whether we are being successful in our exercises. For instance, we might learn that we are much more effective in quieting our minds with eyes closed and engaging imagery than with eyes open and listening to music. It takes some experimentation to learn what works best for us. Armed with that information, we can greatly accelerate our learning curves and become masters of our body's level of arousal.

It's important that we begin our skill development outside of markets, during periods when we're not faced with stress. The idea is to allow repetition to build our competence at staying calm and focused. Once we can slow down and focus on demand, we're ready to apply the behavioral skills to real-life situations. The first step in this process is visualization work, in which we vividly imagine stressful trading situations, imagine our reactions to the stress (racing thoughts, frustration, feelings of tilt), and then commence the breathing exercise to slow us down. *In that way, we're using visualization to provide reps for practice.* We imagine stressful scenarios (losing money, missing opportunities), summon the stressful feelings at those times, interrupt those feelings, and practice our focusing/relaxing activities.

With repeated practice, we can become quite good at recognizing and interrupting stress. Starting with using the breathing and relaxation in response to imagined stresses provides a degree of realism and helps build a sense of mastery. Typically, we'll start by imagining mildly stressful scenarios, such as a position moving against us, and only move to more intense scenarios once we achieve mastery at the lower level. Creating a 'stress hierarchy'—a ladder of situations from minimally stressful to highly stressful—allows us to practice our self-control work gradually and steadily, building our confidence and control.

Once we can stay calm and focused consistently in imagined scenarios, we're ready to bring the behavioral skills to real-time trading. The goal here is to recognize stress and distraction as they're happening, and use that recognition to enter our calm, focused mode with the breathing work. As noted earlier, self-awareness is the key to bringing the behavioral work to real time. We cannot intercept and defuse stress if we don't recognize it. That requires a flexibility of attention, as we shift from tracking markets to focusing on ourselves. One trader I worked with found it difficult to move from the imagery-based behavioral work to real-time use of the techniques. He found it useful to engage in simulation-based trading, tracking his market in replay mode on his platform and entering his orders and monitoring his positions. When he began to feel uncomfortable in the simulation, he was able to recognize it and put himself in the focused, deep-breathing mode. Practice with the simulator helped him gain the experience to bring the behavioral skills to real time.

> **The key to the success of behavioral work is the ability, in real time, to place ourselves in physical, cognitive, and emotional states incompatible with stress.**

In the beginning, as we develop these skills, we may have to interrupt our trading many times during the day to keep ourselves on track cognitively and emotionally. With steady practice, we can bring our focused mind and deep breathing to real time while we're following markets and managing positions. At that point, the new skills have truly become a part of ourselves. The challenge of behavioral work is not that it is so difficult or complex. *Rather, the challenge is that many traders don't take the time to practice the skills each day and reach the point of mastery.* They wait until they get into trouble and, by that time, it's quite difficult—and often too late—to try to cope.

Behavioral methods succeed when they become essential parts of our trading processes, no less than the research we perform or our position management. How we set up our learning and practice determines the success of our work on self-control. We can gradually expose ourselves to trading stressors and train ourselves to respond to them constructively.[130]

The beauty of mastering behavioral stress-management skills is that we can bring them to all facets of life, not just trading. For example, I may reach a point of frustration in my dealings with people I work with or with family members. Having practiced the focus and breathing so often as part of my trading process, it's now become an automatic part of how I deal with stress and physiological arousal. As soon as I feel the frustration, I naturally take a deep breath and center myself. Many times, this has prevented me from reacting—and overreacting—to events and enabled me to respond more constructively.

Just the other morning, one of our cats was very hungry and jumped onto the kitchen island looking for food. He sent plates flying all over the kitchen. I started to become frustrated and stopped myself. I took a breath, reminded myself that he hadn't eaten in a while, and I kissed him before scooping his food. Within the span of a minute, I moved from frustration to focus to empathy. This is exactly the same movement that occurs when I shift gears during adverse price movement, enabling me to relate to what buyers and sellers are thinking and doing.

> What we do to refine ourselves as traders
> inevitably improves us as people.

When we train ourselves to recognize and defuse stress in real time, we gain a life skill that aids our performance in all areas of life.

Positive psychology suggests a promising extension of this behavioral work. *Suppose we use our practice sessions, not just to slow ourselves down and combat stress, but to actively summon feelings of well-being that contribute to an optimal mindset.* Instead of quieting our thought processes, we focus on imagery that brings us feelings of love, happiness, and gratitude. This is a cornerstone of what is known as loving-kindness meditation. It reflects the understanding that meditation acts as an amplifier of whatever we focus upon.

If we fill our minds with thoughts and images of peace while breathing deeply and slowly and keeping our bodies still, we amplify our sense of inner peace.

If we focus on images of joy and love, we amplify our feelings of connection to others—and to the world.

With practice, we can become highly skilled at entering positive mind frames that are incompatible with stress, anxiety, and frustration. This is especially promising because those positive mindsets are the very ones that facilitate our broad, creative thought. From the vantage point of positive psychology, the goal is not simply to lower our stress levels, but to learn to keep ourselves in optimal frames of mind that keep us performing at our peaks.

We can practice evoking these positive mindsets just as we practice quieting ourselves, optimizing our thoughts, feelings, and actions. For instance, early each morning, I engage in a series of stretching and calisthenic exercises working from the top of my body down to my legs. Performing these in rapid succession pumps me up and provides a feeling of well-being and energy. Engaging in a few of these exercises when I get up from the trading desk renews my energy level and mindset and allows me to return to the screen with fresh focus and intention. During these exercises, my mind is highly focused and calm, but my body is working out. It is very much like meditating while exercising, amplifying my sense of energy and well-being. Employed in this manner, behavioral exercises can become a valuable part of our trading routines even when we're not dealing with stress and distress.

Case study: activating our best behaviors

We commonly think of behavioral methods as ways of learning skills that give us control over our negative patterns. As we've just seen, however, we can also use behavioral routines to evoke states of well-being. Derrick was an active trader who wanted to work on becoming the best trader he could be.

A solid performer at a proprietary trading firm that focused on the trading of futures listed on the Chicago Mercantile Exchange, Derrick believed that he had the potential to be a world-class talent. He went through periods of trading very well and feeling on top of his game, only to fall back into trading that was only average.

I asked Derrick if perhaps the problem was that his markets were changing, and he was not adapting quickly enough. He indicated that this was not really the problem, as sometimes his merely average trading occurred during periods when he clearly perceived trends, breakouts, and opportunities. It seemed to him that he was always a step slow at those times. When he felt on top of things, he was active and proactive, leaping at opportunities as they presented themselves. Sure enough, a review of Derrick's performance confirmed his impressions. His best trading occurred when he traded largest and most aggressively. When he traded more cautiously, with modest size, his results were positive, but not outstanding.

As we reviewed his trades and reverse engineered his psychology at those times, it became clear that Derrick's best trading occurred in the flash of an 'aha!' moment. When an opportunity jumped out at him, he took full advantage. At other times of more ordinary trading, nothing jumped out at him. When Derrick was energized for the hunt, he took his best shots. What energized him was the flash of opportunity. *Simply attempting to sustain a quiet, focused mindset did not bring out his killer instinct.* At one point, Derrick made the comparison between a lion that has just eaten and is full and a hungry lion who is on the prowl for food. It's the hungry lion that is most likely to aggressively surround prey and make the kill. Derrick's aim was to always trade 'hungry.'

As we further reviewed Derrick's best trades, it became clear that his big kills occurred when the markets he was trading picked up volume and volatility. In other words, he was skilled at reading other participants and gauging when they were aggressively revaluing their market. Often, it was simply an expanded bar with a wider range between high and low in the context of an overbought or oversold condition that cued Derrick to potential opportunity. One time he was watching the crude oil market and noticed aggressive participants entering buy orders at a certain time of each minute. He was convinced that these were large algorithmic accounts. He used this information to aggressively trade in the subsequent portion of each minute to ride the flows of the large accounts. It was the 'aha' moment of noticing the order flow that triggered Derrick's best, aggressive trading.

I use the term 'triggered' intentionally, because this was a case of a trader operating with a positive trigger. Seeing something in the market that wasn't obvious set off his excitement and stimulated his ability to go after opportunities in size. When he didn't experience that trigger, his trading was good, but not nearly as profitable as when he was the hungry lion on the hunt.

I encouraged Derrick to expand his trading universe, suggesting that his expertise wasn't a detailed knowledge of crude oil, but rather a detailed ability to read market participation. Sure enough, when he tracked more instruments—including several equity index futures instruments—he found more occasions where active market participants tipped their hands.

We practiced visualization exercises of watching multiple screens and quickly gauging when there was unusual behavior in order books and short-term price action. *The behavioral 'therapy' was not to reduce frustration and eliminate tilt trading, but to invoke his best, killer instincts.* With enough markets to follow through the day, he didn't have to worry about any single market turning slow and directionless.

Rehearsing the mindset of a hunter helped Derrick sustain aggressive hunting through the day. Rather than sustaining deep, slow breathing while keeping himself still, he used behavioral rehearsal to sustain an alert mindset in which he was ready to pounce. Doing this repeatedly helped him bring more consistent aggressiveness to his live trading. He found that behavioral methods were not simply tools of relaxation and focus, but also pathways to sustaining optimal states for risk-taking.

My experience is that behavioral methods most help beginning traders by keeping them out of impulsive, frustrated mindsets. As traders gain experience, the behavioral techniques not only dampen emotion, but can be utilized to enhance mindset and improve quality and duration of concentration. For experienced traders, the behavioral framework can provide opportunities to sustain optimal states that are associated with the best practices of trading. This is a nice example of how our trading psychology activities evolve with the growth of our trading. How we work on our heads as novices, how we develop our mindsets as we're growing our trading, and how we strive for optimal performance as experienced traders are quite different. All, however, require us to work as hard on ourselves as we work on our trading, whether we're reprogramming our negative triggers or building our positive ones.

Improving our trading psychology: cognitive methods

Where behavioral methods seek to directly impact our bodies and our emotional arousal, cognitive approaches start from the premise that how we think is the primary driver in how we feel and behave. From this vantage point, going on tilt is not just a physiological event, but a function of what we tell ourselves about our trading. For example, we might be conflicted about entering a trade, waiting for better and better entry points, only to be left behind when the market embarks upon its move. In a flash of anger and frustration, we tell ourselves what idiots we are and how we'll never succeed if we can't take advantage of solid trade setups. To quiet this self-criticism, we chase the market move, only to have our position undergo a normal reversal. At that point, our frustration and self-criticism can feed one another, leading to ever more reactive trading.

Underlying our negative thought patterns is often the linkage of our self-esteem to our trading results. We seek profits to validate ourselves; we fail to take losses because we don't want to feel like losers. Because we need P/L to affirm our worth, we find ourselves needing to trade, and that leads to overtrading. Simply telling ourselves to follow rules and trade selectively misses the point if we're ultimately trading to feel good about ourselves. Indeed, if we become full of ourselves and overconfident after a winning period, that can be a significant threat to our success.

When we have a perspective that treats losing trades, missed trades, and improperly sized trades as opportunities for learning and catalysts for fresh goals and plans to improve, our mindset remains constructive. It's when we have learned—and overlearned—negative modes of self-talk that losses and mistakes can spiral. Cognitive work helps us recognize that negative self-talk in real time and replace it with more constructive ways of approaching our performance. Of course, this is most readily accomplished if all our self-esteem eggs are not in the basket of trading. If we feel good about ourselves and our lives, we're best positioned to take setbacks in stride and actually embrace them as learning experiences.

In cognitive work, we learn to think about our thinking and become better and better observers of how we talk to ourselves. This work on 'metacognition' can be practiced outside of market hours, like the behavioral techniques, and it can become part of our trading breaks, as we make mental resets. I outline ways of engaging in cognitive work in *The Daily Trading Coach*; as mentioned above, *the important initial skill is recognizing our negative self-talk as it occurs.*[131]

One technique I've found to be especially helpful is to think back to someone in our lives who was a particularly negative influence—preferably someone we can't stand—and conduct an imagery exercise in which our critical, angry self-talk is coming from them. Thus, for example, I will find myself disgusted with my trading when I make a mistake and catch myself thinking: *How could I be so stupid?* Immediately, I recognize what I'm doing, quickly take a break, and vividly imagine my nemesis saying that very same thing to me. *That invokes a motivation even greater than the perfectionism driving my self-criticism: the desire to not let that other person dominate my mindset.* I can imagine myself answering that person back, telling them to shut up, and asserting a more constructive self-talk in the situation. Instead of wallowing in frustration, I shift cognitive gears and engage in a wholly different internal conversation: embracing my mistake and making sure I learn from it. Indeed, I can rehearse a radically different mindset in which I say "thank you" to the mistake I made for providing me with a learning experience that will make me better. When I change my mode of thinking and process events in ways that evoke gratitude, I actually energize my efforts and can re-engage trading in a more focused, positive mode.

> **Important positive psychology principle: Instead of trying to eliminate negative patterns of thought and behavior, replace them with stronger, more constructive ones.**

Many times, the way to overcome a pattern of negative thought and action is to draw upon a motivation more powerful than the one driving our negativity. In other words, instead of fighting the negative, we invoke the positive. Instead of trying to reduce our negative psychology, we work on building our positivity.

I learned this principle from our kitten Naomi, who Margie and I adopted from a cattery in California. Naomi was clearly shaken by the flight from California to Newark and immediately spent her time in our home hiding under the bed. Using food as a coax, I was eventually able to get her to come onto the bed, but she kept her distance. Her fear was too great to interact with us. At one point, I got the idea to put my hand under the bedcovers and move it around. Naomi's eyes became large; she was very interested in whatever was moving under the blankets. Before long, she pounced and chased and was interacting with me. Her fear was a strong motivation, but her hunting instinct was much stronger. By drawing upon the stronger motivation, I was able to help her overcome her reticence.

Since that time, I have found this technique to work very well with traders. As we've seen, the trader who becomes self-critical due to perfectionism can reach out to a teammate, for example, and suddenly becomes quite constructive because of the stronger desire to help others. At times I feel discouraged in my trading and feel like packing it in. Instead, I return to my research, notice fresh opportunities, and—like Naomi—find myself ready to pounce. In a very real sense, the problem is often not just the presence of negativity, but our lack of access to our positivity.

Case study: changing the cognitive psychology of overconfidence

One of the trickiest psychological patterns disrupting our trading is overconfidence. Most of us are ready to work on ourselves if we're immersed in negative emotions. When we're winning and doing well, however, we rarely think to make that an opportunity for pulling back and reframing our mindset. We like the feeling of making money, and that can lead us to feel as though we can do no wrong. A common observation I've made in working with developing traders is that their overall P/L is quite good when they are trading small but becomes surprisingly negative when they are taking the most risk. It's when they are small that they are most careful. Often that's during a period following drawdowns. When they are trading large, they are most confident—and most vulnerable to a large loss.

Mimi traded at a proprietary trading firm where there were no salaries. Traders were given access to capital; they paid a desk fee to cover their expenses; and they kept a meaningful share of their profits. That arrangement meant that the way to succeed was to be given more and more capital to trade so that positions could be larger and more numerous. Mimi experienced early success at the firm, trading futures contracts on the Chicago Mercantile Exchange. She was not hesitant to use leverage to size up her positions and quickly became known in the firm as a confident, aggressive trader. Her biggest problem was that her winning streaks led her to get bigger and bigger in her trades until a series of expectable losses drew her account down significantly. By the time she reached out to me, she felt that she was good at making money but not at all good at keeping it.

We explored what was going on in Mimi's thought processes when she was making money, and it became clear that winning triggered a kind of perfectionistic thinking. 'Good enough' was never enough: once she tasted profits, she wanted more and more and more. This took her eye off the objective opportunity set and made her vulnerable to large losses. "I just don't want to be on the roller coaster anymore," she told me.

What was tricky about this situation was that the trigger of the negative, perfectionistic thinking was winning, not losing. On the surface, what Mimi was doing looked positive: she was being aggressive and making the most of her edge. In fact, however, her perfectionism led her to never be satisfied with good results. She always needed *great* results—and markets weren't always in the mode of offering those.

The cognitive work that Mimi and I undertook encouraged her to take a short break when she had gone on a run and started to feel like trading more and more. In that break, she reminded herself that the need to trade more after good gains is what put her on the roller coaster. She slowed herself down with a couple of deep breaths and reminded herself, "This, too, shall pass." Instead of fantasizing that the big moves would continue indefinitely, she prepared a mindset where "trees don't grow to the sky" and "all good things come to an end." In this slowed down mode, she replaced the perfectionistic thinking with a much more constructive alternative: "How can I make sure I hold onto my profits?" On her own, she came up with the idea of automatically taking profits anytime she felt the urge to trade more and more following a winning streak. "This, too, shall pass" became a way of rehearsing "I deserve to celebrate my win." By leaving on a portion of her position—and sometimes restructuring it with options to gain better risk/reward from that point—she locked in a win at the same time that she positioned herself to benefit from a continued move.

This became part of Mimi's planning, so that she spent a portion of her morning identifying where 'good enough' was *truly* good enough and where she would take profits. Her success came not just from fighting perfectionism, but from invoking a positive, appreciative mindset. Overconfidence became an opportunity to step back and celebrate success.

Mimi's example shows us that, as with the behavioral methods, cognitive techniques can be rehearsed daily as part of our premarket preparation. For instance, we can sit quietly and visualize scenarios that tend to invoke our worst self-talk and frustration and then actively rehearse telling ourselves that we refuse to abuse ourselves emotionally. We then visualize a more constructive self-talk, perhaps the way we would speak to a colleague we care about who is in the same situation. If they were to mess up a trade, we certainly wouldn't heap abuse upon them! Rather, we would encourage them to put the episode in perspective, learn from it, and move on with a fresh learning lesson. *Notice how this, too, is an example of replacing a negative pattern and motivation with a stronger and more positive one.* Most of us have the emotional sensitivity and social skill to reach out in a caring way when a trader friend encounters a drawdown. All it takes is imagining ourselves as that friend and we suddenly become capable of recruiting the support for ourselves that we routinely provide to others.

Notice, however, that it is impossible to replace negative thought with more constructive thought if we don't recognize our negativity in real time. A technique that is important in this context is known as 'thought stopping.' In a trading context, this involves catching ourselves processing a market event in a reactive, unhelpful way and immediately telling ourselves, "Stop!" One trader I worked with had a particular gesture he used when he wanted to interrupt his destructive self-talk, banging his trading desk for emphasis. That "stop!" gesture acted as a mental wake-up call, disrupting his negative thinking and cueing him to deal with what was going on in a more constructive way.

> Cognitive work does not necessarily replace negative thinking with positive thinking. Rather, it trains us to always think constructively, so that whatever happens in markets can make us better.

The distinction between constructive self-talk and positive self-talk is important in trading. Let's face it: sometimes we *do* make silly mistakes and undergo needless drawdowns. There is nothing to feel positive about in those situations, and any achievement-oriented, competitive person is going to be frustrated when they let themselves down. One of my favorite recollections from my college basketball days was the reaction of one of the coaches when a player made a thoughtless mistake during practice. He would call the player to the sidelines, look him face to face, and say, "C'mon! You're better than that!" It was a criticism, but it was also an affirmation. Every player knew that the coach was trying to bring out the best in the team, and they responded to the message with fresh motivation. The verbal swat on the behind was not positive talk—no one looked forward to being called over to the sidelines—but it *was* constructive talk.

> Negative self-talk tears down. Constructive self-talk points the way to improvement.

When we fall short of our ideals, the ultimate litmus test of our self-talk is whether it inspires us to correct our mistakes or whether it sets us off and triggers further errors. In coaching ourselves, we want to be like the basketball coach, calling us to the sidelines and reminding ourselves that we're better than our worst mistakes.

How can we make our cognitive work part of our daily trading processes? As I point out in *The Daily Trading Coach*,[132] keeping a journal of our self-talk can be a powerful way of recognizing, interrupting, and shifting our negative thought patterns. A common format in cognitive practice follows an ABCD structure:

> **Activating event:** clearly identifying the situation that triggered our negative thoughts.
> **Beliefs:** spelling out what we're telling ourselves about what happened and what underlies our negative self-talk.
> **Consequences:** elaborating on how those beliefs interfere with our lives and our trading; reminding ourselves of their cost and consequences.
> **Disputation:** challenging those negative beliefs to create constructive alternatives; reframing the situation that has triggered us.

Dividing our journal into the four ABCD columns allows us to write down critical incidents as close to real time as possible, reinforcing metacognition and helping prevent our negative thinking from spiraling. *Journaling is a powerful strategy for shifting cognitive gears, taking us from emotional processing to more reasoned analysis.* In an important sense, when we take the time to complete a journal entry, we change roles, moving from the trading role to the role of trading coach. We move from being immersed in our negative patterns of processing events to becoming an observer of those patterns. An important goal of work on trading psychology is learning to coach ourselves, recognizing and shifting the patterns that interfere with our best decision making.

My experience with journaling is that it promotes spontaneous self-awareness, training us to recognize our disruptive thoughts as they occur. After keeping the journal for a while, traders find themselves engaging in the ABCD process in real time, identifying the ways of thinking that sabotage them, reminding themselves of the consequences, and rapidly shifting gears to challenge the problematic self-talk and begin fresh avenues for processing market events. *The goal is not to eliminate negative thoughts and feelings altogether, but to stop us from buying into them.* We can become better and better at intercepting the self-talk that is associated with our worst trading, expanding our control and turning destructive processing into helpful ways of coaching ourselves. In that sense, the keeping of a journal is a kind of riding with training wheels—a step toward eventually doing the right things in real time.

Note that performance journaling at the end of a day—writing down our ideas about markets from the past session, noting what we did well and what we want to improve, and setting goals/plans for the next day—can also embrace our cognitive work. Whenever we write down our assessments of our performance and our goals, we *are* engaging in self-talk, but we are doing so in ways that get the thoughts out of our heads, framing them constructively. Think back to Mimi. She eventually got to the point where taking profits was part of her planning for the next day's trading. It was incorporated into her trading journal. That made the cognitive work proactive.

One team that I worked with at a hedge fund made weekly journaling a shared process, requiring members to acknowledge each of their teammates and their positive contributions to the member's performance. This ensured that the journals reinforced a sense of gratitude and teamwork, shaping the entire team's self-talk. *It is not well recognized that teams themselves have their own, shared cognitive processes.* Some are quite destructive, as when members blame each other for poor trades and push themselves forward to get credit for ideas that work out. The most effective teams feature members that care about each other and that actively help, mentor, and support one another. Such teams build *an esprit de corps*: a sense of mission and purpose that becomes part of their positive self-talk. It is remarkably difficult for individual traders to sustain positivity amidst a lack of team spirit. Positive psychology suggests that fighting negative thought patterns might be most effective if we place ourselves in situations that bring out our most helpful ways of processing events.

For independent traders, *this highlights the value of being part of a supportive trading community and/or developing ongoing collaborations with peer* traders. A good 'trading buddy' will not allow you to get away with your habitual negative talk, and you similarly can support your partner in staying constructive. The sense of being 'in this together' builds a support framework that intercepts negative thinking well before it becomes a threat to our trading.

Being with people who care about us makes it so much easier to care for ourselves. This lesson was reinforced by our adoption of a neglected blind calico cat, Mali. When I first saw Mali, she had been removed from a setting that failed to care for her and was placed in a veterinarian's office where she stayed in a cage. Her fur was matted, and she did little to take care of herself. When the vet took her from her cage and put her on the counter in front of me, she responded to my petting with eager purring, moving in circles to rub against me and establish closeness. After a bit of petting, to my amazement, she immediately began to clean herself! Feeling love from someone helped her recover the motivation to care for herself. From that point forward, she was a loving friend to Margie and me and kept herself quite well.

> Trading is vulnerable when it is a purely solo activity.
> When we trade with a partner or team who cares
> about us, we cultivate our ability to support ourselves
> and weather the inevitable ups and downs of P/L.

From the positive psychology perspective, we can utilize cognitive methods not only to challenge negative thinking and reframe our views on our trading, but also as a way to actively rehearse and internalize our optimal mindsets. Combining cognitive and behavioral approaches, we can visualize missed trades, drawdowns, and other frustrating situations in vivid detail while we mentally invoke the self-talk that we want to draw upon to handle those situations effectively. Similarly, we can prepare for the market day by calming ourselves, closing our eyes, and talking ourselves through various anticipated scenarios. This is proactive self-coaching: training ourselves to process events constructively before those events impact us. Some of the best coaching occurs proactively, as we anticipate challenges and internalize constructive ways of dealing with those.

One positive psychology application of the cognitive approach that I've mentioned with respect to my own trading draws on the fact that I actively allocate a meaningful portion of my trading profits to causes I deeply believe in. The self-talk I rehearse prior to trading is a kind of pep talk, reminding myself that I am doing this for an important purpose and can't allow myself to mess up because I care so much for the people I'm helping. Sometimes the visualization and self-talk pertain to a charity; sometimes it's visualizing my children and grandchildren and inspiring myself to add to their futures.

On a larger scale, Traders4ACause holds conference events for traders, and a portion of the proceeds goes to organizations doing good work. *The idea is to focus traders on something more important than moment-to-moment P/L. When we view something as part of a worthy cause, we're inspired to give our best.* This, we've seen, is an important dynamic in teamwork, as our self-talk focuses on our very highest and strongest motivation: *to do good things by doing things well.*

Improving our trading psychology: solution-focused approaches

Both behavioral and cognitive approaches to working on our trading psychology start with a recognition of our problem patterns. We learn to identify and disrupt them and then replace them with new states of body and mind. Solution-focused work turns this process around by starting with an analysis of situations in which our problem patterns *don't* occur. The solution-focused coach recognizes that we don't always find ourselves in the midst of tilt trading and the negative processing of performance. Indeed, sometimes we handle drawdowns well. Sometimes we focus very well during our trading, accessing our best ideas. Sometimes we are especially effective in our teamwork. In short, there are occasions in which we are able to access our best selves.

The challenge from this perspective is not engaging in the right mind frames, but *sustaining* that engagement. Instead of working to solve our problems, we should reverse engineer our successes and do more of what works for us. As I point out in *The Daily Trading Coach*, "What did I do better this week than last week?" is an excellent starting point for guiding our self-coaching.[133]

> **The goal, from a solution-focused perspective, is not to correct the worst of our trading, but to identify, understand, and grow our experiences of success.**

Once again, self-awareness precedes meaningful change. We need to be aware of our best trading practices in order to more consistently draw upon those. When we develop market insights, express those well, and manage their risk well, we want to ask ourselves, "How did I do that?"

For instance, analyses of my best trades were what taught me that I am most likely to find promising ideas and trade them well when I'm in a state of prolonged, intense concentration. In that state, I process more and I process better. A major reason I pursued brain wave biofeedback was to more consistently and effectively access 'the zone.' This is a clear application of positive psychology, as the goal was not to eliminate conflicts and negative states, but sustain optimal functioning.

The solution-focused framework suggests that it is every bit as important for me, as a trading coach, to meet with traders after periods of good performance, not just when they are having problems. Similarly, it is important for traders to include in their performance reviews what they did well, not just the mistakes they made. When our trading problems are not occurring, it means we might be drawing upon a hidden strength. Similarly, when we're doing well, we might be engaging in our unique best practices. *Once we identify what is working for us and why it's working, we can become more intentional in drawing upon our underlying strengths.*

A very simple example of this is that I find certain music inspiring. Over time, I've built a YouTube playlist of my most stimulating and meaningful songs and I play this during my market preparation, my writing—anytime I want to perform at my best. Such music places me in a creative state where I'm able to see broader and deeper and make connections that I would miss in other mind frames. I've found that a variety of elements of lifestyle, from sleep quality to exercise, similarly contribute to my optimal mindset in trading. I use the Fitbit watch to monitor these and to ensure that my daily routine keeps me in my physical zone.

Notice how the exceptions to our problem patterns, such as being in states of emotional and physical well-being, can then anchor our daily trading processes. We study, study, study what we did well with the aim of discovering the process elements that contributed to the success. We can then try those out in a purposeful way and, if we continue to find them helpful, we make them parts of our daily routine. The goal of solution-focused work is to identify the ingredients of our success, so that our best trading contributes to our best practices.

The next time we draw down and handle it well, it's worth asking ourselves, "Why didn't I overreact? Why didn't I allow my mistake to sabotage my entire trading day?" Very often, we'll identify states of body, qualities of self-talk, and preparation practices that enabled us to maintain our focus. Over time, these best practices can be assembled in a checklist, so that they become consistent parts of our trading process. *The key to making this solution-focused approach work is to become as vigilant in identifying our trading successes as our mistakes.*

It is very, very common to read the journals of traders and find one entry after another detailing everything they did wrong. If we're always focusing on our shortcomings, how are we supposed to internalize a sense of mastery and competence? Our journals need to educate us about what we do well so that we can observe our cognitive and emotional strengths in action. We are not failing traders looking to improve. We are good traders who fail to consistently do what we do best. No amount of problem focus, positive psychology tells us, can acquaint us with who we are at our best.

Case study: making use of context in our trading

A little while ago, I conducted a review of my trading, focusing on my periods of best performance. What was I doing on those occasions that I might not be doing at other times? The answer was not one that I anticipated. It wasn't that my mindset was better during the good trading periods; nor did I eat, sleep, or organize my time better when I was making money. *Rather, prior to my best trading, I reviewed many macro markets and consulted them before formulating my ideas.* That surprised me, as I'm a short-term trader. My best reviews emphasized two factors:

1. Are macro markets moving in a coordinated, thematic fashion?

In other words, is there a coherent narrative linking what we're seeing in the U.S. dollar, U.S. interest rates, stocks, and commodities? For instance, recent economic statistics might be suggesting growing economic weakness, fueling expectations of central bank rate cuts. This is leading value stocks to outperform growth shares, and it's contributing to downturns in the dollar, commodities, and interest rates. Once I perceive this theme—this overriding correlation among markets—I can ensure that my trades benefit from the thematic pursuits of large, institutional participants.

2. Are markets following clear trends and cycles?

If markets are not trading thematically, that means that idiosyncratic factors might be influencing oil, stocks, the dollar, etc. By breaking down recent price action into two components—trend and cycle—I can anticipate market direction and use movements against the direction to time entries and exits. In the idiosyncratic environment, I can draw upon cycle-based tools such as John Ehlers' adaptive moving averages to specifically look for stocks that are clearest in their cyclicality and trend. These, I found, are most likely to set up the cleanest trades. *The review of my trading found that my best results came, not from the biggest moves, but the clearest ones.* When I waited for the clarity of movement, my hit rate on trades improved meaningfully.

In short, my best process seemed to begin with the big picture and identifying whether we were trading with a dominant theme. If so, I generally traded stock indexes or ETFs best aligned with this theme. If no such theme was evident—i.e., asset classes were not trading in a clearly correlated way—then I looked within the stock market for the 'in play' opportunities of sectors and individual stocks with clear trends and themes. When I followed this preparation process, I traded with a much more settled, clear, and confident perspective. To put it bluntly, I felt like I knew what I was doing. When I did not engage in the process thoroughly, I felt as though I was chasing opportunities, not patiently allowing them to unfold.

> **Our best trading practices both reflect and nurture our best trading psychology.**

In this case, the solution-focused framework was especially effective because it started with an open-minded examination of best trading periods. I did not enter the review with preconceived ideas. Indeed, I expected that what I would find would be more related to lifestyle factors than concrete trading practices. Fortunately, because I kept notes as part of my daily review, I could see that my notes were more detailed during the periods of strong performance and more coherent, linking various markets, time frames, and modes of market behavior (trend/cycle).

The solution-focus encouraged me to do more of what was working for me, and that led to a more detailed structuring of my premarket preparation. Interestingly, as I became more rigorous in my prep, I entered the trading day in a better mindset: more focused and more energized. Our solutions are often found in reverse engineering our trading practices when we're making money. *Our positive trading practices nurture our most positive trading psychology.*

The power of the solution-focused approach is magnified many times over when we trade with a partner or within a trading team. Imagine that you are part of a pod of three traders that prepare for the day ahead each morning, conduct midday and end-of-day reviews, and set goals based upon recent performance. As we have seen, such teamwork creates a trading process that keeps us organized and constructive. Now take the pod concept a step further. Suppose each member of the group identifies what he or she did especially well during the trading day and maps out the best practice behind the good trading. Then, at the end of the day, the teammates share their best practices and each trader makes a specific effort to focus on and incorporate one of those in their next day's trading.

Such a sharing of strengths turns positive psychology into a daily process, as everyone learns from everyone else and accelerates their learning curve. *When trading partners share their best practices, they turn mentoring into a daily part of trading process.* Everyone benefits from the successes and strengths of the others, creating a powerfully inspiring work environment. The key to this approach is to recognize that, every day, we do something, in some way, that avoids our trading problems and affirmatively contributes to our success. *When everyone is learning from what they do well and everyone is learning from the successes of others, the result is exponential improvement in performance and mindset.*

How we trade—and how we approach trading—shapes our psychology. The risk of being problem-focused is that we unwittingly reinforce the notion that we are defective. Once we realize that, in some ways and at some times, we are already the trader we hope to become, then the challenge is not really to change ourselves, but to more consistently access the best of who we are. Few traders recognize this. I'm repeatedly asked by traders how they can avoid tilt, reactive trading, etc. *From a positive psychology perspective, they're asking the wrong questions.* They're assuming that they're broken and need to be fixed. Once they realize that, at times, they implement their own fixes, the challenge becomes one of becoming acquainted with the strengths behind those successes and more flexible in accessing and taking advantage of those.

Our most positive emotional experiences point the way to our strengths—and to where we are likely to find our solutions. *An extension of the solution-focused approach is to identify occasions when we feel most happy and fulfilled in our trading and figure out what we're doing at those times.* In other words, instead of searching for exceptions to our problem patterns, we hone in on periods in the market when we feel most alive, most purposeful, most attuned to markets, most centered, and most focused.

When we are trading in a peak mindset, the odds are good that we're actively doing something to create and sustain that mindset. The issue is not so much one of our P/L, but of our experience of ourselves when we're trading. If our generation of ideas, structuring of trades, and management of risk draw upon what we do best, we're most likely to feel our best—and that fuels our focus, our energy, and our creativity. Many developing traders do not reach their potential, not because they're trading with a poor psychology, but because they're trading with a suboptimal psychology. We are most likely to engage markets successfully when we're fully engaged in markets.

Traders often recognize their solutions when they catch themselves feeling happy, fulfilled, and energized in their trading. From the perspective of positive psychology, the goal of trading psychology is not just a reduction of stress, but an enhancement of the peak states that fuel our best performance.

> Our well-being alerts us to our optimal processes.

I recently worked with a portfolio manager who reached out to me after having hired two team members, both of whom had made an excellent start in their trading. The team was freely sharing ideas, and they were successful in finding opportunities in different markets and strategies. Not surprisingly, the team was performing well and was on pace for a nicely profitable year. The reason the team leader contacted me? He wanted to know what more he and the team could be doing. His intuition was that he and the team still had further to go to reach their potential.

In the solution-focused mode, I asked the PM to tell me about occasions when he felt the team was operating closer to its potential. Everything might not have been perfect, but when had the team functioned at its best in the past month? The PM mentioned a team offsite event in which they socialized and attended a number of learning sessions. When we delved into what was going on during this event, it became clear that the team was at its best when it was learning and sharing in a collegial environment. Being on the trading floor was fine—and necessary at times—but what brought out the best in team interactions was getting away from moment-to-moment business and engaging each other creatively.

Based on that observation, we discussed ways of generating creative 'offsite' time even when the team was onsite. That way, the team could make 'offsites' a standard part of daily trading practice. By conducting the offsites midday, the team effectively broke up the trading day and tapped into activities that were energizing. I've found that many of the most effective solutions for traders and teams have been ones of process, drawing upon activities that are engaging precisely because they engage our trading strengths.

Sustaining our work on trading psychology

In the first two chapters, we explored trading as a performance activity and emphasized the idea that cultivating the best trading psychology comes from exploiting talents, developing skills, and maximizing our mindsets. We also saw how we are best able to maximize our mindsets when we learn trading the right way and give ourselves the opportunity to find markets and strategies that best draw upon our competencies. Trading psychology, we learned, is not something we append to trading, but is developed and sustained in our trading processes. Still, all of us bring our emotional baggage to our trading endeavors. When we react to markets and P/L personally, we lose our freedom to see opportunities and threats clearly and objectively. Behavioral, cognitive, and solution-focused methods are ways in which we can identify and reframe the patterns of thought, feeling, and action that can interfere with even the best trading processes. These methods help us change our disruptive patterns by catching them in real time, disrupting them, and replacing them with more constructive responses. Solution-focused methods naturally bring an element of positive psychology to our self-work, by identifying what we are doing when we are not having trading problems and when we are trading at our best. Once we recognize our best practices, we can draw upon behavioral and cognitive strategies for practicing them and accessing them regularly. In other words, solution-focused approaches alert us to what we do well; behavioral and cognitive methods help us turn those best practices into robust habits.

> The goal of trading psychology is to empower us to serve as our own trading coaches.

Having worked with many developing and experienced traders, my experience is that the hardest part of changing our trading psychology is not the complexity of the methods, but rather the consistency of implementing them. Even short-term approaches to psychological change require repetition and practice. A well-worn principle is that we need to do something new the same way each day for 30 days before it becomes a natural part of us. *From this perspective, the goal is not simply to change how we think or feel, but to create new, positive habit patterns of thought and feeling.* One of my most popular TraderFeed posts described FIGS: Focused, Intensive Goal Setting.[134] We change ourselves by making change a daily part of our lives, day after day after day.

If we have to motivate ourselves to change, we're likely to relapse when our levels of focus and energy decline. Once a change has been repeated sufficiently, it becomes a natural part of us, freeing us to pursue further performance improvements. For this reason, our work on coaching ourselves must be ongoing, regular work, not just occasional adjustments during times of poor trading. We are looking to internalize and expand our best practices, not just correct our shortcomings. *It is the consistency of our change efforts that helps us create positive habit patterns and sustain our improvements.* Life is a gymnasium, offering many stations to build our trading fitness.[135]

Practical takeaways from Chapter Four

1. The key skill essential to working on our trading psychology is self-awareness. We cannot change a pattern in our thoughts, feelings, or behaviors if we're unaware of that pattern. Once we identify that the pattern is occurring, we need to summon the awareness of the destructiveness of the pattern, triggering the sense of urgency to not allow the pattern to play out. It is our full acknowledgment of the consequences of our negative patterns that provides us with the motivation to do something different.

2. Once we disrupt a pattern of thought, feeling, and/or behavior that has interfered with our best trading, we can utilize behavioral methods to shift our state of consciousness and reprocess our stress. Through repeated exposure, we can divest stressors of their emotional impact, making them familiar and non-threatening. It is the repetition of stressful triggers in controlled conditions that gives us control over our most negative trading patterns.

3. Many times, it's what we tell ourselves about market events and not the events themselves that stresses us out and disrupts our trading. Cognitive methods offer a structured format for identifying the events that trigger our negative thinking and the beliefs that are part of our stressed-out self-talk. We can then challenge those beliefs and replace them with more realistic, constructive alternatives, training ourselves to reprocess triggers in real time. Once again, it's the repetition of these techniques that enables us to internalize them as new, positive habit patterns.

4. Solution-focused methods bring our attention to what we are doing when problem patterns are not occurring, encouraging us to identify what we are already doing that is working for us. An examination of our best trading tends to reveal strengths in terms of our coping. Once we're aware of these strengths, we can practice them and proactively utilize them during the heat of trading. By regularly enacting our best practices, we can turn them into standard parts of our trading processes. The goal of positive trading psychology is to improve our coping, but also to grow our trading strengths. Simply correcting our weaknesses will not, in itself, cultivate our strengths.
5. The goal of a positive trading psychology is for you to become your own trading coach, intercepting negative performance patterns and building positive ones. The best use of a trading coach is to help you learn how to become your own best mentor and coach.

As exciting as positive psychology has been, it continues to expand, promising new strategies for improving ourselves and our performance. In Chapter Five we will explore some of these frontiers and what they promise for our trading.

CHAPTER FIVE

EVOLVING FRONTIERS IN POSITIVE PSYCHOLOGY

THUS FAR WE'VE looked at trading as a performance discipline. We've seen how the unique psychological challenges of trading can be addressed through training and development that provides ongoing deliberate practice. We've also explored performance practices that address potential psychological disruptions of trading, including behavioral and cognitive approaches. We've reviewed practices that build our positive psychology by improving our focus on markets, our teamwork, our best trading, and our generation of unique trade ideas. *The intersection of positive psychology and trading psychology suggests that trading success is built upon the information processing and personality strengths we bring to markets.* It also teaches us that successful trading can only occur in the contexts of lifestyles that are grounded in who we are at our best, providing us with energy, fulfillment, closeness to others, and meaningful challenge. My sense is that we have only scratched the surface in terms of the promise that positive psychology can bring to trading performance. In this chapter, we'll explore promising frontiers of positive psychology that will likely reshape trading practice in the years to come.

Two ways to approach markets

Dr. Jason Williams makes the valuable point that trading success must draw upon our personality traits and strengths.[136] If we are to be consistently profitable, how we trade must be an expression of who we are, leveraging what we do distinctively well. This not only includes our emotional makeup and interpersonal traits, but also the ways in which we process market action. As I think about the successful market participants I've worked with, two very different approaches to market opportunity stand out: *short-term trading and position trading*. The key difference between these is that shorter-term traders hold a limited number of positions at one time and typically hold their positions for minutes to hours. Position traders typically hold quite a few positions at any one time and manage them over a period of days and weeks. *These are very different games, and they call upon different strengths.* Most notably, short-term traders and position traders process different information and process information differently. Consider an analogy: On the surface, what the 100-meter sprinter and marathon runner do are similar, but these are distinct sporting events requiring radically different talents. The training each undergoes is quite different, and the psychological challenges differ.

Much of what has been written about trading psychology has been derived from authors' experience with beginning, independent short-term traders. This fails to capture the psychology of experienced, successful short-term traders and it does not address the psychology of profitable position traders. As a rule, beginners wrestle with the emotions of risk and reward and the uncertainties of financial markets. Experienced, successful market participants are much more concerned with cultivating unique ways of identifying and exploiting opportunities in markets.

Once we achieve a degree of emotional mastery, the challenge is to see what others don't see and take actions that elude others. In other words, the arc of development begins with overcoming emotional disruption and continues with a positive focus on cognitive mastery. This mastery requires different forms of perceptual creativity for the short-term trader and the position trader.

> The growth of market participants is a movement from emotional mastery to information-processing mastery. Successful shorter- and longer-term traders process unique information and process familiar information uniquely.

Short-term trading success

Let's begin with short-term trading. As I walk the trading floors of proprietary trading firms, one thing stands out: There are many computer screens active at all times and these screens are tracking different things, from breaking news to chats with traders to charts of markets of interest. Each chart displayed typically carries a wide range of information and the various charts track different time periods. To give a simple example from my own trading, I generally have charts of the S&P, NASDAQ, Dow, and Russell futures markets in front of me, as well as charts of the major S&P sectors, such as energy (XLE); consumer discretionary (XLY); technology (XLK); etc. I track each of these on multiple time frames (minutes to hours) and each chart displays indicators such as volume, overbought/oversold (RSI), and moving average crossovers (Ehlers' adaptive moving averages). Other traders display charts of stocks 'in play': those displaying unusual movement and volume, as well as those responding to news items and/or data releases. These charts also cover different time periods, allowing traders to quickly place shorter-term movement into a longer-term context.

The arc of idea generation for the short-term trader begins with scanning—tracking a broad range of instruments and time frames—and proceeds to pattern recognition and a narrowing of attention. Something will jump out for the trader and suddenly the broad attention to various instruments and time frames will focus on a specific pattern that is setting up. At SMB Capital, for example, each trader develops 'playbooks' of patterns that make sense to them and that they study intensively and trade successfully.[137] For instance, for any given trader, there may be a playbook for stocks breaking out of trading ranges on elevated volume and/or breaking news. There may also be a playbook for reversals of stocks that have moved well beyond their moving averages. The playbook details what to look for, using multiple examples with annotated charts. Clearly, this is training in pattern recognition, immersing the trader in the identification of opportunity.

In short, the broad awareness and open-mindedness of the short-term trader scans and scans until a pattern shows up that fits their particular playbook: their internalized templates for opportunity. Once potential opportunity is detected, there is an important shift as broad, sustained information processing transitions to narrow, intensive focus.

Think of a predator in the wild scanning the environment for prey and then noticing a grazing animal. At that point, there is a rapid shift from breadth of processing to narrowed, intensive processing. The short-term trader then typically moves to a shorter time frame to achieve best execution of the opportunity. For instance, there may be a pullback in price that leads to an oversold level on a short time frame and that finds near-term support at a price level higher than the prior low. The trader may use this as an opportunity to buy the asset and participate in a bounce with excellent reward relative to risk.

Observe how the short-term trader begins with a cognitive telescope, surveying the broad range of opportunities in the market, and quickly transitions to a microscope to focus on a particularly attractive situation. That microscopic perspective continues as the position is managed. Partial profits might be taken at the next overbought juncture, for instance, with a piece of the position held in anticipation of new highs. Implicitly or explicitly, the experienced trader has developed rules for turning promising trades into actual profits. Once the trade is exited, the trader may return to telescope mode, scanning to locate fresh opportunities.

POSITIVE TRADING PSYCHOLOGY

> Successful short-term trading requires unusual flexibility of attention, combining bigger-picture awareness with detailed focus. It also requires an unusual ability to sustain attention over extended time periods.

What we see among especially successful short-term traders is the ability to sustain the telescope mode even as they are tracking positions in the cognitive microscope. For example, the trader may be holding a long position in a stock and might place an order in the market for taking profits and stopping out. That then enables the trader to return to broad scanning to exploit opportunities occurring at the same time. This rapid shifting between idea generation and trade management is especially helpful when a market catalyst creates multiple short-term opportunities. The ability to quickly transition between breadth and depth of processing creates diversification for the short-term trader: the ability to simultaneously pursue and trade multiple, different instruments and time frames.

Perhaps most impressive about this trading style is the real-time blending of sustained concentration and flexibility of focus. The successful short-term trader processes more information than others, does so more quickly, and does so more flexibly. *These are distinct cognitive talents.* To engage in such varied and intensive processing hour after hour, day after day is more than mere 'discipline.' Quite simply, the successful short-term trader is a superior processor of information. Such prolonged, focused processing can only occur if the trader finds what they're doing to be enjoyable, challenging, and meaningful. They possess the curiosity to enjoy the hunt for opportunity, and they possess the competitive mindset to translate opportunities into actual profits. Personality and talent intersect to create unusual success. As Jared Tendler points out, successful traders are "ruthless" about performance, but also "find moments to have fun with the process."[138]

What makes this a frontier for positive psychology is that, due to the ability to see more in markets, successful short-term traders experience more opportunity than the average trader. They thus experience more of the positive thoughts and emotions that accompany the discovery of opportunity. The cognitive strengths of the skilled short-term trader fuel emotional strengths, making trading a sustained process of positivity. If we can train traders in the active skills of pattern recognition and sustained focus—as in the biofeedback training that I described earlier—then we push the boundaries of what's possible both in trading success and in trading mindset. What if, for example, we can train ourselves to become such fertile idea generators that trading becomes a continuous process of discovery and profiting from discovery? Whether it's by augmenting our search for opportunity with artificial intelligence (AI)-driven research or with advances in training superior brain functioning, improvements in information processing promise advances in trading psychology by keeping us forward focused and grounded in evolving opportunity.

There is one additional aspect of short-term trading that accounts for distinctive success. The successful trader is very good at not losing money, and is also quite good at finding occasions to make significant money. Typically, the latter occurs when traders 'size up' positions. The good trader finds favorable risk/reward opportunities; the great trader is able to identify and aggressively exploit situations in which the reward is meaningfully greater than the risk.

When working with short-term traders in Chicago, I found it helpful to conduct reviews of their trading, focusing on the P/L of their largest positions during a given month. Such a review tells us whether sizing up positions occurred as the result of impulse or overconfidence or whether it represented a true discernment of special opportunity. *Invariably, the best traders were distinguished by their profitability when trading largest.* They had a keen ability to pounce when the opportunity was greatest. When I spoke with them about their decision-making process, they often focused on their ability to read other participants in the market. They could identify what the herd was thinking and doing, and they could identify occasions when the herd could move prices. A simple example would be an oversold stock with modest expectations for a coming earnings print.

The print would come in higher than expected and traders would realize that those who had shorted the stock (or who had avoided it altogether) would need to revise their views and enter positions. By acting quickly, ahead of the herd, these traders created superior reward-to-risk situations that could be sized up.

As we've seen recently, Denise Shull emphasizes that an important question for successful traders is what others are likely to perceive in the future.[139] The ability to size up positions requires more than analytic ability and more than pattern recognition. It calls upon a kind of empathy, where the trader can place themselves in the shoes of other market participants and anticipate their actions. *Notice the cognitive complexity involved in such success: tracking multiple instruments, honing in on individual opportunities, and keying in on the actions and intentions of others.* I rarely see this cognitive complexity acknowledged in writings about trading; indeed, there are many attempts to portray trading as 'easy' to lure those looking for a quick buck.

The reality is that success begins with distinctive information-processing talents and is honed through skill development and intensive practice. Great short-term traders read the market, and they also read the traders of their market. They combine intelligence with shrewdness. Shull stresses that, "You make money by correctly predicting the opponent's future perception—not 'the facts'!"[140] "Price," she points out, "reflects perception."[141] This is a perspective built into the Market Profile work of Jim Dalton and colleagues, as time and volume are displayed to reveal the behavioral tendencies of traders in response to price.[142]

Case study: cultivating the killer instinct

The very best and very worst short-term traders I've encountered have been the most aggressive in their risk-taking. Earlier I mentioned the poster in my office depicting a military sniper hiding in the brush. The sniper is quiet and careful, attracting no attention. Then, when the target comes into sight, the sniper becomes very calm and focused and takes the lethal shot before returning to the mode of evading detection. There is no drama to the professional sniper's work; excitement and emotionality will attract the enemy's attention. *The best killer instinct is cold, calculated, and controlled.*

I've found this same dynamic among the most successful short-term traders. The least successful seem to be trading for a thrill and continually hunt for opportunities to take big risk. They're excited to put on the risk and their emotions rise and fall as their positions move. Ironically, it's precisely that distractible, emotional mindset that prevents these traders from experiencing the intuitive sense of genuine opportunity.

> **When we're busy shouting to ourselves, we can't possibly hear subtle market signals and follow subtle market shifts.**

The very successful short-term traders, on the other hand, are good at sitting and waiting. They don't *need* the thrill of getting big, but they are very sensitive to the lining up of opportunity that signals the opportunity to size up. It is precisely because they don't need the big score that they're able to exercise the patience to wait for asymmetric opportunities. The best traders let the best trades come to them.

Stefan was a leading trader in his London prop trading office. He made seven figures a year routinely, but you would never know that from his dress and demeanor. He was friendly and enjoyed talking and joking with others on the trading floor. He was all business, however, when his formal preparation for trading began. He scanned news item after news item, chart after chart, looking for something that jumped out at him. He was receptive to hearing the ideas of others and he often called out what he was seeing and hearing. To watch Stefan, however, was a bit like observing an air traffic controller: processing lots of information at one time and continually juggling priorities. All was routine until something out of line occurred and then it was a quick shift to intense focus.

I had worked with Stefan when he was a developing trader and, at that time, he never traded large. He stood out, however, because his eyes would light up when something in the market made sense to him and signaled a trading opportunity. It was clear that he loved approaching the market as a giant puzzle and gained energy from finding pieces that fit together.

Long before Stefan was a financial risk-taker, he was an intellectual risk-taker. He would become excited about seeing a pattern in what he was observing and would call it out to the group. My sense was that he wasn't calling out his ideas simply to be a good guy and help others. Rather, his enthusiasm compelled him to call out the ideas: he loved assembling the puzzle.

Over time, I noticed that Stefan used a particular tone of voice and body language when he saw his best opportunities. Those trades were invariably good ones that worked out quickly. In our work together, I helped Stefan recognize how these best trades set up, not only in markets, but also in his subjective experience. One of the rules we established was that if he spontaneously called out an idea, that meant he believed in it and should size the trade accordingly. His excitement about what he saw was real information; it was not reflective of a mere need for action.

Over time, he became better and better at sizing up his best ideas because he became better and better at finding market patterns that jumped out at him. Stefan's development was a great example of positive trading psychology, because his success came less from correcting problems and controlling emotions than from recognizing and acting upon his strengths. He looked at more things to trade across different time frames and was quick to identify when patterns lined up and deserved to be expressed in larger trades. Because he didn't *need* to trade big, he was able to size up trades on the most promising occasions.

Over the years, I've worked with a number of successful short-term traders and I've continually found that the best ones process more information than the others. They scan more information than the average trader and are quick to recognize patterns in the information. Because of their love of the hunt, they are able to move rapidly from seeing to doing, pouncing on opportunities out of enthusiasm. For the same reason, they are able to sit back and observe, observe, observe when opportunities don't stand out. Perhaps most impressive of all, they are able to sustain this focus hour after hour, day after day, week after week. Only a love for the process of pattern recognition could sustain such intensive effort.

It was only after working with successful traders like Stefan that I realized that, not only did they process more information than their peers, but they processed higher-quality information. In other words, they weren't simply looking at more chart patterns or scanning more news items; they were looking at things that others did not focus upon. I invariably detected an element of originality to their processing when they walked me through their screens. For example, one trader made special note of how global markets behaved in their opening hours, as these were typically the most liquid periods in which large, institutional participants would show their hands. By watching the opening hours in Japan, London, the U.S., etc., the trader would get a sense for sentiment that helped him pounce on intraday opportunities. Yes, he traded on a short-term basis, but his vision was broader than that of the average day trader.

> Successful traders gather better and more information than their peers and they are better at synthesizing this information.

Positive psychology helps us see that there is an important element of creativity in the work of the best short-term traders. This is what we might call 'perceptual creativity,' as opposed to the kind of problem-solving creativity we often associate with successful entrepreneurs. *Very successful short-term traders see differently than their peers.* They look at different things and connect those in different ways. One stock or sector will behave differently from others in terms of volume, volatility, and/or price directionality and suddenly the trader detects a possible short-term breakout trend. Rate, commodity, currency, and stock markets will move in unison and the trader quickly processes potential new activity among large macro participants. A big part of what holds the trader's interest is the hunt for patterns of interest and the focus on unique patterns.

The use of Market Profile displays, depicting volume at various price levels across different time periods, is a great example of perceptual creativity. Skilled profile traders, such as Jim Dalton, quickly see shifts in volume in different instruments at specific price points, alerting them to changes in market participation.[143] They are literally seeing markets differently from others: as the outcomes of auction processes, not just chart patterns.

A very important consideration, relevant to the frontiers of positive psychology and trading, is the degree to which the performance of short-term traders is state-dependent. In other words, it makes sense that the active trader processing many markets at one time and quickly detecting patterns will suffer in their performance if they are highly fatigued or distracted. *To what degree, however, can these short-term traders hone their abilities to perceive and act upon rapid patterns in markets by building their capacity for undistracted concentration and open-mindedness?*

Recall the work on brain wave biofeedback that I described earlier. Might it be the case that we can literally identify the brain states associated with top traders and train these through biofeedback routines? In one of my Muse sessions, I noticed that I remained highly focused in my brain waves, but still showed a relatively high degree of body movement during the exercise. The movement was subtle; I wasn't even aware of it. As a result, I pursued the rainforest exercise with the aim of minimizing movement while maximizing the state of serene focus.

The combination of very high physical control along with brain wave control resulted in a deeper sense of being in the zone, somewhat akin to self-hypnosis. In such a heightened state of awareness, might subtle market patterns jump out at me? Might I be quicker to respond to such patterns and express them with superior reward relative to risk? Positive psychology, focusing on building strengths and not just ameliorating weaknesses, could lead to entirely new directions for coaching, helping short-term traders become better and better at processing information. Quite simply, we can learn to be more perceptually creative if we can sustain states that are hyper-receptive to subtle shifts in markets. That is an amazingly promising frontier of positive trading psychology that we will explore in detail in the final chapter.

> The trading psychology of the future will leverage new ways of building information-processing strengths as well as correcting emotional and trading weaknesses.

Position trading success

As noted earlier, a major shortcoming in trading psychology texts is that they describe the (largely emotional) challenges faced by beginning (usually day-) traders. Most of my work is with hedge funds described as 'multi-strat,' because they invest in multiple markets and strategies at any given time. These funds actively manage capital to minimize drawdowns and strive for diversification in their portfolios. Because of this, they are able to earn solid risk-adjusted returns: good upside with reduced downside. Such large funds manage capital across global markets, combining quantitative, discretionary, and hybrid strategies. They are thus able to achieve returns that are not highly correlated with large market indices. This makes them attractive to institutional investors, who are looking to exceed passive index returns. If they can do so with high diversification, large funds can find the investment holy grail: superior and unique returns achieved with modest drawdowns.

Notice how such position trading is quite different from the short-term trading we were exploring above. Where the short-term trader looks for what is moving now, the position trader seeks a basket of assets that promise unique movement over time.[144] Where the short-term trader pursues a series of different individual positions over time, the position trader diversifies with a portfolio of multiple instruments. *What makes the position trader active is the continuous reconstruction of the portfolio, as individual positions become more and less attractive, more and less correlated, more and less volatile, etc.* The active portfolio manager always maintains a twin focus: tracking the ups and downs of individual positions and markets and tracking the overall movement of the portfolio.

Rarely if ever do short-term traders talk about portfolio construction. Indeed, at any given time, they hold a limited number of positions, not a diverse portfolio. What makes portfolio management active is the process of continually adding to the book and trimming it as risk/reward shifts for each position and for the entire portfolio. The focus is not just on each position, but on the dynamics of the portfolio as a whole. Basso refers to this process as "filling in the potholes" in one's market positions. By adjusting and minimizing vulnerabilities, we maintain superior risk-adjusted returns and also sustain a more level mindset.

Consider one fund that I currently work with. They are managing over $25 billion of capital, which means that they are too large to participate in common day-trading strategies. They also are too large to participate in relatively small, illiquid markets, because it would cost too much money to get in and out of positions. As a result, the fund has to focus on major asset classes in major economies—interest rates, currencies, large equity and commodity markets—to achieve their returns. Because other, competing funds face the same constraints, the hedge fund has to find unique ways to deploy and manage its capital so that it can stand out from the competition.

Such large hedge funds are really teams of teams, as the capital allocations to portfolio managers become too large for a single person to manage. Hiring a team with diverse experience and talents allows for diversification of positions, which contributes to superior risk management of the portfolio. Over time, the expanding multi-strat hedge fund increasingly looks like a collection of small hedge funds. *It is a team of teams.* The challenge for management is to balance the allocations and risk limits for each team so that the overall fund portfolio can meet its goals of superior, unique risk-adjusted returns. The challenge for team leaders (portfolio managers) is to generate unique ideas and then combine and manage them uniquely to achieve returns relatively uncorrelated with the results from other teams.

Here's what that looks like in practice when I work at a large fund for a day of coaching. There are one or more trading floors and, for the most part, teams sit together to facilitate communication. Separate areas of the floors are dedicated to management staff that oversee risk, execution, and the proper accounting of positions, profits, and losses.

Risk management and support staff are important to the teams, as they make sure that risk is properly accounted for and that transactions proceed smoothly. The team might consist of a leader/portfolio manager, one or more developing assistant PMs who manage smaller 'sleeves' of capital, and one or more analysts who research ideas for the risk-takers. Often, there is a desire among the analysts that they will eventually grow into assistant PMs, and there are ambitions among the assistant PMs that they will grow their capital allocations within the team and eventually merit the allocation of their own capital and the mandate to build their own team. As a result, everyone has an incentive to perform well and earn promotions and capital. The team is truly a business within a business, and it fulfills an important role in developing the next generations of investment talent. At their best, hedge fund teams are talent incubators.

> Once so much capital is managed that trading must take place in teams, people management becomes as important as money management.

This is a very important dynamic in terms of positive trading psychology. Successful PMs need to be effective people managers, even as they are tracking and exploiting opportunity across markets and balancing/rebalancing/sizing/resizing portfolios. *The most successful PMs, in my experience, derive particular satisfaction from the growth and progress of team members*. They are invested in mentoring and spend considerable time and effort to help team members advance in their careers. This commitment builds loyalty among team members, inspiring their best efforts. PMs who are focused largely on their own performance and who view team members as mere helpers in the overall P/L inspire little loyalty and are particularly vulnerable to losing teammates when better offers come their way.

This has been a powerful dynamic recently: with so much capital to manage, funds constantly need to find talent and actively 'poach' promising team members from other firms. Losing team members to competitors is a tremendous loss for a fund, as they invest time and energy to hire and develop up-and-coming talent, only to lose it by failing to secure team member commitment and loyalty. Each team leader is challenged to create the kind of team environment that will not just recruit talent, but retain and grow it.

Right away, it's easy to see that there is a dimension of trading psychology different for position management teams than for short-term traders: the ability to nurture and navigate interdependent relationships. Very successful PMs are very successful in team building and growing talent within the business. The integration of position management strengths and active people strengths is unique, and it's becoming increasingly important as funds grow and their teams grow. This calls for flexibility in functioning and the ability to quickly shift from analytical research modes to trading modes to interpersonal support and development modes. This can only be possible if PMs possess multidimensional strengths and a particular passion for multitasking. It's also only possible among PMs who find unique meaning and challenge in the juggling of money management and people management. *A vital frontier for positive trading psychology is cultivating effective blends of instrumental and interpersonal activities.* The successful hedge fund manager has to be both an intellectual leader and a team leader, continually researching and expressing ideas; constructing and reconstructing portfolios; and engaging and developing talent. This is particularly relevant for individual traders who collaborate with peers within proprietary trading firms and trading communities. We're increasingly seeing individual traders operate within virtual teams, achieving the collaboration benefits of money managers at trading firms.

I have found the solution-focused approach to be especially valuable in working with position managers. The initial period of this work is spent in observation. I interview everyone involved in collaboration and gather their perceptions of what has worked distinctively well and what has fallen short. Recall that the solution-focused perspective is to explore what is going on when the team is *not* having problems. In those exceptions can be found hidden strengths worth identifying and pursuing.

For instance, one team that had struggled for much of the year went through a profitable period. We intensively deconstructed the successful period and found that it corresponded with increased collaboration of team members. This was a bit surprising, as the team members had very different spheres of coverage. What happened, however, is that the members gathered information that was more broadly relevant than they expected. The analyst who subscribed to an external data service tracking patterns of airline demand (number of empty seats on commercial flights) found that these numbers lined up well with overall consumer spending and sentiment, informing analysts studying consumer discretionary companies.

Increased communication within the team kept team members informed and stimulated, and that led to better idea generation and higher degrees of conviction in ideas. By identifying what the team was doing when it was firing on all cylinders, we eventually were able to create lists of 'best practices' that built on existing strengths.

This is an important frontier for positive trading psychology. *Once we reach a certain size of capital, we best develop ourselves as money managers by developing those who can contribute to our money management decisions.* As we become larger in our trading, we need to become better in our ability to work effectively with others. From solo trading to teams to entrepreneurial think tanks: what we're seeing in the multi-strat hedge fund world is the development of creativity factories. With more and more capital pursuing liquid markets and strategies, creativity inevitably wins. Tomorrow's positive trading psychology will be a training ground for creative perception and thought. The shift from short-term trading to position management opens the door to greater collaboration and diversification of positions.

Case study: teams within teams

Once a team grows to ten or more members, any portfolio manager's bandwidth will be sorely tested to adequately supervise and mentor everyone. To make this growth sustainable, senior team members hire junior talent that help them build out their pieces of the business. *This means that the growth of the overall team occurs by developing small teams within teams.* This, we've seen, is an important dynamic, as it provides analysts and assistant PMs with opportunities to cultivate the people skills necessary to their eventual development as full team leaders/PMs.

One of my roles in the development of these teams within teams is to help analysts and junior PMs identify and hire the right talent. Because I can assess the psychological and investment strengths of the team member and also assess the strengths and experience of candidates seeking to join the teams, I am able to help ensure that team building leverages the best of everyone. The cost of a bad hire is quite high in terms of lost time and energy. The advantages of a good hire are multifold, as the right additions to teams make everyone else better.

My role as a trading psychologist is to understand the positive psychology underlying team success and the successes and strengths of the candidates for positions. The goal is synergy—and that only occurs when there is creative compatibility between the team member who is hiring and the candidate for the position. If the team is to sustain positive psychology as it grows through differentiation, it is not enough to hire talent: the goal is to hire talent that yields synergies, making everyone better.

> When working with active investment teams, positive psychology must embrace team/organizational psychology, not just the performance psychology of individual team members.

Mack came to his team as a quantitative analyst, specializing in economic models that track growth trends across different regions, economies, and industries. As he expanded his models to include multiple regions of the world and specialized data from industry trade groups, he recognized that he needed help organizing his databases. He also saw a great deal of opportunity for exploiting new information. He hired a recent computer science graduate with a strong interest in applications of artificial intelligence (AI).

The new grad helped integrate the different databases and create a user-friendly interface for conducting queries. What attracted me to the candidate during the interview process was his initiative in using a recent version of ChatGPT to conduct natural language analyses of documents. Mack followed the research reports of sell-side analysts and industry experts and wondered if it might be possible to use AI to uncover when these sources of information displayed particular confidence in their views. The resulting collaboration between Mack and his new hire led to worthwhile findings, and it also fueled Mack's growth in project management and people management.

One of Mack's key strengths was his intellectual curiosity and love of discovery. By finding a new teammate who shared this strength, Mack was able to create a team within a team that excelled at intellectual entrepreneurialism. Over time, Mack's unit expanded in ways that maintained this spirit and eventually was granted its own allocation of capital within the team. The team within a team now became a portfolio within a portfolio within a fund of portfolios. The focus on positive psychology—the cultivation of complementary strengths and processes that nurtured an environment of exploration and discovery—supercharged Mack's development. This focus on teamwork is very relevant to individual position managers who look to collaboration to expand the range of their idea generation.

As money management increasingly occurs within team contexts, the role of trading psychology expands considerably. Rarely do my meetings at position management firms focus on the mindsets of individual market participants and the emotional mistakes of their buying and selling. Instead, I function more like a team coach, helping team members develop their productivity by playing to their strengths and also helping teams and teams within teams figure out how they most successfully work together. Positive trading psychology is all about figuring out what we do when we are at our best and understanding how we achieve our successes. We create a model of our ideal selves and that model guides our performance and our development. I've often defined my role as being one of "comforting the afflicted and afflicting the comfortable." When position managers go into drawdown, it's important to find the comfort that comes from learning from mistakes, and then it's important to take on the challenges of pushing boundaries and broadening horizons. The best teams study themselves as intensively as they study markets and trades.

> **Failure is a step in the process of growth. Success educates us in our optimal performance.**

Position managers actively invest in themselves and in collaboration. Recall the opening prologue of this book: We are the entrepreneurs of our lives. If we are not getting better and better and if our teams aren't continually evolving, we are sure to be left behind by ever-changing markets. One of my favorite ways of engaging teams is to hold monthly reviews that become ways of identifying individual and collective successes and figuring out how to build upon those. Those reviews are also opportunities to reflect on what could have been done better and how team members can help each other implement improvements.

The best coaching comes from helping team members coach themselves, turning drawdowns into opportunities for greater teamwork and team cohesion. Great position managers and investment teams 'fail fast': they are quick to innovate and quick to learn from the results of their innovations. An important frontier of positive trading psychology is helping PMs and teams sustain the growth mindset that brought them together. The role of the positive trading coach is to never let teams and team members forget who they are at their best. The focus on best practices sustains our best—and most positive—psychology.[145]

Short-term trading and position management: shared frontiers

We've seen that the market activities of short-term traders and position managers are quite different. Where short-term traders benefit from rapid scanning and quick information processing, position managers succeed when they can search and research bigger-picture opportunities in markets, assembling diverse portfolios of unique positions that are managed over time, often with active collaboration. Despite these differences, there are shared challenges among short-term traders and longer-term position managers that call for unique solutions from positive psychology.

As noted earlier, our growth often comes from drawing upon strengths that are latent—not necessarily our core strengths. Indeed, many times traders and investors run into problems precisely because the strengths that they've been relying upon cannot meet the new challenges that have appeared. This is important: *suboptimal performance doesn't necessarily come from mistakes and weaknesses, but from the failure to cultivate the entire range of our strengths.*

If we perform a thorough inventory of our most successful and fulfilling experiences, we invariably come across many strengths that typically work in combination. For example, my analytical interests and abilities are key to my identification of market opportunity, as I track shifts in market breadth across equity markets and sectors. This draws upon my pattern recognition and, as mentioned earlier, also makes use of my ability to carefully listen and detect themes, whether it be in counseling sessions or trading sessions. I can become so focused on those core strengths that I don't make optimal use of other competencies, such as the ability to network with other professionals and identify shifts in their views and sentiment. When I run into trading problems, it's often because I've become so engrossed in the analytical areas of interest that I find myself relatively isolated from the views of others. By doubling down on reaching out to others and incorporating their standout perceptions and ideas, I expand my perspectives and can address where my recent trading has fallen short.

Both short-term traders and position managers easily fall prey to focusing so much on what has worked that they become stagnant and stop drawing upon the abilities that have contributed to their career success. A good example of this is the PM or day trader who becomes locked onto a particular opportunity and stops looking at the broad range of evolving market moves. Recently, the investors I worked with concentrated their attention on U.S. rates markets, given statements from members of the Federal Reserve and expectations of rate cuts. This focus blinded them to equally significant developments—and important moves—in the equity and currency markets of Hong Kong, China, and Japan. At the same time, short-term traders were so preoccupied with the technology stocks that had been relatively strong that they failed to exploit meaningful moves in the real estate and utilities sectors, which had benefited on the shift to lower rates. For these market participants, their core strength of focus and pattern recognition overwhelmed their secondary strength of broad, creative perception. The answer to their performance challenges was not to correct anything negative in their mindset, but to ensure that their daily processes actively drew upon the full range of their abilities to survey a broad range of markets and uncover new, emerging opportunities.

> Often, the focus needed to jump on opportunity and take meaningful risk shuts out our abilities to process information broadly and creatively.

Whether it's in my trading or the trading of those I work with, positive psychology reminds us that success can be a trap. We can keep doing the same things until we inevitably run into market situations that call for new things. Very, very often it's our latent, secondary strengths that can open the door to adaptation and fresh opportunity.

Yet another psychology frontier is helping position managers and active traders juggle the demands of work life and personal life. It is not at all unusual that longer-term traders have to follow news and market developments outside standard trading hours. They also need to spend time outside those trading hours to conduct and review research, update views, etc. Similarly, short-term traders typically need to track their markets during premarket trading, especially during active periods of economic data releases and earnings reports. Savvy traders recognize that how markets trade overseas provides important clues to larger-picture demand and supply from international institutional participants.

Tracking markets intensively during the day and then also in the evening and early morning can take a toll. It becomes very difficult to switch off, and this impacts one's quality of life. Exercise and healthy eating are frequent casualties, and family life can suffer. Burnout destroys our ability to think quickly and uniquely: we become less creative as we grow more tired and overwhelmed. *What this means is that drawing upon our strengths in markets is necessary for success, but not sufficient.*

We also need to understand what brings us enthusiasm and passion outside of markets, so that our personal lives keep us energized and at the top of our game at work. This is more than simple 'work-life balance.' Positive psychology tells us that we want *work-life optimization*, drawing upon the best of all our lives' endeavors. This is an important frontier for trading psychology across different types of market participation.

Few of us consciously engage our personal lives to bring out the best in our trading and even fewer engage their trading in a way that fuels their relationships and personal pursuits. Simply correcting trading problems as they occur does not make us stronger across life spheres. When we begin our work in markets in energized, clear-headed states, we want to figure out what we might have been doing right in our personal lives. When we feel fully engaged at home, we want to review what we were doing in our trading that helped us stay positively focused. *Our positive focus in one area of life inevitably fuels other areas.*

Case study: work-life optimization

A PM I worked with at a macro hedge fund, Bob, seemed unusually happy and energetic whenever I spoke with him. His P/L could be up, down, or flat and he always seemed to maintain a positive attitude. It wasn't anything false or forced; he naturally seemed unflappable. During one period of drawdown, he reached out to a PM at a nearby desk and asked how he was doing. He knew that the PM had positions similar to his and must be drawing down as well. The two of them brainstormed and figured out how they would manage their positions from that point. They were informing each other, but also supporting each other. After collaborating, Bob suggested that they meet up with their spouses after work for a bite to eat. The PM readily agreed, eager for a respite from the difficult markets.

When Bob returned to his desk, he explained the foundation of his personal process: how he optimized his life activities. He said that, "I always try to make sure I have something specific to look forward to." Before he went to bed, he planned new market research that held considerable promise. Before he went home after a difficult day, he planned an enjoyable get together after hours. Each week, he set a goal for his trading that grabbed his interest and enthusiasm; each quarter, he and his wife planned a unique vacation. Always, always something to look forward to: Bob optimized work and life by making sure he was never stuck in a coping mode that drained energy, but instead was planning activities that would inspire and excite him. For him, positive psychology was an ongoing activity.

To repeat a theme that has appeared throughout this book: trading psychology is so much more than correcting the problems that beset beginning traders. When we open ourselves to insights from positive psychology, we find new frontiers for making the most of our market participation. Simply improving our mindsets, accepting risks, and maintaining discipline in taking profits and losses is not going to connect us with the best of who we are. Nor will corrective work help us recruit our unique strengths in each phase of the trading process and during each phase of life outside of markets. Positive psychology challenges us to find our frontiers and discover ways of translating our talents into unique skills and processes.

An additional frontier of positive trading psychology lies at the *intersection between* short-term trading and position management. The ability of short-term traders to read patterns of price and volume and detect subtle shifts in volatility and correlation is extremely helpful to position managers in getting the best prices for their entries and exits. Similarly, the ability to synthesize a broad range of fundamental and price data that are central to the position manager's idea generation and portfolio construction can also aid the short-term trader in identifying the most promising areas of market opportunity (i.e., those most likely to attract large market participation). Getting good prices for entries and exits allows investors to size up positions; taking advantage of institutional money flows enables short-term traders to ride the most meaningful market moves. Integrating the strengths of other market approaches challenges us to expand our strengths. The longer-term trader must become better at fast processing and pattern recognition; the short-term trader must grow their ability to analyze and synthesize information. It's a great example of how we grow by cultivating areas of latent strength to broaden the application of our talents and skills.

What does positive psychology offer the developing trader?

If you are relatively new to trading, the best thing you can do is surround yourself with those who are genuinely successful. Whether in trading communities, proprietary trading firms, or hedge funds, exposure to the thought processes and trading practices underlying success will provide role models for your own development. As we've seen, simply taking courses, watching videos, and reading books cannot substitute for real-time mentoring. *Many of the emotional challenges faced by new traders are a function of the improper structuring of their learning processes.* They would face similar emotional frustration if they attempted to teach themselves saxophone playing, ballet dancing, or shotput throwing. Positive psychology for the developing trader begins with observation of different professionals and a search for the trading approaches and markets that best draw upon our talents and skills. It continues with structured, deliberate practice that provides experiences of learning and mastery. The goal of the early learning curve is to discover and develop one's niche in markets. *That* is what builds confidence and clarity.

Consider the format of the mentoring that I described earlier in my collaboration with Jeff Holden and SMB Capital. The developing traders met in the morning to identify stocks that were displaying unusual movement. They then traded these opportunities in the morning session with small size and met as a group with Jeff midday to review how the trades unfolded and how they were best traded. This process of prepare-trade-learn then continued in the afternoon. Journals maintained by the trainees tracked their progress, identifying what they did right and what needed improvement in their performance. The trainees were encouraged to interact with one another, so that there was an opportunity to benefit from the experience of others. Think of how many more 'reps' these traders were getting compared to someone attempting to learn in a solo, unstructured environment.

When I first learned trading many years ago, sophisticated simulation platforms were not available and so I printed out short-term and medium-term charts at the end of each trading day. The charts tracked the movements of various equity indices and they also captured volume, overbought/oversold indicators, and the NYSE TICK. Day after day, I reviewed the charts and began to see patterns within and across markets. I did this every day for a number of months before ever placing a trade. Though I did not realize it at the time, I was training myself in the pattern-recognition skills that I so enjoyed in working with people as a psychologist. The learning process was effective because it played to my strengths and nurtured a positive psychology separate from P/L.

In *The Playbook*, Mike Bellafiore references my description of the learning process in trading[146] and stresses the importance of having fun while building mastery. The important question, he emphasizes, is whether we are better today than the day before.[147] What supercharges the development of beginning traders is the energy and enthusiasm of improving every day in an area of work that draws upon their greatest skills and talents. *The learning process will only succeed if it provides a gateway to our most positive psychology.* It is vitally important to structure our learning so that our reviews and work on improvement *give* us energy.

Sometimes aspiring traders become so enamored of the possibility of making a living from trading that they quit their day jobs and spend all their time trying to make money. Invariably this leads to disaster. Even in well-developed training programs, it takes many, many months—and usually a year or more—for a trader to become consistently profitable. When you consider the length of the learning processes in other performance fields, you can appreciate that this amount of time is not unusual. It is important to have a financial cushion during one's learning period, so that the *need* to trade and make money doesn't overwhelm the need to trade well. If we feel pressured to make money, it will be impossible to access our most positive emotions and strengths.

> If we don't love the process of developing as traders, we will never get to the point of actually succeeding as traders.

All of us have distinctive learning styles. Some learn best interactively, sharing ideas and experiences with others. Some learn best through hands-on trial and error. Some learn best intellectually and conceptually. Our learning styles reflect cognitive strengths. How we structure our learning plays an important role in how engaged we'll ultimately be in the learning process. Again and again, the lesson is clear: we maintain the best and most positive psychology when we figure out how we are wired and play to those strengths. This is equally true for shorter- and longer-term traders.

Case study: learning our strengths by experiencing our weaknesses

Most of my learning as a developing trader took place during morning hours when I had free time in my work schedule to follow markets and place trades. Of necessity, these were short-term day trades. Over time, I was successful with this trading and learned how I performed best and worst. For instance, if I placed trades very early in the morning session shortly after the NYSE open, on average I lost money. If I placed trades after the first half-hour of market action, my trading was profitable. The reason for this taught an important lesson for my development.

The reason I placed trades in the first 30 minutes was that I entered the day with a view. I was eager to profit from this anticipated movement and thus placed my trades early in the session. *When I began the day in an open-minded way and let trades set up, I was much more focused and much more likely to profit.* The problem was not simply that I experienced

FOMO when I had an opinion and needed to trade early in the day. Rather, I was not playing to my strength: my best thinking is inductive, not deductive. What I'm good at—as a psychologist and as a trader—is gathering information and letting patterns come to me. If I impose a predetermined view on a counseling client or on a market, I'm much less flexible because I'm less inclined to listen carefully. *I had to experience my weakness to fully appreciate my strength.*

I learned this same lesson when I attempted to expand my time frame and hold positions for days rather than intraday. With the longer time frame, I lost the intimate connection to unfolding market data and completely lost my feel for the market. I had to experience failure as an investor to appreciate what made me successful as a trader. Similarly, I found that my trading results were best in the morning, worst midday, and in between late in the day. Those results showed me that I was most successful in markets where I could detect the activity of larger market participants and ride their coattails. If volume was low and there was little volatility, I generally didn't find meaningful signals.

More recently, I found that my traditional focus on stock index futures kept me from exploiting strength in particular stock sectors that occur in rotational markets. When I only traded the ES (S&P 500) futures, I left significant money on the table. By broadening my data collection to include breadth information from each market sector and each equity market, I became able to identify opportunities specific to segments of the market. I also more readily identified when rotational markets were transitioning to trends and vice versa. It was only by seeing the weakness of my narrow focus first hand that I was able to embark upon an expansion of my trading.

> Some of our most positive learning experiences come from our most distinct shortcomings. Every weakness is an opportunity to expand a strength.

The developing trader always, always needs to keep score. Only detailed review enables us to reverse engineer what we do best and leverage our trading strengths. It is detailed review that also uncovers our greatest shortcomings so that we can grow fresh areas of strength. Sometimes we need to experience our greatest weaknesses to uncover our highest strengths. For the developing trader, every victory and every setback are invitations to learn and grow and thus become part of our positive psychology.

I recently wrote a blog post with the title, 'Why Can't I Improve My Trading?'[148] If you reflect, it's really quite remarkable: There is so much material disseminated each week, month, and year—all devoted to making traders successful. This has been going on for year after year and still traders find themselves unable to achieve consistent positive returns. The emphasis of the blog post is that developing traders are learning in the wrong modalities. *Our trading problems—and our best trading performance—are state-dependent.* We best retain experience if the states of mind and body during our performance mirror those during our study. If we learn trading ideas and practices when we're in the cool mode of the classroom, it's unlikely that we'll be able to recruit those lessons when we're in the heat of the trading moment.

The example I use in the blog post is parachuting from a plane or helicopter. We could learn all about packing and deploying a parachute during classroom sessions, but would that adequately prepare us for our first jump? No, we learn parachuting by engaging in safe practice jumps (where we're tied to a secure line) and then gradually moving toward actual small jumps and then larger jumps. By rehearsing our skills in the midst of real-time pressure—training ourselves what to do when the adrenaline is pumping—we prepare ourselves for our eventual leap from the copter. Similarly, we can study market 'setups' and research market patterns in the calm of after-hours review, but are we truly training ourselves to focus on the right things and make the right decisions when we're caught in moving markets and the risks and rewards of P/L?

Much of what is offered under the guise of trading psychology and coaching is advice. It is not training. Advice does not instill the right thoughts and actions at the right times. We learn trading by doing trading: entering the modes of uncertainty, risk, and reward and training ourselves to do the right things at those times. State-dependent learning means that we are most likely to internalize the right mindsets and skills if those are practiced in conditions of progressive challenge.

Where positive psychology intersects state-dependent learning is by anchoring our training to optimal cognitive and emotional states. If we engage in our training only once we've entered deep states of focus and energized mindset, then we are best prepared to draw upon our learning when we sustain focus and energy during our real-time trading. In other words, work on our performance in optimal states of mind and body enables us to draw upon our learning once we recruit those optimal states in our trading.

> If we perform best in optimal mind and body states, then our learning and practice need to be conducted in these states. It is because learning is state-dependent that it's vital to rehearse our skills in the same positive frames of mind and body that we want to be in during our trading.

Most traders attend to their psychology when they're trading, not necessarily when they are reviewing their trading and learning from mentors. Bringing real-time psychology into our training is a promising frontier for positive trading psychology. Our states during learning and practicing must mirror our optimal states during trading if we're going to maximize our performance.

Case study: evidence-based trading psychology

Together with my colleagues at SUNY Upstate Medical University, I recently wrote a chapter for a standard reference work in psychiatry.[149] The chapter covered brief approaches to psychological change, drawing upon the evidence of recent research and practice. *An important conclusion from that chapter is that emotion is necessary to change emotion.* Simply distancing from our psychological difficulties will not help us overcome them. When traders attempt to get away from frustration, negative thinking, overconfidence, etc., their first inclination is to take a break and get away from the state that can hurt their trading. That can be helpful, but will it actually *change* our psychology?

A powerful technique, grounded in the research literature, is to replace (unwanted) emotion with (more desirable) emotion. More specifically, we can undo negative emotional states by actively evoking their opposites. For instance, let's say I miss a trade and begin to blame myself and become caught up in destructive self-criticism. If I can recognize what I'm doing in real time and actively invoke the opposite state, I not only reduce disruption, but reinforce the ideal mindset for performance going forward. Thus, when I'm engaged in self-criticism, I might stop, recognize what I'm doing and how it hurts me, and then actively visualize successes I have experienced that bring a sense of gratitude and appreciation. I can vividly evoke occasions when correcting a mistake brought me learning and greater profits going forward and I can feel inspired by the ability to learn and bounce back. Once I've immersed myself in the positive perspective after having been frustrated, my energized state makes it easier to internalize that positivity so that it will stick with me.

It's tempting to assume that the path to changing negative emotionality in trading is to remove emotionality from trading. Research evidence suggests otherwise. Emotion is our gateway to change. By moving from negative emotion to positive emotion, we train ourselves so that, eventually, that transition becomes automatic.

Frontiers of positive psychology research

As mentioned earlier, a wealth of research is conducted each year that highlights dimensions of our optimal functioning. Here are a few areas that are likely to impact trading psychology in years to come:

Hardiness

Compton and Hoffman cite the work of Kobasa regarding psychological hardiness, the ability to weather stress without experiencing physical distress and illness.[150] People with a high degree of hardiness experience better overall well-being than their counterparts, because they feel they have greater control over their lives. This is partly because they interpret sources of stress as challenges rather than as crises and because they display a high degree of commitment to supportive relationships and meaning systems that make sense of sources of threat. The research suggests that hardiness can be learned, helping people cope better with stress. It is quite likely that training people to be hardy can help them display greater hardiness in challenging trading situations. Learning to replace negative emotion with positive experience, as described earlier, can become training in hardiness.

Post-traumatic growth

Zelenski reviews research studies that document how traumatic events can lead to growth and eventual well-being.[151] Very often, this growth follows from deriving a sense of meaning and purpose behind the challenging events. Indeed, a number of studies find that more than half of all people report some positive outcomes to their traumatic setbacks. Clearly this is related to hardiness, and it suggests the possibility of training traders to handle losses and frustrations. A solution-focused perspective, examining how each trader has already been able to weather setbacks, may be useful in a more comprehensive training for dealing with trading upheavals. In that vein, Zelenski emphasizes that the most effective training is fostering actual coping strengths, not simply convincing people to look at setbacks through rose-colored lenses.[152] Asking "How is this setback going to make me better?" and then implementing a concrete improvement plan turns traumas into growth opportunities.

Mindfulness

Cheavens and Feldman review a wide range of research that documents how training in mindful self-awareness increases our capacity for attention and regulation of emotion.[153] Indeed, it appears that mindfulness activates brain areas involved in decision making (the prefrontal cortex) and deactivates brain areas responsible for emotional response (the amygdala). Mindfulness interventions thus help people improve their problem-solving capabilities as well as improve their mood.[154] As mentioned earlier, this is precisely what I have found through the use of brain wave biofeedback (neurofeedback). We can train people to control their brain functioning to optimize focus, concentration, and problem-based coping. Such brain training may be the most efficient way of developing traders, both in their idea generation and in their position management. Per the aforementioned case study, a tremendously promising frontier is studying brain wave patterns associated with positive emotional experience and training the brain to remain in optimal psychological modes.

Creativity

Sawyer and Henriksen offer a wide-ranging review of research on creativity, both among individuals and groups. They point out that creative ideas are most likely to occur when we maintain a broad awareness of relevant and related information.[155] By connecting these connected pieces of information, we are able to generate insights that help us see the world in new and promising ways. Interestingly, these insights are typically not flashes of awareness, but rather the accumulation of many small insights over time that draw upon different cognitive processes, such as analogies and causal analyses.[156] *In other words, we're most creative when we look at many things in many different ways over a period of time.* This is especially true of creativity in groups and teams, where innovation occurs over time as the accumulation of contributions from multiple members.[157] Trading psychology has become so dominated by the emotional issues facing newer traders that it has largely ignored the creativity challenges faced by established traders and teams.

> The trading psychology of the future will focus on building processes that help experienced traders (who have overcome their rookie errors) become consistently profitable performers.

Positive deliberate practice

When traders review their performance, they often focus on mistakes they have made. If they are doing deliberate practice well, they then translate those observations of mistakes into goals for correcting the errors and improving performance going forward. As indicated earlier, there are many missed opportunities to review trading strengths and successes and then turn those into positive goals for repetition and expansion. It is by studying and growing our strengths that we cultivate our best practices and anchor trading processes in what we do best. Positive deliberate practice for teams allows for members to learn from each other's successes and accelerate their growth. Peterson points out that intuitive decision making underlies over 90% of all our choices.[158] By exposing ourselves again and again to our best intuitive decisions, we hone our abilities to "listen without thinking" and anchor our trading in what we do best.[159] This is a promising frontier for trading psychology, as we focus on the building of success, not just the correction of failure.

Positive emotional experience

Rarely do traders and teams of traders consciously structure their practice and performance time to maximize positive experience. Diener and Biswas-Diener review research suggesting that challenges are experienced as more doable when we're happy.[160] They also point out that productivity increases when we're in positive states, in part because happy people tend to be more creative.[161] This is an important reason why teamwork can be valuable to trading performance, even for solo traders who constructively network with peers. When we are with others who are in states of well-being, we experience more energy and positive support. Trading processes need to be structured for learning and growth—and they're most likely to achieve their ends if they are also meaningful and fun. *An important frontier of positive trading psychology is positive trading experience.* Even during periods of drawdown, trading can bring fulfillment for those invested in learning, growth, and social engagement. In that context, every trading day can bring a positive emotional P/L.

Resources for positive trading

In the trading literature, we're seeing a growing body of work describing the successes of established traders and coaches. From these works, we can identify best practices that we can adapt to our own trading. When we read the works of multiple experienced, profitable traders, we can synthesize their ideas and practices into a trading style that fits with who we are and what we do best.

Positive trading models

There are many resources available from successful traders that offer positive role models for developing professionals and those seeking to expand their repertoires. Mark Minervini, in his book *Trade Like a*

Stock Market Wizard, breaks performance down to a process of trading with the trends and fundamentals of individual stocks that display the characteristics of performance leaders and locating trades with specific entry point analysis (SEPA).[162] He expands on successful trading practice in his subsequent text *Think and Trade Like a Champion*, emphasizing trade planning, risk management, market timing, and optimal position sizing.[163] He addresses issues related to trading psychology in *Mindset Secrets for Winning*,[164] outlining best practices for maintaining a competitive mindset and structuring rehearsals for peak performance. Minervini offers ongoing mentoring to stock market traders, allowing them to tap into his best practices, learn in classes, and track trading progress over time: an unusually complete training platform.[165]

Mike Bellafiore of SMB Capital, in his book *One Good Trade* describes the process for finding stocks 'in play' by reading and identifying opportunity from shifts in bids, offers, and short-term price and volume behavior.[166] In his subsequent text, *The Playbook*, he describes the process of developing detailed game plans ('playbooks' that capture best trading practices in terms of stock selection and trade execution).[167] SMB offers a number of videos on best trading practices on their YouTube channel.[168] They also offer training and mentoring sessions delivered by experienced, successful traders, most of whom I know personally and can vouch for, including SMB partner Steve Spencer.[169] Their collaboration with Lance Breitstein has been especially instructive in illustrating the thought and action patterns of an established and highly profitable trader.[170] Lance has developed a Magnum Opus of his training lessons and videos, which provides a rare opportunity to get inside the head of a very successful proprietary trader.[171]

Especially helpful have been the trading contributions of Rolf Schlotmann, who offers extensive trader education via the Tradeciety site, including courses and videos.[172] Of particular value is the Edgewonk trading journal developed by Schlotmann and colleagues, which enables traders to track their results, identify areas for improvement, and hone in on strengths.[173]

Edgewonk links with a large number of brokerage platforms, making it relatively easy to track one's trading.[174]

In *The Logical Trader*, Mark Fisher outlines his ACD methodology, which identifies trading opportunities by tracking price action with respect to opening ranges and pivot ranges from prior time periods.[175] These price levels provide reference points for decisions regarding buying and selling, making discretionary trading more rule-based.

Jim Dalton's classic work on Market Profile, *Markets in Profile*, describe a tool for visualizing volume behavior at various price levels.[176] He illustrates its use in creating rules for trading market breakouts and reversions to trading ranges. Dalton builds on this work in his recent text *Markets and Momentum*, illustrating how traders can draw upon time, price, and volume to capture market movement.[177]

Brian Shannon's book *Technical Analysis Using Multiple Timeframes* breaks markets down into stages of behavior at different time frames, enabling traders to derive rules for buying and selling that integrate shorter-term opportunities with bigger-picture perspectives.[178] His text *Maximum Trading Gains with Anchored VWAP* illustrates how this unique tool, applied across market time frames, can help identify promising trading opportunities and keep traders in their trades as they work out.[179]

Drawing upon a variety of technical tools from simpler to more complex, Anne-Marie Baiynd's *The Trading Book* describes ideal trade setups and rules along with checklist items to guide decision making.[180] Her work effectively combines trading psychology with trading methodology.

Andrew Aziz, in his book *Advanced Techniques in Day Trading* offers a range of day-trading strategies employed in his trading community, Bear Bull Traders, including ways of finding stocks that are in play and exploiting advanced patterns among technical indicators.[181] Aziz and Sheehy-Kelly, in *TradeBook* share their adaptation of Bellafiore's playbook concept, helping traders clearly structure their trading edges.[182]

A longer-term perspective is offered by Eve Boboch, Kathy Donnelly, Eric Krull, and Kurt Daill in *The Lifecycle Trade*, who have studied patterns in 'super growth stocks' among IPOs.[183] They point out that, by tracking the 'lifecycle' patterns of these high-growth opportunities, traders and investors can participate in particularly promising longer-term returns.

An unusually clear and practical view of portfolio management comes from Tom Basso's *The All-Weather Trader*,[184] which breaks down a 'complete trading strategy' in terms of process components and then adds the ingredients of investing to turn short-term trading into active investing,[185] thereby 'filling in the potholes' in our trading strategies.[186]

Positive perspectives on trading

A number of successful traders and trading coaches have also summarized the lessons they've learned in their development. Linda Raschke, in *Trading Sardines*, describes her growth as a highly profitable trader, finishing each chapter with wisdom she has learned.[187] This nicely complements her classic text with Laurence Connors, *Street Smarts*, which highlights strategies that have made her a Market Wizard.[188]

Indeed, the *Market Wizards* series of five books consists of interviews with successful traders and author Jack Schwager's commentaries on what has made them special. The first in the series was especially helpful in my development, providing fresh perspectives on the management of risk and opportunity.[189]

Tom Hougaard's text *Best Loser Wins* is particularly effective in describing the thought processes that underlie winning trading, including the need to embrace failure and cultivate unique mindsets.[190]

In a similar vein, Yvan Byeagee's *Trading Composure* captures in detail how embracing the uncertainty of markets frees traders to make sound decisions in a constructive mind frame.[191]

In an especially unique framework, Steven Goldstein captures trading performance as a cycle in *Mastering the Mental Game of Trading*, enabling traders to track their psychology across the various elements of their processes.[192] He also offers coaching for traders based upon the ideas in his book, drawing upon the experiences of both institutional and individual traders.[193]

Denise Shull's *Market Mind Games* explores the thought processes underlying trading and what we need to do to preserve and build our mental capital, including an understanding of our unconscious thought processes.[194] Jared Tendler, in *The Mental Game of Trading*, explores such common emotions as greed, fear, and frustration and helps traders understand where they come from and how to master them.[195] Steve and Holly Burns explore trading psychology in their book *Complete Guide to Trading Psychology*, explaining how we can overcome our egos to stay grounded in our trading processes.[196] Gary Dayton, in *Trade Mindfully*, explores the relationship between our states of consciousness and our trading success, emphasizing the need to maintain mindful self-awareness in our deliberate practice and trading.[197]

A number of classic texts have been instrumental to my development. Ari Kiev, in *Trading to Win*,[198] *Trading in the Zone*,[199] and *The Mental Strategies of Top Traders*,[200] captures a range of strategies employed by successful professional traders, including some of the success elements touched upon in this book, such as creativity and teamwork. Particularly enlightening for me has been Victor Niederhoffer's *The Education of a Speculator*[201] and his text with Laurel Kenner, *Practical Speculation*.[202] More than any other author, Niederhoffer has a gift for extracting insights across a variety of fields and applying those to financial markets.

Finally, I would be remiss if I did not acknowledge the original catalyst for my development as a psychologist and trader, the works of novelist-philosopher Ayn Rand. It was my exposure to *The Fountainhead* in my sophomore year at Duke University that set me on the path of positive psychology.[203] "Anyone who fights for the future," Rand observed in *The*

Romantic Manifesto, "lives in it today."[204] The quote at the opening of this book is my acknowledgment of her personal and professional influence and inspiration.

Among the books that I have written, *The Daily Trading Coach* has specifically described psychological techniques for improving performance;[205] *Enhancing Trader Performance* describes in detail how to develop trading expertise;[206] *Trading Psychology 2.0* delves into ways of playing to our strengths and drawing upon creativity in developing our own best practices;[207] *The Psychology of Trading* captures the overlap between psychological change processes and changes in our trading;[208] and *Radical Renewal* explores the role of spiritual development in trading success.[209]

All of the books listed here—and indeed referenced in this book—sat in front of me as I wrote *Positive Trading Psychology*. They have been sources of information and insight in my own trading and in my work with traders. It may seem expensive and time-consuming to acquire and read many books, but when you consider the potential return for our trading, reading is a phenomenal investment. Just one valuable idea from each book, applied diligently to our trading processes, can compound into significant learning and growth.

> We contribute to our positive psychology by fueling our own positive development.

Resources for my current trading

My own trading process incorporates elements of investing, quantitative analysis, and big-picture thinking with detailed short-term rules for trading with superior reward relative to risk. I have found the research services sentimentrader.com and quantifiableedges.com to be especially helpful for back-tested idea generation. I also make use of the data services at barchart.com, stockcharts.com and marketcharts.com sites, tracking indicators across multiple markets and equity sectors and also downloading information for my own analyses. Excellent mentoring resources include the SMB Capital training program at www.smbtraining.com; the Market Profile-based work of Jim Dalton found at jimdaltontrading.com; and the training resources and trading ideas of Brian Shannon at alphatrends.net.

My approach to trading is to first define current market patterns and back test them for past performance. The goal is to always trade with a historical edge. If a clear edge has been identified, I then drill down to short-term price and volume behavior and identify the setups that provide solid reward relative to risk in trading those historical patterns.

For example, let's say that I see that breadth in the technology sector is much stronger than that for the overall market during a recent move higher. I then examine over the past five to ten years how technology stocks have tended to behave subsequently. If there is a demonstrable momentum edge to the upside, for example, I'll then look for a short-term pullback in the XLK (tech) sector to enter a long position as soon as I see a bounce, setting the previous low as a stop. This approach to trading draws upon my interests and strengths in mathematical analysis and also my earlier-mentioned strength in pattern recognition, creating a blend of quantitative and discretionary decision making that keeps me positively engaged in markets. The resources for my current trading, listed above, have been instrumental in helping me find the bigger picture edges that guide my shorter-term trading.

Practical takeaways from Chapter Five

1. Positive psychology is a growing area of research and practice, and its development as a discipline can fuel our development as traders. There are challenges unique to short-term trading and position trading: the two require different cognitive and emotional strengths. Learning from the strengths of each form of market involvement can very much improve our overall performance.

2. A key strength underlying success in short-term trading is pattern recognition: seeing how price and volume shift over time and how the market we're following is behaving relative to other, similar markets. The ability to sustain focus throughout trading days is essential to profitable short-term trading.
3. A key strength underlying success in position management is the ability to identify longer-timeframe opportunities, often through an understanding of market fundamentals and researched market relationships. Operating at longer time frames helps the trader carry multiple positions, providing the possibility of diversification and a smoothing of returns over time. The longer time frames also free the trader up to not be glued to screens and engage in non-trading priorities.
4. The resources listed in this chapter will be especially helpful for those looking to develop their own approaches to trading that leverage what they do best. This may well be the most exciting positive trading frontier of all. What grabs your interest, what makes sense to you, what challenges and excites you: that is where you are most likely to find your trading edge. Your most positive psychology will further your most positive development as a trader. We need not develop in isolation; there are many resources that can support our trading growth and the growth of our trading psychology.

CHAPTER SIX

THE POSITIVE PSYCHOLOGY OF MENTORING

BRETT STEENBARGER AND JEFF HOLDEN

OUR FIRST CHAPTER emphasized that trading is a performance activity, similar in many ways to sports, performing arts, military and police work, and the helping professions. All draw upon our native talents and hone those through intensive training and mentoring. It is difficult to think of a competitive performance field where top performers simply train themselves or expect to achieve great things by taking classes, watching videos, and reading books. Research in psychology is very clear: We change through the medium of positive relationships, learning from emotionally impactful experience.[210] This is how professionals develop at successful investment banks, hedge funds, and proprietary trading firms. When developing traders join talented teams, every day becomes an opportunity to absorb the ingredients of success.

For a number of years, I have worked with active traders at SMB Capital. I am not employed by the firm, but I've worked long enough there as a trading coach that I have witnessed first hand the development of many successful traders through day-to-day mentoring. Many traders who I first worked with as beginners are now experienced traders mentoring a new generation of traders. *What has impressed me in their mentoring is how their guidance of new traders has not only imparted good trading practices but also positive trading psychology.*

I am grateful that a number of the SMB mentors have summarized best practices of their training in this book. This provides us with a rare opportunity to learn from traders and mentors who are on the front lines of trader development every single day. In this chapter, Jeff Holden and I share their best practices as they have written them up and then add our own perspectives. Jeff, as Director of Training at SMB, is a successful trader himself who mentors many new traders. Our hope is that this chapter will take the trading psychology topic well beyond the usual focus on controlling emotions and following trading plans and illustrate the lessons learned from the best practices of successful mentors.

Jeff Holden, director of training

My best practice in mentoring is to challenge developing traders to be more specific.

What's truly amazing, when talking with anyone who is passionate about the market, and especially about trading, is that everyone has a unique view and those who have been trading for even a little while often know more than even they believe they do.

When we discuss an idea, it might seem just like a normal idea, but if I challenge the trader to be more specific—to highlight the key elements of the trade that were present or to describe what they saw or felt or experienced—the details of what they have observed or experienced start to emerge. Through discussions about those details, we can often not only unlock the edge that was present in this trade, we can also begin to get a sense for when and where that edge might be present in the future. It's powerful how much we all know; we just have to be more specific!

This is a great example of a best practice that is simple, but profound. The idea that we know more than we can verbally express is called 'implicit knowing' in the psychology research literature. Often, this tacit or implicit knowledge shows up as a hunch or a gut feeling. If we're focused externally—on the ups and downs of markets and P/L—we typically miss what we know but don't *know* that we know. Jeff's prod to be more and more specific with an idea pushes the trader to put what is known into words, making the implicit explicit.

Let's say that I believe a particular stock is going to be moving higher and I'm thinking of buying. Jeff will then challenge me to explain why the stock might go higher and how I could recognize when the directional move is beginning. I would then make reference to several charts that show how the stock has been trading in a range following a move higher on positive earnings. On Jeff's prod, I will look at the shortest-term chart and note the skew in recent volume, with shares trading on increased volume during price moves higher. That could lead to an execution idea to wait for a pullback on modest volume and then buy when it appears that selling has exhausted. The focus on specifics helps translate the trade idea into a great risk/reward trade.

The best practice doesn't necessarily end here, however. Suppose someone in the training class hears my focus on the specifics of the trade and observes that the dynamics occurring in my stock are also setting up in the broad market. This now leads to a vastly increased opportunity set, as the class focuses on recent relative strength and the market sectors in indexes best fitting the trade setup. In the team context, being specific stimulates ideas for all present, acting as a catalyst for creativity. As Jeff points out, once we drill down with specifics and see how the idea sets up across stocks and indexes, we're then prepared to note this pattern in the future and take advantage of the new edge. If the trader had not elaborated the idea, it might have made a profitable trade, but would not have stimulated the development of a broader edge.

Pushing for specifics prods us to make the implicit explicit, increasing our confidence in the idea and also placing us in a mindset that is active and proactive, not reactive. Laying out the specific factors that contribute to a good trade idea immerses us in an opportunity mindset: a great example of how sound mentoring also promotes a positive psychology.

Seth Freudberg, director of options trading

The options income trading desk at SMB is primarily composed of traders who deploy systematic options trading strategies with long-term edge. The major realization that we have had over our years of training options income traders is that most untrained retail traders have never actually gone through a rigorous analysis to determine if their trading styles in fact have edge. Hard as it may be to believe, many times traders continue to trade strategies, sometimes for years, that have a negative expectancy, and then wonder why they are not making any progress towards their trading goals.

As professional traders we have learned that an entirely different approach has to be taken to assure long-term options trading success. After determining that our traders have the proper understanding of options trading fundamentals (by completing our options training program), we then require each of our traders to back test every strategy that they propose to trade with our capital. This is a powerful process for many reasons. Not only does the back test prove whether the strategy has long-term edge, but, perhaps more importantly, the back test acts as simulated practice of trading the strategy. That simulation is crucial for the trader to build the 'muscle memory' for the protocols of the strategy. And more significantly, when traders prove to themselves that a strategy works if adhered to strictly, they are much less likely to bail out on a perfectly legitimate strategy after a minor setback. The back test gives them the courage to endure drawdowns—a major psychological challenge for any systematic trader—allowing the trade to play out just as it did in the back test.

Seth offers a great example of a best practice in trading that also generates a positive psychology mindset. We saw that Jeff challenges traders in training to be more specific and drill down to details that illustrate the edge of a trade idea. Seth accomplishes something similar by challenging traders to back test their strategies before using them to put capital at risk. Performed properly, such a back test helps identify when the strategy works and when it doesn't, contributing to further understanding and confidence in the idea.

For example, one short-term strategy that I tested worked best in lower- to medium-volatility market environments and also worked best with holding periods of three to five days. Understanding these dynamics enabled me to employ the strategy only when volatility was in its sweet spot. It also helped me hold a portion of my position (often in options form) for the several-day holding period. The back test was key to knowing when to size up the trade and also was instrumental in getting the most out of the trade. With a deeper understanding of the strategy, I was more confident in trading it.

Testing strategies is especially important in options trading, because results depend not only on the right movement of the underlying asset, but also on the changes in its volatility. This is especially relevant if the option is close to expiry and is being held for several days. The decay in volatility can overcome any favorable price movement in the underlying stock or index. A proper back test will highlight the volatility environments in which the trade works and can also identify when the idea works especially well as both price movement and volatility benefit the position. The back test thus identifies potential opportunities to size up positions.

Seth makes the important point that developing traders, in their desire to not lose money, will often exit a trade at the first sign of adverse price movement. The back test, however, may suggest that the trade is worth holding for a more extended period. In such situations, the trader could end up taking small profits only to see the position move much further in their direction. Knowing how the trade behaves historically can be very valuable in holding the position through a minor countermovement and can even help traders add risk on such pullbacks. The back test is instrumental in providing the positive mindset to follow the trade plan. Once again, drilling down to understand the trade provides us with the positive psychology that comes from a sense of mastery.

Before I formally, statistically test a trade idea, I simply scan historical results. I maintain historical databases of the variables that I use to frame my index trades, such as breadth across different time frames; number of stocks generating buy and sell signals on various technical trading systems; volatility; volume; price change, and then examine forward price movement over the next 1–20 days. The databases go back at least four years to capture a variety of market conditions. As I describe in *The Daily Trading Coach*, the data are maintained in Excel sheets and I use the database functions within Excel to sort through the data.[211] If the average profitability of a pattern (both in terms of absolute average size and number of winners vs. losers) does not jump out at me, I won't bother with any further analysis. If the results look promising, I'll drill down to identify the conditions in which the pattern has been most profitable. I will also test the pattern on other market and sector indexes to see if it is broadly successful and where it might perform best. This is invaluable information in developing a plan for trading the idea.

One advantage of working at a firm like Seth's is that back testing resources are readily available to the firm's traders. There are also mentors at SMB who can guide traders in the back testing process. Perhaps most helpful of all, the firms where I work maintain clean historical databases so that it becomes easy to explore the historical behavior of trading patterns. Over time, testing many ideas gives traders a feel for which patterns perform best in particular market conditions, helping idea generation. This is an important part of what Seth calls the building of 'muscle memory.' Interestingly, performing more and more analyses feeds our intuitive feel for market patterns—yet another way in which sound trading practice fuels positive trading psychology.

Steve Spencer, partner and senior trader

Creating a pre-market game plan will dramatically improve a trader's probability of being profitable each day. Why is this the case? Because making money as a short-term trader has two requirements: The first part is developing various trading skills; the second part is stock selection.

If you have developed trading skills but not good stock selection your consistency will be lower and you will be unable to scale your trading to bigger size.

Stock selection involves identifying the stocks with the strongest money flow and other properties that allow you to control your risk. When larger market participants are heavily buying or selling an individual stock it will create higher volatility as well as greater liquidity. This creates trading opportunities for those who have trading skills.

Please make sure you read Steve's blog post on this topic at www.smbtraining.com/blog/why-i-game-plan-every-day. In this post, Steve provides very specific examples of his pre-market game planning. *One important idea behind this planning is that what you choose to trade is every bit as important as how you trade.* The how-to-trade is what Steve refers to as "trading skills." This includes being able to read very short-term price/volume action (sometimes referred to as 'reading the tape') as well as placing daily price behavior in the context of the medium and longer term. As I mentioned earlier, in my own trading, I create short, medium, and longer-term charts of a market such as the ES (S&P 500) futures, where each bar represents an amount of volume traded. Looking at my screen currently, I have charts where each bar represents 2,000 contracts traded; 5,000 contracts traded; and 15,000 contracts traded. Overlaid on these charts are moving averages and indicators highlighting moving average crossovers. Seeing how the market is behaving over various time periods helps me place shorter-term price action in context. A short-term move higher, for example, may represent a breakout of a medium-term range within a longer-term uptrend. The trading skills represent the ability to place market action in proper context and frame ideas for sizing and holding period.

THE POSITIVE PSYCHOLOGY OF MENTORING

Once a trader has those skills, Steve points out, the ability to identify stocks in play can very much help maximize the value of the skills. After all, if one sector of the market is trading with healthy trend and momentum and another is lodged in a narrow range with low volume, the same patterns on charts will likely yield extremely different results. Steve explains that good stock selection helps with the consistency of trading and enables traders to trade with larger size. This results in a distinctly positive mindset: every day's preparation is a kind of treasure hunt where we see what is moving well and moving meaningfully. Preparation thus acts as a builder of real-time trading psychology as well as game planning for the day's trade.

In the blog post, Steve mentions that his planning employs a "combination approach," where he tracks multiple trading opportunities at one time. This enables him to see how the trades in each of the stocks are evolving, so that he can take advantage of what is moving best and moving now. Notice that this means that Steve begins his day with analysis and opportunity-finding and then moves to the real-time tracking of the opportunities to identify the best trades here and now. The psychological benefits of this preparation are significant, as he feels more prepared each day, but also energized by the trade ideas he has uncovered. To no small degree, Steve's game planning is also his way of building his positive trading psychology.

Observe the interesting practice at the end of Steve's blog post. If fewer than half of the ideas he uncovers in the morning actually work out, that triggers a broader review. *When well-formulated ideas are not profitable, that is often an early sign that markets are undergoing important changes.* Of course, it could also mean that we're doing something wrong in pursuing the ideas, so a clear-headed review of our trading practice is important. When market regimes change, the setups that had been working well in the most recent period may fail to yield profits. This early warning allows the trader to step back, review how different markets are behaving, and adapt to changing conditions. Open-minded review of trading and markets when we are not making money can help us become flexible and adaptable, preventing temporary losses from becoming trading slumps. Trading psychology thus becomes preventive and proactive and losses are dealt with constructively.

Garrett Drinon, team leader and senior trader

I communicate with traders the same way I communicate with myself. Whenever I share insights on trading, as a mentor, team leader, or collaborator, I draw from universal themes that have proven vital to my own trading. I focus on these themes every day. When I make a trading mistake, I draw on this experience to help get to the next level.

In my practice, every facet of research, playbook development, review, and preparation funnels into a singular goal: maintaining an excited mindset anchored in the present. I trade at my best when focused on the present and excited about the next opportunity. I can then hear what the market is trying to say. How often have we forced trades or missed opportunities by dwelling on the past or worrying about the future? I know I have. If I'm not focused on the present, my trading breaks down.

When a trader is frustrated, maybe from a forced trade or a missed opportunity, I try to help them refocus their attention on the present. I like to share this solution: The better our preparation, the more we can focus on the present.

What does this mean?

The more data we have on a setup, the clearer the key variables, the more detailed our execution and trade management methodologies, and the more effective our screening processes, the easier it becomes to operate in the present. Think about it. It becomes easier to wait when we know exactly what we're waiting for. It becomes easier to put on size when we know the exact variables that make an A+ setup. It becomes easier to trade without the fear of missing out when we have ways of being alerted to these setups. The easier things become, the more bandwidth we have left over for listening to the market.

Notice how, in Garrett's best practice, there is a link between focusing on universal themes in trading and "maintaining an excited mindset anchored in the present." As he notes toward the end of his writeup, a detailed awareness of what goes into our best trading naturally anchors us in the present. Instead of becoming distracted by past P/L or future concerns, we ground ourselves in the details of trading process: screening, trade selection, execution, and position management. Once we are focused in the present on the steps of best trading practice, we have "more bandwidth… left over for listening to the market." This is subtle, but very important. Being process focused keeps us from distraction and provides us with greater awareness of what is happening in the market here and now. That is precisely what provides us with that 'excited mindset.' We cannot be energized in pursuing evolving opportunity if we are distracted with our thoughts and feelings in the present.

In a team context, this focus is powerful. Garrett starts by explaining that he communicates with other traders the way he communicates internally. In other words, he is as present-centered and opportunity-focused in sharing information with colleagues as he is in his own trading. This means that his interactions with other traders possess the 'excited mindset,' so that everyone is energizing everyone else. If there are multiple sets of eyes intensely focused on the present, from the screening of trade ideas to the management of the resulting positions, trading psychology becomes a team effort. Focus highlights opportunity and opportunity fuels excitement. Our psychology is embedded in what we do and in how we interact with others. Positive talk—internally and with others—gives rise to a positive trading psychology.

Finally observe Garrett's observation that trading mistakes are meant to help us get to the next level of our performance. The same detail orientation that keeps us present-centered in our trading goes into our trade reviews, focusing us on what we did well and what needs improvement. When we view our trading mistakes as our path to our growth as traders, we maintain the energized mindset. Today's mistake is tomorrow's trading goal. What keeps us in the positive mindset is not an absolute P/L number, but the focused awareness that we are always growing, always getting better. As part of his best practice, Garrett included a quote from basketball great Kobe Bryant:

> It sucks to lose, but at the same time, there are answers there. There is a constant process. It's exciting when you win, it's exciting when you lose because the process should be exactly the same whether you win or you lose. You go back and you look and you find the things you could have done better. You find things that you have done well, that worked. You figure out 'How did they work?', 'Why did they work?' and 'How can you make them work again?' But the hardest thing is to face that stuff. That's a really, really tough challenge. The mistake you made in the game… you have to do the hard stuff and watch that game, and study that game to not make those mistakes over again…

The "really tough challenge" is to take as detailed a look at our mistakes as we do with our market preparation. No one likes to dwell on their setbacks, but it's the detail of our reviews that prepares us for improvement, just as the detail of our prep sets us up for profitable trading. When we're focused on improvement, Bryant points out, it's exciting when you lose *and* when you win. That is the mindset of a champion, and it's the hallmark of a positive psychology.

Ryan Hasson, senior trader and training mentor

One of the most essential best practices for new traders is the ability to remain open-minded and absorb knowledge from those who have already achieved success. Too often, novice traders enter the market with preconceived notions about what strategies will work, or with an over-reliance on complex indicators. These traders often struggle because they fail to set aside their biases and embrace proven strategies. Trading is not about being right or wrong; it's about developing positive expectancy and the discipline to follow consistent, well-defined rules and processes. New traders who align themselves with experienced mentors are more likely to achieve long-term profitability, as these mentors can provide insights and practical wisdom based on their own success.

In addition to this mindset, I emphasize the importance of starting small and experimenting with various strategies in the early stages of a trading career. By trading with small size for the first three to six months, new traders can protect themselves from significant losses while exploring different approaches to the market. This period allows traders to gather data, analyze their performance, and identify where their edge lies. Once they've discovered what works, I encourage them to refine their strategies, cutting out what doesn't yield results and doubling down on what does. By further researching and understanding the strategies that show promise, traders can gain confidence and categorize setups based on historical performance and expected value, leading to more calculated and informed trading decisions.

Ryan points to an important element of success for developing traders: open-mindedness. Many come into trading for ego reasons and want to trade *their* ideas and *their* style. This makes them less open to observing and learning from others. In almost all performance fields, training begins with mimicking a mentor, learning their way of succeeding, then learning under another mentor and absorbing their lessons, and so on. It is only over time that the experienced student is able to draw upon the parts of the learning/mentoring that best fit their talents and skills to develop their own style. The early part of the learning curve is really a process of copying the masters and internalizing their practices. Sound training means encountering a market situation and asking, "What would my mentor be thinking here? How would my mentor trade this market?" Circling back to the mentor allows for identifying when you've followed the mentor well and when you've fallen short of their example. Your initial goal is not P/L; it's performance-based learning. *Before we can find our own greatness, we have to absorb what is great in others.*

Note the important point Ryan makes: In following the experienced, successful trader, the developing trader cultivates "the discipline to follow consistent, well-defined rules and processes." In other words, it is not just a set of entry and exit rules that a new trader is learning. The structured learning process builds discipline, rule-following, and a process mindset. Once again, we see that well-designed training builds our trading psychology. In learning to follow a mentor, we hone the discipline to follow markets. In mimicking the rules of a senior trader, we learn to be more rule-governed in our future trading.

This is why online podcasts, webinars, and courses can only go so far in moving us toward competence and expertise. Telling someone what to do in the abstract is different from role modeling the right actions in real-time situations. When a medical student begins their clinical education, they shadow senior students, interns, senior residents, and attending physicians on their medical rounds in a hospital. There they observe how their mentors think about their patients and develop appropriate treatment plans. Seeing many cases and following many mentors creates an immersive learning environment. "See one, do one, teach one" is the mantra of medical education: first you observe, then you try it yourself under supervision, then you share and cement what you learned with a new student. Ryan wisely observes that the same process applies to becoming a successful trader.

Ryan also makes an important point regarding "starting small." Early in a learning curve, we're likely to make many mistakes. Indeed, making mistakes is an essential part of performance learning, which is why entrepreneurs often emphasize the need to fail fast. As developing professionals, we have limited financial capital, and we have limited psychological capital. If our need to make money overwhelms our need to learn markets the right way, we will take too much risk and inflict severe drawdowns on our accounts. We will also inflict real trauma early in our learning process, derailing our development.

THE POSITIVE PSYCHOLOGY OF MENTORING

As I've mentioned in my previous writing, there is much to be said for starting one's trading in pure simulation mode. We can trade real markets in real time and track our results without putting any money at risk at all. This is like a basketball or football team playing scrimmage games to hone their strategies and skills. Eventually, of course, it's necessary to put real capital to work and deal with the ups and downs of actual P/L. If this is done slowly and size is bumped up gradually, only following extended periods of success, the learning curve can reinforce success and mastery and avoid shock and trauma. Ryan also points out that this period of small trading and limited risk-taking enables traders to refine their methods, identifying what works and what doesn't in various market conditions. *Trading small allows the trader to put their learning P/L ahead of financial P/L during their learning curves.*

Indeed, experienced and successful traders I've worked with will dramatically reduce their size if they notice major changes in markets, giving themselves an opportunity to adapt to new market regimes without undergoing major loss. As Ryan emphasizes, such a process of adaptation builds confidence, keeping trading psychology positive even as we face market challenges.

Lance Breitstein, senior trader and mentor

While I managed Trillium's Chicago office, I implemented a concept that I call "one up, one down." Each trader in the office was assigned both a mentor and a mentee. The mentor, one experience level above, would provide advice and guidance to the trader on how best to reach the next step in their growth process. The trader would then also get to solidify their own learning while passing on their knowledge and best practices to a mentee, one experience level below them.

Not only did this give traders extra ownership and accountability, but it made sure that each person in the office was providing support as well as receiving it. New trainees with nobody below them would return the favor by doing research and some of the more menial tasks for the rest of the office. All of this led to a powerful reciprocal dynamic where everyone in the office was invested in the success of each other. This is a concept I now help to implement with the traders at SMB Capital.

As soon as I received this best practice from successful trader and mentor Lance, I emailed him and commented on how his idea of "one up, one down" is mirrored in medical education. The key idea in medical school is that learning occurs by teaching as well as by following the example of mentors. Over time, the student experiences many mentors with different areas of specialization and also passes along what they've learned to multiple junior students. The net result is a high-performance learning culture where new things are always learned and shared.

As Lance points out, this also creates accountability and a support structure. In the learning culture, we're evaluated on how well we help others on the team, just as we benefit from team support. As described earlier, this is very much the culture within hedge fund teams. Each junior team member is tasked with doing research and sharing ideas with those who are risk-takers and each risk-taker shows the junior members how those ideas are implemented. This is very different from a hierarchical model where junior people simply do work for the more senior ones. It is more similar to an apprenticeship model, where each work project becomes an opportunity for role modeling and teaching. This is what Lance describes as the "reciprocal dynamic." The most junior members are helping the more senior ones and benefiting from seeing their work applied in real time.

Online trading communities are valuable learning resources, especially for traders who are located far from the usual centers that house trading firms, such as Chicago, New York, and London. These communities typically charge a membership fee, providing traders with access to mentors and courses. For developing traders who otherwise would be on their own, this is a unique opportunity to learn from multiple mentors and interact with other learners.

The downside of many trading communities is that they lack the accountability described by Lance. Someone can join and simply pick off the best ideas of members who share in forums and contribute nothing of value to the community. Because there is no expectation of "each one, teach one," it is easy for the community to fall into the trap of becoming a group of learners who don't teach.

Following Lance's reasoning, a best practice for those joining trading communities is to make a special effort to connect with those learners who are taking advantage of the opportunities to share their learning in forums *and create virtual teams within the community*. These teams can operate with a commitment to preview markets together, share ideas and observations during the trading day, and review trading after markets close. The teams would also share experiences in applying the learning from the community mentors, so that everyone is getting the most value from the classes and discussions. An ideal situation would be for a trading community to evolve into a team of teams, where there would be a "one up, one down" dynamic between more junior and more senior teams.

I have also found a kind of "one up, one down" framework to be useful in my own individual development as a trader, as well as in the trading of professional money managers. There are markets and strategies that are my bread and butter and that take up the lion's share of my risk. However, I always want to be expanding my trading and cultivating new edges. This might be accomplished by adapting my methods to a new asset class or a new set of instruments within my asset class; it might be accomplished by taking a portion of my trading to an entirely different time frame.

A good example would be the research I conduct daily on patterns of sector and market breadth in U.S. equities. Some of this research points to momentum and mean reversion effects that typically last several days. The great majority of my trading has been intraday, catching swings that are aligned with these bigger-picture opportunities. I realized, however, that I was leaving money on the table by not holding these swing trades overnight. At the same time that I worked on sizing up my basic intraday trading (one up), I began to take small overnight positions that were supported by the research (one down). My smaller trading kept me focused on the big picture in markets and helped me manage the intraday trades, and the intraday trading alerted me to situations in which the longer-term, historical edge was playing out.

In a very real sense, my short-term market activity was mentoring my longer-term efforts, and the swing trades were guiding (and helping me size up) the intraday trading.

At one hedge fund where I work, a PM has a purely systematic, quantitative book of trades and a set of tactical, discretionary trades. The feedback from each informs the other, creating a kind of "one up, one down" learning process: the "reciprocal dynamic" highlighted by Lance. With learning coming from multiple directions in real time, it becomes easier to maintain an energized and positive trading psychology. I encourage traders to follow Lance on social media (search for @TheOneLanceB) and on his website (theonelanceb.com), where he teaches his ideas and also incorporates lessons from others: one up, one down in real time.

Justin Spero, senior trader and trading mentor

When I work with a developing trader, I encourage them to execute on their favorite strategy as they normally would so we can identify their strengths and tendencies before putting together a tailored game plan. Once we have a feel for how they trade, we develop strategies that align with their trading personality—whether that means focusing on high-probability, quick scalps for aggressive, fast thinkers or longer, more measured plays for those with a more analytical approach.

I emphasize starting each session with the big picture, using the daily chart for context, and zeroing in on specific setups that work intraday and are proven over time at SMB. This approach—focusing on the broader context combined with a few core setups—helps newer traders avoid overwhelm and build confidence. I also stress the importance of clear risk management, guiding traders to wait for full confirmation before entering a trade to teach patience, accept the risk on each trade and reinforce quality over quantity.

Another key part of my mentoring is post-trade reviews. I have traders go through their trades out loud, annotate their charts, and write up high-quality trade examples. This process builds muscle memory and helps them recognize patterns more clearly in real time. Overall, our sessions aren't just about providing a trade setup—they're about creating a process that strengthens their judgment and adaptability, giving them the tools to make confident decisions on their own.

Justin's best practices highlight some of the nuances that go into effective mentoring. Note that he does not begin by telling a developing trader how to trade. Rather, he observes the real-time trading efforts of the student and gains insight into their "strengths and tendencies." In other words, Justin assesses the talents and skills of the trader before offering guidance. The goal is not to help the new trader become a clone of Justin, but rather to blend Justin's experience and the trader's strengths to find a style of trading that will work for that particular student. Some developing traders, Justin notes, are faster thinkers who thrive in active, short-term trading. Others are more analytical thinkers who are best trading bigger-picture ideas over longer time frames. *Mentorship is thus tailored to the student*, creating a blending of the developing trader's natural talent and the skills learned from Justin.

By exposing traders early in their learning curves to the ideas and patterns that have worked for SMB traders, Justin focuses their development even as he adapts the learning to the traders' talents. Notice how this ensures that the training sets up the developing trader for learning that is doable and likely to succeed. From a positive trading psychology perspective, Justin creates experiences of mastery for the new trader, which "avoid overwhelm and build confidence." The role modeling of risk management is crucial to this effort, as it helps avoid losses that could damage confidence and the learning process. When training is designed to "avoid overwhelm and build confidence," emotional, undisciplined trading becomes far less frequent.

One thing I have noticed among the mentors at SMB is that they make particular efforts to ensure that learning will be active and hands-on. This is very different from how many new traders attempt to develop. Recall the lesson mentioned earlier: Passively watching videos and reading ideas cannot cement skills. Justin requires new traders to talk their ideas out loud and to write up what they did, how they did it, and how well they did it. Justin's goal is to instill muscle memory: an active processing of performance that allows lessons to be internalized. Teaching is thus more than describing setups. It models ways of thinking that can be applied across trading circumstances. The goal is to help traders "make confident decisions on their own" by internalizing processes that have been honed over years of experience.

Finally, notice that Justin's mentorship is multimodal. So often, when developing traders attempt to learn, they restrict how they process market information. They read, they look at charts, but they don't necessarily play to their own information-processing strengths. With Justin, they are hearing ideas from him, discussing trades with him, talking trades out in real time, annotating charts, and writing up their ideas. *Ideas processed in multiple ways are learned more deeply: they are internalized.* By making the learning process active and interactive, Justin helps transform explicit lessons into internalized muscle memory. It is this internalization that helps traders make confident decisions on their own.

Dan Godlewski, senior trader and team leader

I'd like to focus on mentoring through the trading of joint accounts. JAs are a very useful tool for two types of mentoring relationships: between senior traders and skilled, profitable mid-level traders ('performance JAs') and between profitable traders and hard-working junior traders ('training JAs').

The idea of a 'performance joint account' is to bring together skilled traders who are looking to collaborate more closely and integrate more of their preparation, trade management, and review processes. Each person on such a JA is a skilled and consistent money-maker, and the expectation is that each is able and willing to take the lead on an opportunity for the JA when it aligns with their skills and track record. Others on the JA then learn from the processes and confidence of the trade-leader, while also contributing their own useful feedback which can shape the overall trading decisions and risk allocation. As such, the account gains from the varied skills and track record strengths of the individuals, each of whom acts as a trade-leader at different times. And even the trade-leaders get valuable feedback from their skilled peers, helping them to see their own strength areas with new perspective.

The idea of a 'training joint account' is to pair a skilled and consistently profitable trader with a hard-working but not yet consistently profitable junior trader. The main purpose of such an account is to establish a flow of process knowledge and of P&L from the senior trader to the junior trader. The senior trader is expected to model best practices in idea selection, risk allocation, trade management, and review, though much of the modeling is expected to be through instruction to the junior trader, with the junior trader then 'pushing the buttons' and implementing the practices. The benefits to the senior trader include the building of a longer-term collaborative relationship with a hard-working individual who might eventually become a star innovator, a fostering of team-building that motivates everyone to deliver their best, development of a new positive-EV income stream that is not perfectly correlated with existing trading, and an ability to engage with trading ideas by handing off some of the planning and execution mechanics to a capable understudy.

There is a powerful lesson in the joint account (JA) work described by Dan: *The structure of mentorship is every bit as important to the development of traders as the content of mentorship.* In other words, how mentors work with learners plays a crucial role in the effectiveness of the learning.

In many ways, the performance joint account mirrors the learning environment in many of the hedge funds where I've worked over the years. Indeed, when a PM allocates a sleeve of capital to a developing trader, that allocation becomes a joint account. The PM and developing trader discuss the ideas that go into the account, and the trader's management of the positions serves to update the PM about conviction in the ideas being traded.

The allocated account also becomes an opportunity for the PM and trader to review performance in a real-life context. Where Dan's implementation of the joint account goes beyond even the collaboration at hedge funds is that everyone on the performance JA can take the lead for the team when the trade falls into their area of expertise. That means that, quite literally, everyone on the performance JA is a mentor and a learner. Moreover, the JA structure ensures that everyone has skin in the game. Conversations and reviews are not about theoretical ideas or setups, but real-life ideas that are being traded. As Dan points out, this makes the team leader every bit as much a learner as the members of the performance JA.

Note also how the very structure of the performance JA creates a level of urgency in the mentoring. There is real P/L associated with the JA, so it is in everyone's self-interest to learn lessons quickly and effectively. Teaching/mentoring is not an altruistic activity conducted in the senior trader's spare time; nor is it a one-way commercial activity where the student pays a fee and the instructor teaches a course. The real-time context of trading with shared risk on the line ensures that mentoring will occur each day with the ups and downs of the account. Everyone teaches, everyone learns, every day, every trade.

The training joint account that Dan describes is a collaboration between the senior trader and a relatively inexperienced learner. This also occurs at hedge funds, as junior members of the team engage in some of the basic research and trade execution that go into the positions in the portfolio. In such an arrangement, as Dan points out, the senior trader acts as a model for the learners, illustrating how ideas are generated, expressed as trades, and managed as positions. The learners are not mere observers, because they are actively involved in the basic tasks of implementing the trades and monitoring the positions. On one team that I've worked with, the junior members of the team keep track of multiple markets and symbols, scanning for news and for ideas shared among colleagues at various firms. The learners thus act as the eyes and ears of the team leader, keeping everyone abreast of breaking developments and ideas from the team's professional network. An important part of the learning on that team is seeing how real-time information is processed and utilized in the management of the team's positions. This once again creates a sense of urgency to the mentoring process as everyone contributes to the team's profitability.

As Dan notes, the training JA becomes a breeding ground for talent that can grow into the performance JA. In other words, the team/JA structure creates a career path for the developing trader and also serves as an investment in the growth of the team for the team leader. Again, this means that everyone has skin in the game and is motivated to make learning and performance improvement a daily priority. Adding developing traders from the training JA to the roster of the performance JA diversifies the senior trader and enables everyone to profit from the unique skills of everyone else. This contributes to a positive team psychology of mutual goals and shared growth: the learning culture and performance culture reinforce one another.

Carlton Bryan, director of risk management and mentor

Effective risk management is essential to long-term success in trading. A key component of your trading plan should be clearly defined loss limits at the daily, weekly, and monthly levels. These limits serve as guardrails, ensuring your trading business stays in business!

There are two best practices for adjusting risk when trading well:

1) 10-trading-day risk review plan

Assess your trading performance every two weeks. If your net profit exceeds two times your daily stop and you've adhered to all the rules in your trading plan, consider increasing your risk allocation by 20%.

2) 20-trading-day risk review plan

Review your trading stats monthly. If your net profit exceeds four times your daily stop and you've followed your trading rules consistently, bump your risk by 20%.

Note: Traders should select the review plan that best aligns with their trading style and individual needs. This structured review helps align risk adjustments with consistent performance.

There are also best practices for reducing risk when trading poorly. Traders often make the mistake of holding risk constant or increasing it during periods of underperformance. A more disciplined approach involves reducing risk when trading poorly. Below are best practices to help you recover while maintaining discipline:

1) Utilize a 'soft lockout' mechanism

If you lose a set percentage of your daily stop, pause your daily trading. Use this break to reassess your strategy and focus on quality over quantity in subsequent trades.

2) Implement weekly risk reductions

If you hit your weekly stop, reduce your risk exposure by 50% until you recover your losses. If the weekly stop is breached again, cut risk by another 50%. If the stop is hit a third time, shift to paper trading until you demonstrate a positive P/L slope, ensuring you regain confidence and consistency before reintroducing risk.

3) Monthly risk adjustments

Should you reach your monthly stop, slash your risk allocation by 50%. Maintain this reduced level until you've recouped the losses incurred that month. If the monthly stop is hit a second time, the risk is reduced by another 50%. If breached a third time, move to paper trading until you achieve a positive P/L slope, signaling readiness to return to live trading.

By integrating these practices into your trading routine, you can adapt your risk exposure to market conditions, reduce variance in your P/L curve, and safeguard your capital and confidence.

Notice that, for Carlton, risk management is about growing size and expanding profitability and not just about minimizing losses. He provides two rules for growing risk-taking by 20%. Both require the trader to be profitable and also to be consistent in following the rules of the trader's trade plans. The important idea here is that *consistency precedes growth*: before we are entitled to trade larger, we have to demonstrate consistency of process and the ability to make money. The profitability metric of two times the traders' daily stops over a 10-day period or four times the stop over 20 days sets a meaningful hurdle, but not an impossible one. Because of ever-changing markets, developing traders can't be expected to maintain a high win rate and high Sharpe ratio indefinitely. Periods of drawdown are to be expected. For that reason, initial daily stops will be modest and sizing of positions will be modest. If the trader can make significantly more than their daily loss limit over a 10- or 20-day period, the bumping up of risk limits is 20%. This means that trade P/L will become more volatile, but not in a disruptive fashion. Carlton's framework thus makes the growing of size and risk-taking psychologically successful. The risk-management process contributes to a positive psychology and is not experienced as onerous.

Of course, if a trader makes money but does not hit their profitability goal over a 10- or 20-day period, trading size and risk limits remain the same. This gives the trader the opportunity to adapt to current market conditions and make necessary improvements in their trading. The growth of risk-taking (and thus the growth of P/L) becomes a stairstep process by which consistency is rewarded first and foremost. *Consistency of performance leads to consistency of mindset which leads to trading growth.* Carlton's risk framework is one that develops traders sustainably, so that trading yields confidence and a sense of mastery. When I have worked at SMB, I have noticed Carlton reaching out to junior traders who might be struggling on a particular day and also acknowledging good trading performance.

During my work with traders in Chicago, I had a risk screen and could see what each trader was doing at any given time of day. That helped me identify when a trader was trading differently from their norm—perhaps overtrading or sizing too small or large—and gave me a real-time opportunity to check in with them. Knowing that someone is watching their trading and cares about their trading is quite helpful to the developing trader. Carlton's role is not just to clamp down on traders performing poorly, but to encourage their best performance as a mentor who cares about them.

The risk-taking framework that Carlton describes is especially powerful when traders are losing money. If a meaningful percentage of one's daily stop, such as 50%, is lost during the day's session, the trader agrees to take a trading break. During that break, the trader can review markets and review trading performance and make necessary adjustments. Very often, a trader will return from such a break by initially reducing their size and risk limits until they regain a sense of mastery and begin making money back.

This is similar to a sports team taking a time out when things aren't going well. It's an opportunity to revisit the game plan and adjust to any unforeseen circumstances. For instance, a trader might be overconfident in a morning opportunity and lose a decent amount of money. The time out enables the trader to recalibrate confidence and wait patiently for good setups and regain profitability. The risk advice I've passed along to active traders is to never lose so much in a morning that you don't have a reasonable chance of becoming profitable by day's end. Similarly, don't lose so much in one day that you can't end the week in the black, and don't have such a large losing week that it prevents you from being profitable on the month. It is demoralizing to dig such a deep hole that future profitability feels impossible. Carlton's rule regarding taking a trading break is designed to make sure that normal losses don't become deep holes.

Notice also how Carlton's trading rules require traders to cut their size/risk by 50% if they hit their weekly or monthly stop levels. This is a significant consequence. If I lose my limit of X and have to cut my trading size in half, it means that I will have to earn 2X on the smaller size just to get out of the hole. That consequence provides me with a powerful incentive to avoid hitting my weekly and monthly loss limits. Indeed, it provides an incentive to start each week and each month with a focus on the very best trade ideas/setups and build enough P/L cushion that hitting those loss limits is unlikely to occur.

In Carlton's framework, a second occasion of hitting weekly/monthly loss limits leads to yet another 50% reduction of risk and a third occasion requires the trader to return to simulation (paper trading) mode. These are powerful incentives to make money the right way, emphasizing consistency over swinging for the fences. The goal becomes to focus on one's best trading opportunities and take measured swings, so that profitability becomes consistent and losses are kept in check. While the consequences of risk reductions may seem punitive, they in fact are designed to keep the developing trader from blowing up and derailing their careers. The role of the risk manager is to help traders lose money the right way, so that they have plenty of opportunity to learn and make the money back.

Brett's observations on the SMB mentoring best practices

1. *Notice how each of the above mentors takes a different approach to mentoring and helping developing traders.* What dramatically improves a trader's chances of becoming consistently profitable is the availability of many experienced mentors. The opportunity to hear from multiple mentors every day provides a wealth of role modeling. It also creates a structure where traders can learn from the mentors who are best aligned with their strengths and trading approaches. Whether this is achieved in a trading firm or in a trading community, the diversity of role models allows for diversification in trader development—a real benefit to the trading firm.
2. *Note the difference between training and education.* The mentors do educate, but they provide much more than knowledge. They actively observe and provide feedback for developing traders and they provide real-time role modeling through their own trading. Trading success is a developmental process; mentors guide that development. No amount of coursework, tweets, or seminars can substitute for the ongoing guidance provided by daily involvement in markets. Education is necessary for performance expertise, but it is never sufficient. Mentors guide the processes by which knowledge is translated into practice and skill building.
3. *Psychology is rarely directly taught by the mentors, but it is a powerful byproduct of the mentoring process.* Mentors provide experiences of success and performance-based learning. That contributes to a mindset of mastery and confidence. The positive psychology that fuels optimal learning and performance is created and maintained by mentoring activities that bring out the best in developing traders.
4. *The best mentoring develops the mentors as well as the traders.* When developing traders add to the mentor's trading and the mentor guides the efforts of learners, everyone wins. That creates a team

dynamic that further enhances ongoing trading psychology. At its best, trading is a team sport. The quality of teamwork shapes the quality of trading and both shape the quality of trading psychology. This is equally observable at hedge funds and at proprietary trading firms.

5. *Very often, trading psychology problems are the result of learning in the absence of active mentoring.* No one learns a performance domain in isolation. When we try to learn by ourselves and mentor ourselves, it is easy to become overwhelmed and stressed. Much of the emotionality experienced by developing traders occurs because they are developing the wrong way. Teamwork makes the dream work. You are most likely to achieve success if you operate in the framework that Lance called "one up, one down." There should always be traders you are mentoring and who contribute to your trading. There should always be traders who mentor you and expand your horizons. Always be a student, always be a teacher. Always learn; always grow; always adapt.

6. *There is much we can do to mentor ourselves.* In a recent blog post, I emphasized two best practices in self-mentoring:

    a. Make sure that everything we study in the market and everything we study about our performance is processed in multiple ways and in great detail. Many times, traders look at charts and write down quick notes in a journal and never process information in depth. What we encounter multiple times in multiple ways is more likely to stick in our minds and much more likely to influence our subsequent actions.

    b. Make sure that everything we study in the market and everything we study about our performance is processed with energy and enthusiasm. Think of the atmosphere in a locker room before game time. There is a last review of the game plan and there is a pep talk by the coach. This is one of the key lessons of positive psychology: a positive, energized mindset is most likely to engage in peak performance. Passionless preparation for the day's trade and cursory review of performance cannot possibly fuel our best efforts in markets.

What I took away from the best practices of the SMB mentors is the importance of being actively and fully engaged in learning and in performance. We're most likely to succeed if we're active and proactive: deeply focused on markets and deeply focused on ourselves.

Jeff's observations on the SMB mentoring process

There is not much we need to do outside of the summary provided by Dr. S above; he is known as the best in the world for a reason! He just gave us six clear, actionable summaries we all can adopt and put into practice over time. These disciplines are really just skills to develop: not all at once, but methodically. The best learning means tackling one skill at a time until we have made it a part of who we are as traders.

One thing that sets apart the people who follow through on building these skills into their trading is the consistency and the quality of their actions. This determines the impact they have on our trading performance. It also shapes the expectations we have for the impact these skills will have on our trading performance (and our P/L).

We have seen different traders come (and some go) on our desk at SMB, but one trader stands out in his implementation of these skills. The impact of these specific skills, methodically added to his trading over a period of time, created a learning curve that has been shorter than many would expect.

Shred is a trader who did not stand out initially. In fact, he was struggling so much very early in his time with us as a trader that we were forced to ask ourselves if he was the right trader for our desk, if he was going to continue on as a trader, or if he would be forced to take some of his skills and pursue something else. Shred was known for being passionate about markets; he would lose himself in them. He remarked that when he was trading, or focusing on trading, it seemed like time stood still—he would look up and two or three hours would have passed, and it felt like it had been no time at all. He wanted to be a successful trader because he understood the upside from a P/L perspective, but more just because he could not imagine doing anything else!

Unfortunately, bringing that desire and passion to the markets does not make a trader successful, and Shred struggled with that. He would make some money, then lose it. He would go through periods where he felt he was trading well, then find his way into a period where he just felt he could not do anything right.

But then a subtle, almost unremarkable shift occurred in his mentality, his approach, and most of all in his trading. He started by setting a goal for himself every day. When he would finish his trading day, he would write down his goal for the next day. The first thing he would do as he started the next day was simply read his goal. His goals were never P/L focused: they were always process and skill-development focused.

Shred started with the first skill we challenge you to develop: he started being more specific with his preparation. He would hear a scalp idea from someone and then work his own process of specificity, asking himself what observational variables would make that trade a good or bad trade. What was the catalyst driving the stock? What was the setup the stock was trading in, the bigger-picture technical setup? Then what different trades that presented with that catalyst and setup made the most sense to him?

After developing that skill, he was able to use some of the resources mentioned to back test some of the ideas he had generated. He would gather data on the variables in his observations and test if—and how much—those variables (such as volume, location in higher time frame range, and type of bigger-picture setup we were trading in at that time) mattered to his trades. This back testing skill allowed him to organize his trading day more effectively. His premarket game planning improved significantly, and he was able to better communicate those premarket plans with others as a result. We would start to hear greater confidence in his voice when he presented ideas in the morning meeting. He wasn't guessing as much as to what could happen. Instead, he was planning for what could be a big opportunity each day. This improved his psychology. He spent far less time needing to remind himself to be present, and far more time just being present, focused on the opportunity. Sidestepping so much of the self-judgment and lack of presence that had led him to miss or undersize the best opportunities and oversize the other trades, he learned faster from his mistakes. Mistakes still happened—they happen for every trader at every level on our desk—but the impact of the mistakes was less and the speed at which he learned to let go and recover from those mistakes sped up drastically. That increased the confidence in his voice, reflecting a growing belief that he was here to do something great.

As a result of this confidence slowly but distinctly increasing, he was able to engage in better conversations with traders both one level up from him and one level down. He was asking better questions, talking about examples with more specificity, and sharing his information and experience with others more frequently. Over time, he attracted the type of people he wanted to work with to him through his efforts instead of just hoping to be able to get noticed.

Armed with this higher level of collaboration, Shred learned faster from the experiences of others. For example, he would ask a senior trader about a trade they had made, and quickly make small, but impactful, adjustments to the way he traded that opportunity, further improving his performance. He was also better able to learn from the mistakes others had made by recognizing when he was in a situation where that mistake had been made previously, sidestep the mistake, and keep pressing forward. As he attracted the attention of higher-level traders, he maintained the one up, one down communications, steadily moving up the overall development curve of traders. This allowed him to open his first development joint account with a senior trader, which quickly led to his first performance joint account with that same senior trader and another senior trader.

This work is helping Shred quickly recognize and adjust his risk taking in various situations. Armed with a daily focus on his risk, he is working to improve his trading results even further by developing the skill and ability to press the gas in bigger opportunities when he is trading well and very quickly pump the brakes when the market opportunities are shifting and not meeting his expectations.

The skills illustrated by Shred build on themselves, but methodically. This chapter can help demystify the growth path of traders, serving as a road map of best practices. Take this road map, understand the landmarks along the way of your trading journey. Build each of these skills with a relentless desire on your trading journey, and—like Shred—watch yourself achieve more than you thought possible.

Readers can find further mentoring insights from Jeff and many other SMB Capital traders on their YouTube channel: www.youtube.com/smbcapital. Gaining insights from different traders with unique trading styles is a powerful way to identify approaches that can expand and refine your trading.

Practical takeaways from Chapter Six

1. Because markets are ever-changing, every trader is a developing trader. Every trader should have someone they learn from; every trader should have someone they're teaching; every trader, formally or informally, should be part of a team imbued with the spirit of each one, teach one. Continuous learning turns positive psychology into an ongoing mindset, fueling accelerated development.
2. As I described earlier, one of the best decisions I made when I first tackled markets was to identify, each day, the best trade of the day in the S&P 500 Index. I printed out a variety of charts of the

market on different time frames and relevant indicators that struck me as promising. I reviewed the charts in detail, burning into my mind the patterns that stood out. I 'role played' how I would enter the trade, how I would size it, where I would take profits, where I would exit, where I would stop out. Day after day, every day, I immersed myself in opportunity and how to identify and trade opportunity. Of course, I was also rehearsing an opportunity mindset. To this day, more than 20 years later, those charts—and that mindset—stick with me. Through deliberate practice, we can mentor ourselves.

3. Developing your trading the right way develops your best trading psychology and helps develop the best within you. That is what positive trading psychology is all about. There is an important difference between training and education. Taking courses and reading books can inform and inspire, but it is daily training that helps us internalize the skills that leverage our talents.

4. The right trading psychology is a byproduct of effective mentoring. Learning from multiple mentors helps us develop our own approaches to trading: the ones that best leverage our interests and abilities. Learning with other traders helps us internalize their gains and accelerates our development. When we see the breadth of mentoring at a training setting such as SMB, we can appreciate that the greatest contributor to trader failure is an impoverished learning environment.

CHAPTER SEVEN

THERAPY FOR THE MENTALLY WELL: NEW DIRECTIONS FOR TRADING PSYCHOLOGY

IN THIS FINAL chapter, I would like to sketch fresh, promising directions for developing our trading psychology. The common assumption among traders is that sound trading is hijacked by emotion and emotionally driven behaviors. That naturally leads to the conclusion that calming ourselves, ridding ourselves of emotional arousal, and improving our attitudes will allow us to trade in planned, successful ways. These assumptions miss an important dimension of elite performance. *Success in trading—as in any deliberate activity—depends, not on a taming of emotion, but on an intensification of consciousness and the resulting increased capacity to sustain purpose.* Once we are able to sustain purposeful focus, emotionality and impulsivity no longer become issues in trading.

Intentionality: the capacity to sustain purpose

If we could operate with complete free will, trading psychology—and indeed any form of performance psychology—would cease to exist as a discipline. With a full ability to sustain purpose, we could select and pursue our goals with consistency and persistence. We would be able to flexibly move from one activity to another based upon our choice, not because of distraction or impulse.

Conversely, there could be no performance psychology if we lacked free will entirely. Animals cannot pursue trading and the improvement of trading performance. They cannot plan their lives and work toward ideals. What makes trading psychology necessary is the ability to direct our activities *and* the challenges of sustaining effort in the pursuit of those activities. We are blessed with a degree of free will—and we are cursed by our incomplete will. The capacity to sustain directed effort varies from person to person; note the difference between those with significant attention deficit disorders and those who can sustain effort and purpose across a variety of life domains. The paradoxical challenge of developing our will is that it takes ongoing sustained effort to build our capacity to sustain effort! Doing what comes naturally maintains the status quo; it does not expand our capacity for self-determination.

The successful performer achieves success, not by dampening emotion and restraining impulse, but by maximizing intentionality. We see this in the development of the military sniper. An experienced, trained sniper can sit in the hide for hours on end, waiting for the high-probability kill shot. This requires immense self-control not only to avoid detection, but to maintain the focus and slow breathing pace needed to take the ideal shot when the target presents itself. Most of us can only maintain a meditative exercise for minutes at a time. Distractions eventually get the better of us. The sniper demonstrates lengthy periods of superior focus and self-control: every action while in the weeds is devoted to the aim of taking the right shot. With such a highly developed intentionality, the sniper does not go on 'tilt' or veer from purpose.

> **Our trading can never be more disciplined than our thought processes.**

Indeed, we observe this superior intentionality across performance fields. Imagine the focus needed by the ballerina who must maintain physical self-control for hours at a time, performing complex, flawless actions in a synchronized fashion. Consider the surgeon immersed in a complex operation where any single mistake can prove fatal and where time may be limited to complete the procedure. Do we see elite ballerinas and surgeons going on tilt or wrestling with emotions and stray impulses? Of course not. Their extensive training incorporates training in sustaining focus and effort. A large part of performance training is training of intentionality. We learn to sustain performance by practicing, practicing, practicing the effortful pursuit of goals. Elite performers hone their skills, and they hone their ability to sustain the application of those skills. *Effective performance training is training of the will.*

Imagine that I receive some basic training in deploying and maintaining an assault rifle and engage in a few weeks of shooting practice and instruction in evading detection. I'm then thrust into the middle of an intense battlefield, where I'm given the instructions to avoid capture and take out the commander when the enemy troops appear. With only the practice in non-battlefield conditions to guide me, it's understandable that I would fall prey to many doubts and fears. Would I be able to maintain hours upon hours of quiet and remain focused on my mission? Would I be able to take a steady shot toward my target amidst my anxiety and concern? Without extensive training and practice in realistic conditions, I could never sustain my purposeful intent—and I certainly could not maintain ideal performance.

Note that, in the above situation, no amount of talking with a psychologist or coach could, by itself, improve my performance. Only ongoing training of the will would make it possible to sustain effortful intent for a prolonged period. Emotionality and impulsivity are the results of the problem; not the problem themselves. The problem is an underdeveloped intentionality. The philosopher G. I. Gurdjieff taught that the majority of people operate in relative states of 'sleep.' Without sustained intent, we drift from thought to thought, activity to activity. Gurdjieff asserted, "Man's possibilities are very great. You cannot conceive even a shadow of what man is capable of attaining. But nothing can be attained in sleep."[212] The training of elite performers is not so unlike the training of mystics: both teach people to sustain unusually high levels of effortful activity. It is in cultivating purpose that we awaken from the randomness of sleep and find our "possibilities."

Our challenge is that, as we sustain mental effort, our willpower typically diminishes. Dr. Kelly McGonigal points out that "Neuroscientists have found that with each use of willpower, the self-control system of the brain becomes less active. Just like a tired runner's legs can give out, the brain seems to run out of the strength to keep going."[213] She cites research suggesting that willpower is highly sensitive to the energy available to the brain, as self-control is "one of the most energy-expensive tasks the brain performs."[214] Even simple self-control exercises, such as controlling our diet, can generate significant increases in our capacity to sustain will by "training the willpower muscle."[215] As Gretchen Rubin explains in her book *Better Than Before*, "We manage what we monitor."[216] This turns desired actions into habit patterns and conserves our willpower, saving it for new challenges. If we could never turn new effortful acts into eventual habits, we would never be able to sustain ongoing development.

As Gurdjieff found, however, intentionality is not static. We can cultivate the capacity for purposeful thought and action. Dr. Charles Tart explains in his book *Waking Up* that "knowledge and action in any particular state must be tempered by the knowledge gained in other states of consciousness."[217] What we know is relative to our state of awareness. In one state, Dr. Tart observes, we can be angry at someone and want to attack them. In a different state, we might even empathize with them. A great step in our development occurs when we can recognize our 'sleep'—our automatic reactions—and shift ourselves to a different level of awareness.

This alarm clock capacity to wake ourselves from automaticity is something that we can develop. Dr. John Ratey, in *A User's Guide to the Brain* points out that "As we gain more attention and consciousness we can better evaluate actions and consequences and be less impulsive than our current selves."[218] Overcoming impulsivity is thus not a matter of dampening our emotions, but of growing our attention and conscious awareness. By training the willpower muscle across many life activities, we can gain control of our actions and consequences. The combination of 'challenge' and 'variety' in what we tackle maintains and increases our brain health.[219]

Colin Wilson points out that our willpower typically fades long before we truly exhaust our capacity for effort. If we push past our initial fatigue, we can access a second wind of consciousness that enables us to sustain focus and productivity. The extra effort of directed intent opens our reserves of will. A good example of this is the student who studies for a final exam for a couple of hours and feels tired, but realizes that there is much more material to cover. The desire for the good grade inspires an extra effort and suddenly the student is able to study well into the night. I've seen exhausted traders who suddenly notice opportunity and immediately perk up and remain focused in tracking and trading their market. Wilson explains that "it is the act of concentration itself that causes this intensification of consciousness."[220] Indeed, "a steady effort of willed concentration can remove the slackness from the controls and produce an expanding sense of meaning." This is important: our ability to process meaning comes from our "intensification of consciousness."

Baumeister and Tierney summarize a wealth of research that finds that willpower can be trained, impacting a wide range of life activities and contributing to happiness and well-being.[221] The "steady effort of willed concentration" described by Wilson enables us to find meaning in our experience, directing us to opportunities in markets and in life that we otherwise would miss. Wilson observes that "when the mind falls below a certain energy-level, its capacity to *receive meaning* drops abruptly."[222] If markets don't make sense to us, perhaps the issue is not with how our market is moving, but with how well our minds can sustain the ability to "receive meaning." *The training of the brain ultimately is a training to sustain the concentration needed to perceive meaning in our experience.*

A standout quality I have observed among successful intraday traders is the ability to sit in front of screens for hours at a time and remain focused and alert for opportunity. Yes, they take occasional breaks and mix their market observation and trading with conversation, but they spend a significant portion of their trading day switched on. When I first began working with traders in Chicago, whose holding periods were often for only a few minutes at a time, I noticed that many of them had a successful background in playing video games. Indeed, many of them continued their gaming even after long days of trading. Two things became clear to me:

1. Video gaming served as a kind of training of concentration and will, enabling them to sustain a high degree of attention for hours at a time.
2. Their ability to sustain focus was domain specific and did not apply to all activities.

For instance, if I asked them to read a philosophy text, they would likely lose attention and interest quickly. *What helped them trade with sustained intentionality was a passion for active competition and the accumulation of experience that served as a training of the will.* Similarly, I have observed portfolio managers at hedge funds trade throughout the night during active markets and sustain a high level of concentration across multiple markets and many open positions. Where the average person would quickly become fatigued and need to get to bed, the portfolio manager is sustained by the drive for achievement and a trained capacity to work with multiple markets over time.

This suggests that superior intentionality begins with passionate interest and is cultivated by repeated experience. At the gym where I belong, I have observed unusually buff individuals sustain active workouts long after others would become exhausted. The natural assumption is that they can sustain the workouts because they are highly physically developed, but that is not the whole story. It is because they achieve a high degree of satisfaction and energy from working out that they are driven to come to the gym day after day. Over time, their training is not just a training of muscles, but a training of the will.

Passion + Purpose = Performance

Focus breeds creativity and insight

In the case of trading, there is an additional dynamic at work that links training and performance. The sustained concentration that is necessary for active trading filters out distraction and allows us to more readily discern patterns in market data. *Intuition flourishes in a state of focus; ideas come to us far more readily when we have clear, laser-sharp minds.* These ideas can connect different markets, as when we detect a move in interest rates impact the dollar, and they can connect time frames within a single market, helping us see how short-term volume and volatility are connected to a longer-term breakout. *The intuitive insight born of singular focus manifests itself as conviction: we feel strongly what we see clearly.* A highly intentional state is fertile ground for creativity. From this perspective, the greatest enemy of trading performance is distraction. Focused minds are not swayed by emotional impulse. We cannot have confidence and conviction in a trading or investment idea unless we are in a state of mind that facilitates insight. Many skilled traders and portfolio managers underperform their potential, not because they make so many mistakes and bad trades, but because they cannot sustain the focused awareness that would tell them when it's time to make a significant bet.

Case study: idea generation through brain wave training

I have a particular interest in brain wave biofeedback, also called neurofeedback. A new generation of portable biofeedback devices makes it possible for any person to measure their physiological state in real time and learn strategies for altering and controlling their physical and emotional states. As I described earlier in the book, the device I use, from Muse, is a band that goes around the head, sending brain wave information to an app. The app then provides real-time information about the wearer's brain state. For example, in my favorite routine, the rainforest, relative states of distraction create sounds of rainfall in the app. If one becomes more distracted, the rainfall becomes more intense. As the wearer sustains concentration, the rainfall decreases and eventually stops. At high levels of calm focus, the wearer can hear the chirping of birds. The app collects information during the brain workout regarding amount of time spent in high and low rainfall and the number of bird chirps achieved. Over time, it's easy to track progress in sustaining focus for longer and longer periods.

A unique feature of the Muse device is that it does not separately measure each of the five types of brain waves: delta (.5–4 Hz); theta (4–8 Hz); alpha (8–13 Hz); beta (13–30 Hz); and gamma (30–100 Hz). Rather, it makes use of a machine learning algorithm that identifies the optimal combination of these waves for three basic states: active, neutral, and calm. The active state is one in which we are processing different information in real time, moving from one thought to another. It is a relatively distracted state, one that typifies much of our moment-to-moment life. The neutral state is a relaxed state of consciousness, such as we might experience when closing our eyes and listening to music. The calm state is our most focused state, where we operate in a zone of concentration, such as when solving a problem. Before beginning a brain training exercise such as the rainforest, Muse requires an initial calibration period in which the wearer sits quietly and breathes slowly. This establishes a baseline level of brain activity for each person. The feedback received by the increased/decreased rain and

THERAPY FOR THE MENTALLY WELL: NEW DIRECTIONS FOR TRADING PSYCHOLOGY

bird chirps thus reflect changes in brain activity relative to the baseline readings.

One of my most striking findings was that my normal meditation routine, sitting still, controlling breathing, and mindfully observing my breath as I visualized a peaceful image, did not increase the proportion of time I spent in the 'calm' state. The Muse app measures 'stillness' in addition to brain waves and, indeed, my stillness increased during my meditative activity. But I was not more focused, according to the Muse algorithm. The actions I needed to take to increase my zone state, which involved intensely focusing my vision (even with eyes closed), actually decreased my stillness score. The lesson from my Muse experience is that being relaxed is different from being super-focused. While my usual meditative routine helped center me during busy periods, it was not necessarily training me for greater degrees of intentionality. What brought me to unusual levels of focus—from the Muse 'neutral' state to the 'calm' state—was sustained, intensive concentration.

Interestingly, after relatively short periods of the Muse 'calm' state during my neurofeedback workouts, my perception seemed clearer and my mind was quieter. That had not been happening after my usual meditative routines. In the Muse state of calm, I felt like an observer of the world around me, detached and clear-headed. I recognized this state from my best periods of trading. Without realizing it, I had been spending some of my trading time distracted, some of it relaxed, and some of it with laser/calm focus.

> **What we do to reduce our arousal is not necessarily what we need to do to achieve optimal brain functioning; a reduction in stimulus input does not typically lead to an intensification of focus.**

Once I had made progress with the neurofeedback training, I began to make the Muse exercise part of my preparation for trading. Prior to reviewing what markets were doing and before going over my previous day's review and goals, I worked with the rainforest app and maintained a high level of focused activity, as demonstrated by the percentage of time I was in the 'calm' zone and the number of bird chirps I achieved. *I only began my preparation for the trading day when I felt the quiet, detached, focused state.* In quick sequence, I reviewed what various markets were doing: interest rate markets (short and long term); currency pairs (USD and non-USD); commodities; stocks (U.S., Europe, Asia); stock market factors within the U.S. (growth shares; value shares; large cap; small cap); and individual sectors within U.S. equities (XLY/consumer discretionary; XLP/consumer staples; XLE/energy; XLF/financials; XLB/materials; XLC/communications; XLV/healthcare; XLRE/real estate; XLU/utilities; XLI/industrials; XLK/technology). In viewing the sectors, I was particularly attentive to volatility: which sectors were moving more than the day/week previous and which were moving more than the others.

Two things were important to this review process:

1. I proceeded in a steady but unrushed pace, moving from chart to chart, sustaining my focused state.
2. I didn't think about trades unless and until an idea came to me with particular clarity. *In other words, ideas had to jump out at me before I thought about trades to place.* I was content to continue reviewing markets, news, and charts until clarity was achieved.

The ideas that emerged from this focused review changed based upon market conditions. Sometimes it was clear that growth stocks were outperforming other shares, setting up a possible trade where I could be long the strongest growth sector (perhaps XLK) or involved in a pairs trade that was long growth stocks (SPYG) and short value shares (SPYV). Other times, it became clear that investors were selling the U.S. dollar versus other currencies and also versus gold, setting up a trade that was short U.S. stocks and long stocks overseas. I did not trade unless and until I detected a theme across markets and/or market sectors. Only then did I consider drilling down and looking at the specific instruments/stocks that I wanted to trade. The ones that were in play with respect to market themes typically stood out with their degree of movement and volatility.

At no point during this work did I work on my trading psychology by trying to control emotions or restrain any overtrading. With a high degree of calm concentration, my focus was entirely on the markets and the ideas that came to me. Interestingly, the 'zone' that I felt in this state was very similar to the intense focus I feel when I'm working with a client in therapy. The optimal mindset, I recognized, is one of deep listening. If we are processing information in the right brain state, the right actions come to us out of intuitive understanding. It is that way for a therapist, and it is that way for an active trader. Being relaxed was necessary, but not sufficient. What I had thought was an ideal mindset based upon my meditative routines turned out to lack the important dimension of intense focus.

Note that the work on my applying my brain state to my trading could only proceed once I was familiar with markets and what moves markets. *Education precedes training*. For instance, if a consumer price index (CPI) report comes out showing rising prices, I know to quickly look at short-term interest rates to see if the data might lead Treasury bill investors to price in possible rate hikes. If this is the case, I'll then look to rate-sensitive stock market sectors most likely to be impacted by such hikes, such as real estate.

Performing the brain training does not substitute for understanding market relationships, but it does make our processing of those relationships far more efficient. Once we know what to look for, we can see it and act upon it quickly when we are highly focused.

Of course, if I were a high-frequency trader and drawing my ideas primarily from action within the order book for, say, stock index futures, I would be focusing on very different information. If I were a short-term/intraday trader looking for breakouts of ranges, I would similarly seek out different information. The same dynamics regarding information processing, however, would pertain. *Whatever we look at to generate our ideas can be most efficiently processed if we are in a state of enhanced concentration.* It is in the calm focused state that we are most open to intuition and pattern recognition. When we achieve the clarity of that state, we don't look for trades; trade ideas naturally come to us. The goal is not to rein in our emotions, but to enhance our capacity to operate within the zone.

I believe that brain training is the single most promising frontier for trading psychology. Many, many traders fail, not because of a lack of desire or effort, but because they cannot sustain the intensity of concentration needed for creative idea generation and pattern recognition. As we've seen, the ability to operate in the zone depends on the degree to which we are passionately engaged in the activity. Successful traders are not motivated solely by P/L; they have a thirst to understand and master financial markets. That inquisitive drive keeps them going even during periods of drawdown. It also helps ensure that they will sustain high-quality market exposure and more readily internalize market patterns and signals.

Whatever we do in life that passionately holds our interest and keeps us in our zone is most likely our direction in life. That direction may or may not involve trading. If our highest levels of concentration are sustained in other performance domains (such as my ability to focus on people and their communications during therapy), perhaps those other domains are where our efforts need to be directed, not financial markets. (This is why full-time trading has never been my occupation.) If optimal concentration can be sustained only for short periods even though we find trading challenging and meaningful, then perhaps what we need is training to sustain the information-processing capacity that makes the most of our talents and skills. Brain training is therapy for the mentally well, helping us make the most of our ability to perceive and act upon opportunity. This is why the enhancement of willpower is closely connected to the enhancement of emotional and physical well-being.[223]

THERAPY FOR THE MENTALLY WELL: NEW DIRECTIONS FOR TRADING PSYCHOLOGY

Using brain training to maximize life outside trading

The greatest enemy of trading success is distraction. With a limited capacity to sustain focus, we fall prey to a variety of distractions and can no longer read markets and respond to their patterns with our full attention and intention. In a very important sense, brain training is training in freedom of will. We cannot pursue our chosen ends unless we can sustain the paths of our choices. Our willpower is only as strong as our mind power.

This is why our lives outside of trading are vitally important to our trading success. It benefits us little if we work on our focus during trading and then live our personal lives aimlessly, in a relative state of 'sleep.' Suppose we were to approach each day of life with a very specific vision of what would make our morning, afternoon, and evening meaningful and successful. Imagine further that we began each morning, afternoon, and evening with exercises to keep ourselves in the zone, so that we could use the time each day to make the most of our relationships, our work, and our leisure. Each part of the day would have the potential to be fulfilling and meaningful. Over time, how might that boost our energy levels and our self-confidence? How might that positivity spill over to our trading? Our relationships? Our family lives?

> A positive trading psychology springs
> from intentional living.

We know from research in psychology that subjective well-being—a sense of happiness, fulfillment, energy, and affection—is associated with positive health, successful relationships, and work productivity.[224] Such well-being springs from activities that are intrinsically rewarding to us. When we immerse ourselves in what we love—our relationships, our work—the result is a deep sense of satisfaction and the energy of inspiration. How can we immerse ourselves in the parts of life that we don't love, however? Not all trading is fun and exciting. If we cannot sustain states of immersion during the most laborious trading, can we expect to generate our best ideas and truly trade what we see? By definition, distracted activity cannot be the deeply rewarding activity that sustains well-being. When we pursue markets with reduced focus, we can never experience the level of involvement that sustains our positive psychology—and our best trading.

This is why our personal lives are vital to our trading success. *Everything in life is an opportunity to train intentionality and build the willpower to achieve our ends.* How we live our lives outside markets determines the level of immersion we can bring to markets. We are always training the brain, sometimes for the worse, sometimes for the better.

Imagine eating purposefully, exercising purposefully, resting and sleeping purposefully, and being highly intentional in terms of how we interact with our colleagues, our friends, our children, and our spouses. Every activity would be brain training. Living life in the zone prepares us to trade in the zone.

Case study: intentionality in our relationships

As I am writing this, Margie and I will be celebrating her birthday with our children and grandchildren. The occasion is particularly meaningful, because she went through a very serious illness and has bounced back well. That has made each day together special. In planning the birthday celebration, I left nothing to chance: where we would go out to eat with our children, the card I would give her, the birthday celebration after our outing, and of course her gifts. One of those gifts is a newborn Siamese cat who she has named Nomi Lyn. Siamese cats have been part of Margie's life since childhood and have very special meaning for her. Nomi will be a treasured reminder, linking her early life to our current life together.

Another gift is a black opal pendant I selected for her, representing the shining light that has emerged from the darkness of her period of illness.

I'm confident that each time we interact with Nomi Lyn and when I see Margie wearing the pendant, we'll be transported to a special time—and a special mindset. Love thrives in an environment of meaning and purpose.

A while back I wrote about a successful team leader at a hedge fund who periodically held a surprise celebration with the team at the end of the trading day, with food, drink, and comradery. During the celebration, he went around the room and pointed to each person in turn, citing from memory their contributions to the team's success. Everyone felt visible; everyone felt appreciated. The team felt like a team. Their time together felt *special*.

Recently, during my morning exercise, I sat in the massage chair while two of our cats lounged in the room. I noticed the laser pen that I had taken out earlier and turned it on, creating a red dot of light that they could easily see. Suddenly they sprang to attention and chased the light furiously. I moved the light to different parts of the room, and they became hyperalert, looking for where the light would appear. It was a lot of fun for me, as well as for them. The next day, when I sat on the chair, they looked up at me in eager anticipation. They remembered the laser pen. So, I turned it on and, sure enough, they went bounding around the room chasing the light. Fast forward and now the cats make a point of joining me for each exercise session, waiting patiently for me by the massage chair. Now I find myself looking forward to our game together, giving me an additional reason to pursue my early morning workout. The relationship motivation fueled the motivation to stay in shape.

Our challenge is to make each day, each week, each month and year special in how we engage those we care about. Relationships die, not so much out of conflict as out of neglect. Love cannot flourish in the midst of endless routine and habit. Eventually, withering love leads to frustration and that becomes a breeding ground for conflict. Negative emotions enter our lives for the same reason they enter our trading: we lose our sense of mission and purpose and drift from day to day, falling short of our potential. When we live intentionally—as in the case of planning Margie's birthday—our efforts *give* us energy. What we do inspires us because it's special and meaningful. What if we woke up each day with a plan to make our important relationships special in some fashion? What if others did the same with us? The training of our will is not just practice and preparation for trading. It is a mode that enables us to live the fullest lives possible, expanding our capacity for sustaining intention.

Whatever we do, we can do intentionally, fully activating our brains and our will. As in the case of Margie's birthday, it starts with immersing ourselves in meaningful activity and meaningful relationships and having a goal and purpose for what we are doing. I recall taking my little kids, Devon and Macrae, to a playground for an outing. I typically asked myself how this could be the best possible time together: how I could be fully present to be part of their fun. This made the time together special. I recently had a conversation with a trader who called me in distress, having lost a chunk of capital. Immediately I recognized the gravity of the situation and asked myself: How can I make this the best possible interaction to help turn things around? I had been tired and ready for a cat nap when the trader called. In a flash, I was fully alert and engaged. When we live intentionally, each of our daily activities has a purpose and can be approached in a state of focus. In that way, life itself becomes a breeding ground for brain training.

Using the trading journal as training for the will

Imagine that you maintain a weekly trading journal in which you review performance and make note of what you did well in the past week, what you failed to do well, and what you did that was new and unique and how well that went. The entries are detailed, emphasizing the specifics behind what you did profitably, unprofitably, and uniquely. From this journal, three sets of goals and plans emerge:

1. What you will do specifically to extend what you did well and apply it to new market opportunities.
2. What you will do specifically to correct what you didn't do well and how you will implement those changes in upcoming market opportunities.
3. What you will do to improve and/or expand what you did that was new and different and how you will implement those refinements.

The idea is to use the review process as 'game planning' for the week ahead. Each week, you want to learn from what you did well and what you can improve. You also want to learn to become better and better at defining and implementing changes to your trading that help you exploit fresh opportunities. Each day begins with process-oriented goals that provide an expanded vision for how you will make changes in how you identify opportunities; how you express and size them; how you execute them; and how you manage their risk.

This kind of journal naturally creates a vision for each day of trading, underscoring your performance priorities. Instead of reacting to markets without clear goals and plans, you approach each day—and each trade—with intention, so that everything feeds into your improvement. No trade, no trading day or week, is random. Everything is done purposefully.

> Just as a football team goes into a huddle
> before each play, your journal is your way of
> huddling and planning your next actions.

An active trader will journal daily and even intraday during midday breaks. Active investors might journal each month. *The idea is to create cycles of learning and innovation, so that performance improvement becomes a central trading process.* Such journaling is training of the will, as it requires that we focus our efforts and approach each trading day—and each trade—with intention. The trader who regularly reviews, sets goals, makes plans, and implements those plans becomes an engine of innovation. The idea is to both do more of what works and change what doesn't work—and also constantly look for new ways of doing things. The switched-on trader is always on the hunt for new ways to identify market opportunity, new ways to express market views, and new ways to manage risk/reward. That helps ensure that adaptation to changing markets is ongoing. If innovation is not part of our ongoing trading experience and process, we inevitably grow stale and cannot sustain our optimal levels of focus. The trading journal is our way of sustaining intention, ensuring that we always operate in a purpose-full mode.

Now imagine that we are trading with a team, as we saw at SMB Capital in the previous chapter, or trading with others within a trading community. Each week, each trader reviews performance, keeps a journal, sets goals, and makes plans—*and then shares their journal with at least one other trader*. This means that each trader has the opportunity to learn from the 'huddling' of the other traders and make use of best practices and efforts at improvement. Sharing trading journals also allows each trader to observe the innovations pursued by colleagues, broadening each person's vision for change.

When traders are committed to sharing their journals, there is accountability built into the review process. We now operate in a team context and are responsible for helping our colleagues succeed. If each trader simply developed one improvement and one innovation from their partners each month, consider the cumulative performance impact of that learning.

Of course, such a culture of shared journaling also expands the development of intentionality within a team, community, or organization. Greatness is most likely to develop within an environment committed to performance improvement and achievement. It is easy to become so caught up in the day-to-day movement of markets and the ups and downs of P/L that we lose sight of our larger purpose in developing ourselves. Yes, routine and process are essential to success. If they become our sole focus, however, we quickly run out of emotional fuel. Our work on sustaining purpose and improvement is also our work on sustaining an optimal mindset of inspired focus.

Case study: journaling to learn a new market or trading strategy

Keeping a journal to review and improve performance is an important way to ensure that we improve what we do, but journaling can also help us expand what we do in markets. I find that this broadening of our trading is best accomplished with annotated charts, detailing how a particular move unfolded in a market we're interested in trading. One idea that came to me after a brain training session was that breadth thrusts occur on all time frames. In the stock market, of course, we can track breadth thrusts by seeing how many stocks participate in a particular move. A broad move indicates broad-based buying/selling from large market participants, which is not likely to immediately reverse. Daily advance/decline data and data on the number of stocks making short-term new highs/lows can be valuable in identifying such thrusts.

Suppose, however, we want to identify breadth thrusts for stocks on intraday time frames. Now we would need real-time intraday measures of advancing/declining and highs/lows to gauge the breadth of any particular market move. As I've written in the past, the NYSE TICK serves as one such measure for my trading, showing numerous times each minute how many stocks are trading on upticks and how many on downticks. If many stocks are moving all at once, that broad-based buying/selling is sending an important message about supply/demand.

The idea that came to me after a Muse session was that of the breadth of breadth thrusts. In other words, what if we saw broad buying or selling not only among the NYSE stocks, but also among small caps? What if we observed broad buying/selling among the Dow Industrial shares, but not elsewhere? What if we saw simultaneous broad buying/selling among growth stocks and value shares? Do the breadth of breadth thrusts predict continuation of moves and reversals of moves?

The journals I kept were intraday charts annotated with the breadth moves of the various TICK measures. I made note of patterns among the breadth indicators and observed subsequent price action across different trading instruments. Over time, the journal became more detailed, focusing on time-of-day and market volatility as variables that impacted the likelihood of continuation/reversal. This became a journal of pattern recognition, engaging my curiosity and desire to learn. Over time, I began to notice new patterns, such as shifts in the volatility of the TICK measures themselves.

Keeping the journal and hunting for fresh patterns engaged my motivation and made each new day an adventure in seeing whether or not the patterns would play out. It was like reading a great novel, where you can't wait to turn the page and see what happens. The journal kept me involved in markets regardless of whether I was trading and regardless of my P/L on a given day. When we make growth in performance a focus, we grow our ability to sustain focus.

I often hear from traders that they would like to maintain a trading journal, but have trouble sustaining the effort. The journal becomes one more task added to others. Our challenge is to find ways to make journaling—and learning more broadly—exciting, interesting, and stimulating. Sharing journals with others, using journals for creative thinking, and finding unique formats for journals (record them as videos?) are ways in which we can turn journaling into a tool for building will and mindset.

Brain training for sleep

Thus far we've focused on training the brain for improved processing of information and performance in markets. An important application of neurofeedback, however, is in the improvement of the quantity and quality of our sleep. McGonigal cites a range of evidence that we've become "an increasingly sleep-deprived nation," with negative implications for our functioning.[225] Specifically, she notes, a lack of sleep impairs the functioning of the brain's prefrontal cortex, creating impairment of attention and concentration, as it "interferes with how the brain and body use energy."[226] Ironically, we can take the drive for performance improvement too far, creating stresses that disrupt sleep and actually diminish our ability to process information and sustain effort. Simply stated, quantity and quality of sleep is necessary for sustaining peak performance in other areas of life.

Portable EEG devices make use of a variety of meditative routines to promote brain activity that helps wearers get to sleep more easily. The 'digital sleeping pills' offered by Muse are meditative programs that become softer as the wearer gets closer and closer to sleep. Wearing the headband during sleep allows for a monitoring of sleep/awake time, time it takes to fall asleep, heart rate, and more. The idea is that we can train the sleep state just as we train the focus state, using real-time feedback to keep ourselves in our desired zone.

I have found the sleep monitoring of the Fitbit watch to be quite helpful, as it provides a sleep quality score after each night. Some of the factors that I have found to lead to better sleep quality include: the amount of exercise during the day (number of steps taken); the amount of time spent during the day in the elevated heart rate of aerobic activity; the time of getting to sleep (earlier is better); the timing of eating before going to sleep (refraining from eating too late is better); and the comfort level in bed (warm is better than feeling cool/cold).

'Sleep hygiene' is the term often used for the practices that maximize quality and quantity of sleep. It is very common for traders to be so involved in markets (and social activity) during the day and evening that it takes a toll on the amount of sleep and the amount of time spent in deep sleep. I've found the Fitbit sleep score to be useful in assessing the quality of sleep and have noticed a distinct correlation between the quality of my sleep and my ability to sustain work effort the following day. I've also noticed that discontinuing eating early in the evening reduces my need to get up during the night to use the bathroom, and it also keeps my blood sugar lower during sleep. More than that, I've even observed a correlation between lower blood sugar levels and the amount and vividness of my dreaming. Both are associated with better sleep scores.

Sleep quality is an investment in the quality of our trading.

The takeaway here is that every individual concerned with peak performance is like an Olympic athlete. The Olympian knows that everything they do has a role in their success: their diet, their exercise regimen, their preparation for events, etc. Because everything the athlete does is intentional, directed toward their success, athletic training becomes a training of willpower. A trader operating in peak performance mode similarly approaches life as a training ground. Even something as seemingly inconsequential as sleep quality ends up being a target for development. Very, very few traders view themselves as Olympic athletes. The whole idea may seem silly. But why? Why are the career efforts of a trader, investor, or professional in other fields automatically less worthy of training than the efforts of the athlete? Too much of trading psychology has been devoted to coping with the results of a lack of training. A positive trading psychology begins by developing the elements in life that promote peak performance.

On the horizon: brain-guided coaching

Technology continues to evolve and that evolution will bring fresh innovations for positive trading psychology. Hemoencephalography (HEG) is a form of brain biofeedback (neurofeedback) based upon the measurement of blood flow to the brain's frontal cortex. In passive infrared (pIR) HEG, sensitive heat changes are detected in the forehead, reflecting greater or lesser degrees of blood flow. In near infrared (nIR)

HEG, red and infrared light is sent into the tissue of the forehead to see how much of each is reflected. Changes in the ratio of the light reflected reflect shifts in frontal blood flow. The idea is that high levels of blood flow to the frontal cortex reflect use of the brain's intentional functions, such as reasoning. Decreased blood flow to the cortex suggests activation of brain areas associated with fight/flight/adaptive responses. By monitoring blood flow through HEG, we can identify the degree to which we are responding to situations with distraction and stress vs. calm planning/problem solving. This has been quite helpful in the treatment of attention deficits, as well as emotional disorders that interfere with normal information processing.

Note that HEG is measuring something different from brain waves. HEG tells us about the overall activation of the brain; the brain wave data tell us what kind of activation is going on. If a trader is interested in reducing or eliminating stress in trading, the blood flow feedback is particularly relevant and helpful. With real-time feedback, the trader can learn to sustain frontal activity, even during hectic markets and drawdowns. The latest version of Muse, called Athena, makes use of Functional Near-Infrared Spectroscopy (fNIRS) to assess oxygen levels in the frontal cortex. An app similar to the rainforest described earlier involves keeping an owl in flight based upon mental effort. Through the real-time feedback, the user can learn to sustain longer and longer periods of effortful cognitive activity, similar to how a marathon runner might increase endurance. In the past, HEG was cumbersome to measure and could only be accomplished in a lab. The development of wearable devices to measure brain blood flow means that we can literally conduct our own brain coaching.

Here's a straightforward example of what such brain coaching might look like. In *The Daily Trading Coach*, I described a variety of approaches to psychological change, such as exposure-based behavioral therapy and cognitive therapy, that could be adapted to the needs of traders.[227] Imagine now, however, that we conduct our behavioral or cognitive work while wearing a device that provides real-time HEG data. For example, I could visualize a variety of challenging trading scenarios and imagine my responses to them. While conducting those visualizations, the neurofeedback device would tell me how successful I am in avoiding flight/fight modes and keeping my frontal cortex activated. Moreover, I could engage in those exercises for longer and longer periods of time and work on sustaining the endurance of my frontal activity. Similarly, I could engage in simulated and practice trading while wearing the neurofeedback device and see how well I stay grounded in my 'right mind.' The real-time data would also help me identify specific trading situations and challenges that reduce my brain's oxygenation, targeting those areas for specific work.

It's not such a far reach to imagine wearing a neurofeedback device during everyday trading, using the information to help us take breaks and identify problematic situations before they crash our P/L. It may seem strange to wear a feedback instrument during our trading, and it may even seem distracting to a trader who wants to focus solely on markets. In response to that concern, I would point out that all of us drive cars that provide us with real-time feedback about our fuel levels, speed, and vehicles approaching us. That feedback does not interfere with our driving and, indeed, makes us more effective in getting from point A to point B. I believe the trader of the future will be able to track mental performance in real time just as easily as they track real-time P/L. This will support real-time coaching, helping traders maintain focus for longer periods. Indeed, feedback during a variety of life activities could help us maximize the value of our sleep time and our productivity outside of markets.

Language as a window into our trading psychology

Yet another innovation that promises to revolutionize trading psychology is linguistic analysis. The language we use is a window onto our mindsets. Increasingly, we can analyze our language and learn a great deal about our psychology. The work of Drs. James Pennebaker and Joshua Smyth finds that the very act of expressive writing facilitates health and overall well-being.[228] For example, when we are going through emotional difficulties, voicing our experience provides a cathartic benefit and helps us gain perspective on our situations. The LIWC (Linguistic Inquiry and Word Count) software categorizes the words we write or speak, informing us of their positive and negative emotional content, their cognitive complexity, their degree of authenticity, and much more. For example, I entered the paragraph above (starting with "It's not such a far reach") into LIWC and discovered an above-average positive content relative to other formal writing and a very high degree of authentic tone, suggesting unfiltered, spontaneous thought. I then entered a text from a blog that I recently wrote and LIWC identified an unusually high level of positive language.

This opens a new and promising door to understanding our trading psychology. If we talk our trading journals aloud—our summaries of our performance and our market ideas—speech-to-text software can provide us with material we can use for linguistic analysis. Over time, we can see how our language changes when we have genuine confidence in our views and when we don't. We can see how we talk when we prepare for our successful days vs. our language preceding our less successful days. Suppose we talk aloud our ideas about several possible trades. Does the amount of language we use indicate greater idea depth? Does the emotionality or complexity of the language suggest anything about the idea quality? The content and structure of our language become tools by which we can assess what we're thinking about and how we're thinking about it.

Pennebaker and Smyth's work suggests that talking aloud helps us process difficult and even traumatic experience. Talking out our journals may be effective ways to literally get things off our chest and free our minds to focus on markets. Imagine wearing the brain training devices to measure brain waves and frontal cortex blood flow while talking ideas aloud. Now we have brain data and language providing insight into our mindsets. How we talk to ourselves may help shape our brain functioning, just as our brain states can prime our self-talk. By becoming aware of both, we gain valuable tools in coaching ourselves for improved performance.

What we measure, we can master.

Practical takeaways from Chapter Seven

1. Each of us can learn what helps us enter and stay in the zone of optimal focus, building our capacity to process information, respond to market changes, and perceive fresh opportunities. We are most likely to sustain learning when we pursue strategies that actively engage our curiosity and cognitive strengths. This helps us build intentionality, the ability to sustain effort.
2. Journaling can become a tool for the development of willpower, as it structures our self-development and builds our ability to sustain intentional effort.
3. A new generation of wearable brain training devices help us sustain focus, improve sleep quality, and alert us to distraction before it can interfere with decision making. This opens the door to exciting new ways in which we can coach ourselves based upon the performance information we collect.

Consider that trading in the future will make increasing use of artificial intelligence (AI) to identify patterns in market data. Our brain feedback and linguistic information from our journaling can then help us make the most of this information. To no small degree, the trader of the future will be a human/machine hybrid, and the team of the future will be a collection of traders who share their enhanced ideas with each other in enhanced ways. The trading psychology of the future will be a true positive trading psychology: a vehicle for achieving our potentials, not just a means of overcoming our worst impulses. As I emphasized in my interview for *The SharpBrains Guide to Brain Fitness*, we should "think of life as a gymnasium and the obstacles we encounter as the weights we must lift to get stronger. When you can view challenges as resources toward development and not as unfortunate obstacles to be avoided, you'll be well along the path to brain fitness."[229] What we do to sharpen our abilities to process and act upon information can revolutionize our trading: that is a vital message of positive trading psychology.

CONCLUSION

THIS BOOK BEGAN with the observation that you are the entrepreneur of your life. It follows that you're also the entrepreneur of your trading business. Success will not come, in life or in markets, simply by reducing mistakes and correcting weaknesses. Each of us has a distinctive positive psychology anchored by our greatest strengths and our deepest interests. The goal of positive trading psychology is to draw from the best of who we are, so that our trading truly comes from the soul and not primarily from the ego.[230] It is then that we derive energy from every phase of the trading process—from generating ideas to structuring trades—fueling our productivity and our creativity. *The best trading mentor is your trading success.* If you study what you do well and identify the best practices specific to your profitability, you will uncover the building blocks for a thriving business in financial markets.

As I emphasize to the traders I work with, at some times and in some ways, you are already the trader you want to become. Don't try to make yourself different. Make yourself a better and better version of who you already are at your best.

As I mentioned earlier, a recent research review of short-term approaches to behavior change has been published that captures the conclusions that my colleagues and I have drawn over many years of practice and study.[231] *A major conclusion is that it takes emotion to change emotion: we can reverse our destructive emotional patterns by evoking our most positive patterns*. When we intentionally rehearse and review trading in the mind states of focus, opportunity, and appreciation, we cement those states and anchor them to our real-time trading practice. Trading psychology, no less than trading itself, requires training and practice. When we understand the cognitive and emotional states that underlie our best trading, *that* is when we can truly become more and more of who we are at our best. In his book *The All-Weather Trader*, Tom Basso encourages us to "enjoy watching the movie of your life."[232] It's when we stand aside from the ups and down of life and enjoy the progress that we make over time that trading—and life—become most fulfilling.

One welcome consequence of writing this book is that I've rekindled a commitment to my own trading, particularly by applying the lessons I've learned working with successful traders and investors. I will share those lessons on the TraderFeed blog, bringing the ideas from this book to real-time trading. I hope you'll join me there. In the meantime, thank you for your interest and support over the years and best wishes for your positive development in all spheres of life.

Brett Steenbarger, Ph.D.

ACKNOWLEDGMENTS

THE TRADERS AND trading firms I've worked with and learned from are too numerous to list, and they certainly deserve their confidentiality. But they know who they are, and I want them to know that they have been my greatest teachers over the years. The best way to learn about elite performance is to work with elite performers—and those whose development is taking them on an elite path.

I owe a special acknowledgment to SMB Capital and the many ways I have learned from their teams and traders. I'm especially indebted to Jeff Holden for his sharing of training and mentoring insights in this book and to Mike Bellafiore and Steve Spencer for their dedication to positive trading performance. My inclusion of the resources section in Chapter Five is my way of acknowledging the many market professionals who provide the resources to take our trading performance to the proverbial next level.

The most special acknowledgment, however, is to my wife Margie, who has been my greatest support and inspiration for over 40 years of marriage. She and our amazing children, Debra, Steve, Laura, Devon, Macrae and their wonderful families, have been my greatest source of positive psychology over the years. Finally, a shout out to our amazing cats, who have kept me company through this writing, and can be found at paytoncat.com. Thanks to all TraderFeed readers who have reached out over the years to offer their mentoring and support!

NOTES

1 Compton, W.C., and Hoffman, E. *Positive Psychology: The Science of Happiness and Flourishing, 3rd ed.* (Thousand Oaks, CA: Sage), 2020.

2 Diener, E., and Biswas-Diener, R. *Happiness: Unlocking the Mysteries of Psychological Wealth.* (Malden, MA: Blackwell), 2008.

3 Steenbarger, B.N. *Enhancing Trader Performance: Proven Strategies from the Cutting Edge of Trading Psychology.* (Hoboken, NJ: John Wiley & Sons), 2007.

4 Murphy, S., and Hirschhorn, D. *The Trading Athlete: Winning the Mental Game of Online Trading.* (NY: John Wiley & Sons), 2001.

5 Schwager, J.D. *Market Wizards: Interviews with Top Traders.* (Hoboken, NJ: John Wiley & Sons), 2012.

6 Ericsson, K.A. *The Road to Excellence: The Acquisition of Expert Performance in the Arts and Sciences, Sports and Games.* (Mahwah, NJ: Lawrence Erlbaum), 1996.

7 Duckworth, A. *Grit: The Power of Passion and Perseverance.* (NY: Scribner), 2018.

8 smbcap.com.

9 www.investorsunderground.com.

10 traderlion.com.

11 bearbulltraders.com.

12 myinvestingclub.com.

13 www.topstep.com.

14 Cheavens, J.S., and Feldman, D.B. *The Science and Application of Positive Psychology.* (Cambridge, UK: Cambridge University Press), 2022.

15 Steenbarger, B.N. *Trading Psychology 2.0: From Best Practices to Best Processes*. (Hoboken, NJ: John Wiley & Sons), 2015.

16 Bellafiore, M. *One Good Trade: Inside the Highly Competitive World of Proprietary Trading*. (Hoboken, NJ: John Wiley & Sons), 2010.

17 Bellafiore, M. *The Playbook: An Inside Look at How to Think Like a Professional Trader*. (Upper Saddle River, NJ: FT Press), 2014.

18 Cheavens, J.S., and Feldman, D.B. *The Science and Application of Positive Psychology*. (Cambridge, UK: Cambridge University Press), 2022.

19 Fredrickson, B.L., and Branigan, C. 'Positive emotions broaden the scope of attention and thought-action repertoires.' *Cognition and Emotion*, 19, pp. 313–332, 2005.

20 Fredrickson, B.L., and Losada, M.F. 'Positive affect and the complex dynamics of human flourishing.' *American Psychologist*, 60, pp. 678–686, 2005.

21 Isen, A.M. 'Some ways in which positive affect influences decision making and problem solving.' In M. Lewis, J.M. Haviland-Jones, and L. Feldman-Barrett (Eds.), *Handbook of Emotions, 3rd ed.*, pp. 548–573. (NY: Guilford Press), 2008.

22 Van Cappellen, P., Rice, E.L., Catalino, L.I., and Fredrickson, B.L. 'Positive affective processes underlie positive health change behavior.' *Psychology & Health*, 33, pp. 77–97, 2017.

23 Seligman, M.E.P. *Flourish: A Visionary New Understanding of Happiness and Well-Being*. (NY: Simon and Schuster), 2012.

24 Cheavens, J.S., and Feldman, D.B. *The Science and Application of Positive Psychology*. (Cambridge, UK: Cambridge University Press), 2022.

25 Zelenski, J.M. *Positive Psychology: The Science of Well-Being*. (Thousand Oaks, CA: Sage), 2020 (p. 138).

26 Ibid (p. 146).

27 Compton, W.C., and Hoffman, E. *Positive Psychology: The Science of Happiness and Flourishing, 3rd ed.* (Thousand Oaks, CA: Sage), 2020.

28 Sheldon, K.M. and Lyubomirsky, S. 'The challenge of staying happier.' *Personality and Social Psychology Bulletin*, 38, pp. 670–680 (2012).

29 Compton, W.C., and Hoffman, E. *Positive Psychology: The Science of Happiness and Flourishing, 3rd ed.* (Thousand Oaks, CA: Sage), 2020 (p. 95).

NOTES

30 Steenbarger, B.N. *Trading Psychology 2.0: From Best Practices to Best Processes.* (Hoboken, NJ: John Wiley & Sons), 2015.

31 Minervini, M. *Think and Trade Like a Champion: The Secrets, Rules, and Blunt Truths of a Stock Market Wizard.* (Paso Robles, CA: Access Publishing), 2017 (p. 3).

32 traderfeed.blogspot.com/2024/05/focusing-on-quality-of-your-reps.html.

33 Dalton, J.F., and Dalton, R B. *Markets and Momentum: How Profiling Gives Traders an Advantage.* (Hoboken, NJ: John Wiley & Sons), 2025.

34 Shannon, B. *Maximum Trading Gains with Anchored VWAP – The Perfect Combination of Price, Time, and Volume.* (AlphaTrends.net Publishing), 2023.

35 traderfeed.blogspot.com/2024/06/how-elite-performance-actually-occurs.

36 jamesclear.com/marginal-gains.

37 traderfeed.blogspot.com/2024/10/how-to-coach-yourself-to-trading-success.

38 Dewan, M.J., Steenbarger, B.N., Greenberg, R.P., and Antshel, K. *Brief Psychotherapies. In Tasman's Psychiatry,* 5th ed., pp. 3625–3653. (NY: Springer), 2024.

39 Lamothe, M. *The Trading Mindwheel: Eight Essential Skills for Trading Mastery.* (Hoboken, NJ: John Wiley & Sons), 2023.

40 Ibid (p. 177).

41 Ibid (p. 197).

42 Baiynd, A. *The Trading Book: A Complete Solution to Mastering Technical Systems and Trading Psychology.* (NY: McGraw-Hill), 2011.

43 Ibid (pp. 143–4).

44 Topstep.com.

45 Baiynd, A. *The Trading Book: A Complete Solution to Mastering Technical Systems and Trading Psychology.* (NY: McGraw-Hill), 2011 (p. 191).

46 Tendler, J. *The Mental Game of Trading: A System for Solving Problems with Greed, Fear, Anger, Confidence, and Discipline.* (Philadelphia: JT Press), 2021 (p. 5).

47 Ibid (p. 6).

48 Ibid (p. 186).

49 Ibid (p. 42).

50 Zelenski, J.M. *Positive Psychology: The Science of Well-Being*. (Thousand Oaks, CA: Sage), 2020 (p. 311).

51 Steenbarger, B.N. *The Psychology of Trading: Tools and Techniques for Minding the Markets*. (Hoboken, NJ: John Wiley & Sons), 2003.

52 Steenbarger, B.N. *Enhancing Trader Performance: Proven Strategies from the Cutting Edge of Trading Psychology*. (Hoboken, NJ: John Wiley & Sons), 2007.

53 www.smbtraining.com.

54 Douglas, M. *The Disciplined Trader: Developing Winning Attitudes*. (NY: Penguin), 1990.

55 Steenbarger, B.N. *Radical Renewal: Tools for Leading a Meaningful Life*. leadingrenewal.blogspot.com, 2019.

56 Hougaard, T. *Best Loser Wins: Why Normal Thinking Never Wins the Trading Game*. (Petersfield, Hampshire UK: Harriman House), 2022 (p. 207).

57 Goldstein, S. *Mastering the Mental Game of Trading: Harnessing the Power of the Inner Self to Fuel Trading Outperformance*. (Petersfield, Hampshire UK: Harriman House), 2024.

58 Ibid (p. 34).

59 Raschke, L.B. *Trading Sardines: Lessons in the Markets from a Lifelong Trader*. (Wellington, FL: Daughters Press), 2018.

60 Schwager, J.D. *The New Market Wizards: Conversations with America's Top Traders*. (NY: HarperBusiness), 1992.

61 Niederhoffer, V. *The Education of a Speculator*. (NY: John Wiley & Sons), 1997.

62 Minervini, M. *Think and Trade Like a Champion: The Secrets, Rules, and Blunt Truths of a Stock Market Wizard*. (Paso Robles, CA: Access Publishing), 2017 (p. 22).

63 Schwager, J.D. *Stock Market Wizards: Interviews with America's Top Stock Traders*. (NY: HarperBusiness), 2001.

64 Fisher, M.B. *The Logical Trader: Applying a Method to the Madness*. (Hoboken, NJ: John Wiley & Sons), 2002.

65 Raschke, L.B. *Trading Sardines: Lessons in the Markets from a Lifelong Trader*. (Wellington, FL: Daughters Press), 2018 (p. 39).

NOTES

66 Bellafiore, M. *The Playbook: An Inside Look at How to Think Like a Professional Trader.* (Upper Saddle River, NJ: FT Press), 2014.

67 sentimentrader.com.

68 Kahneman, D. *Thinking, Fast and Slow.* (NY: Farrar, Straus, & Giroux), 2013.

69 Bellafiore, M. *One Good Trade: Inside the Highly Competitive World of Proprietary Trading.* (Hoboken, NJ: John Wiley & Sons), 2010.

70 Douglas, M. *The Disciplined Trader: Developing Winning Attitudes.* (NY: Penguin), 1990 (p. 105).

71 Ibid (p. 109).

72 Minervini, M. *Mindset Secrets for Winning: How to Bring Personal Power to Everything You Do.* (Paso Robles, CA: Access Publishing), 2019 (p. 6).

73 Boboch, E., Donnelly, K., Krull, E., and Daill, K. *The Lifecycle Trade: How to Win at Trading IPOs and Super Growth Stocks.* (Westmont, IL: Blanca Graciela), 2019 (p. 130).

74 Burns, S., & Burns, H. *Complete Guide to Trading Psychology.* (Gulf Breeze, FL: Stolly Media), 2022 (p. 36).

75 Ibid (p. 39).

76 Ibid (p. 70).

77 Goldstein, S. *Mastering the Mental Game of Trading: Harnessing the Power of the Inner Self to Fuel Trading Outperformance.* (Petersfield, Hampshire UK: Harriman House), 2024 (p. 113).

78 Ibid (p. 198).

79 Minervini, M. *Trade Like a Stock Market Wizard: How to Achieve Superperformance in Stocks in Any Market.* (NY: McGraw-Hill), 2013 (p. 5).

80 Lamothe, M. *The Trading Mindwheel: Eight Essential Skills for Trading Mastery.* (Hoboken, NJ: John Wiley & Sons), 2023 (p. 111).

81 Schwager, J.D. *Market Wizards: Interviews with Top Traders.* (Hoboken, NJ: John Wiley & Sons), 2012 (p. 410).

82 Aziz, A., and Baehr, M. *Mastering Trading Psychology: Improve Your Trading with Firsthand Reports by Real-Life Traders.* (Vancouver, CA: Peak Capital Trading), 2020 (p. 29).

83 Byeagee, Y. *Trading Composure: Mastering Your Mind for Trading Success.* (NY: John Wiley & Sons), 2024 (p. xii).

84 Aziz, A., & Baehr, M. *Mastering Trading Psychology: Improve Your Trading with Firsthand Reports by Real-Life Traders.* (Vancouver, CA: Peak Capital Trading), 2020 (p. 273).

85 Kiev, A. *The Mental Strategies of Top Traders: The Psychological Determinants of Trading Success.* (Hoboken, NJ: John Wiley & Sons), 2010 (p. 81).

86 Hougaard, T. *Best Loser Wins: Why Normal Thinking Never Wins the Trading Game.* (Petersfield, Hampshire UK: Harriman House), 2022 (p. 210).

87 Steenbarger, B.N. *Trading Psychology 2.0: From Best Practices to Best Processes.* (Hoboken, NJ: John Wiley & Sons), 2015 (p. 217).

88 Ibid (p. 10).

89 Pruden, H. *The Three Skills of Top Trading.* (Hoboken, NJ: John Wiley & Sons), 2007 (p. 179).

90 Hougaard, T. *Best Loser Wins: Why Normal Thinking Never Wins the Trading Game.* (Petersfield, Hampshire UK: Harriman House), 2022.

91 Burns, S., and Burns, H. *Complete Guide to Trading Psychology.* (Gulf Breeze, FL: Stolly Media), 2022 (p. 53).

92 Steenbarger, B.N. *The Daily Trading Coach: 101 Lessons for Becoming Your Own Trading Psychologist.* (Hoboken, NJ: John Wiley & Sons), 2009 (p. 283).

93 Hougaard, T. *Best Loser Wins: Why Normal Thinking Never Wins the Trading Game.* (Petersfield, Hampshire UK: Harriman House), 2022 (p. 84).

94 Ibid (p. 84).

95 Kiev, A. *Trading to Win: The Psychology of Mastering the Markets.* (NY: John Wiley & Sons), 1998 (p. 30).

96 Dayton, G. *Trade Mindfully: Achieve Your Optimum Trading Performance with Mindfulness and Cutting-Edge Psychology.* (Hoboken, NJ: John Wiley & Sons), 2015 (pp. 152–154).

97 Shull, D. *Market Mind Games: A Radical Psychology of Investing, Trading, and Risk.* (NY: McGraw-Hill), 2012 (p. 198).

98 Ibid (p. 200).

99 Dayton, G. *Trade Mindfully: Achieve Your Optimum Trading Performance with Mindfulness and Cutting-Edge Psychology.* (Hoboken, NJ: John Wiley & Sons), 2015.

NOTES

100 traderfeed.blogspot.com/2024/08/how-to-coach-yourself-to-trading-success.html.

101 Steenbarger, B.N. *Trading Psychology 2.0: From Best Practices to Best Processes.* (Hoboken, NJ: John Wiley & Sons), 2015 (p. 322).

102 Ibid (p. 323).

103 Steenbarger, B.N. *The Psychology of Trading: Tools and Techniques for Minding the Markets.* (Hoboken, NJ: John Wiley & Sons), 2003 (pp. 292–293).

104 Dayton, G. *Trade Mindfully: Achieve Your Optimum Trading Performance with Mindfulness and Cutting-Edge Psychology.* (Hoboken, NJ: John Wiley & Sons), 2015 (p. 103).

105 Steenbarger, B.N. *Enhancing Trader Performance: Proven Strategies from the Cutting Edge of Trading Psychology.* (Hoboken, NJ: John Wiley & Sons), 2007 (p. 166).

106 Kiev, A. *Trading in the Zone: Maximizing Performance with Focus and Discipline.* (NY: John Wiley & Sons), 2001 (p. 25).

107 Dayton, G. *Trade Mindfully: Achieve Your Optimum Trading Performance with Mindfulness and Cutting-Edge Psychology.* (Hoboken, NJ: John Wiley & Sons), 2015.

108 Bellafiore, M. *One Good Trade: Inside the Highly Competitive World of Proprietary Trading.* (Hoboken, NJ: John Wiley & Sons), 2010 (p. 125).

109 Bellafiore, M. *The Playbook: An Inside Look at How to Think Like a Professional Trader.* (Upper Saddle River, NJ: FT Press), 2014.

110 Dewan, M.J, Steenbarger, B.N., and Greenberg, R.P. *The Art and Science of Brief Psychotherapies: A Practitioner's Guide, 3rd ed.* (Washington, DC: American Psychiatric Press), 2017.

111 Ibid.

112 Steenbarger, B.N. *The Daily Trading Coach: 101 Lessons for Becoming Your Own Trading Psychologist.* (Hoboken, NJ: John Wiley & Sons), 2009 (p. 15).

113 Ibid (p. 16).

114 Aziz, A., and Baehr, M. *Mastering Trading Psychology: Improve Your Trading with Firsthand Reports by Real-Life Traders.* (Vancouver, CA: Peak Capital Trading), 2020 (p. 332).

115 Bellafiore, M. *The Playbook: An Inside Look at How to Think Like a Professional Trader.* (Upper Saddle River, NJ: FT Press), 2014 (p. 73).

116 Kiev, A. *The Mental Strategies of Top Traders: The Psychological Determinants of Trading Success*. (Hoboken, NJ: John Wiley & Sons), 2010 (p. 19).

117 Shull, D. *Market Mind Games: A Radical Psychology of Investing, Trading, and Risk*. (NY: McGraw-Hill), 2012 (p. 40).

118 Ibid (p. 118).

119 Dayton, G. *Trade Mindfully: Achieve Your Optimum Trading Performance with Mindfulness and Cutting-Edge Psychology*. (Hoboken, NJ: John Wiley & Sons), 2015.

120 Byeagee, Y. *Trading Composure: Mastering Your Mind for Trading Success*. (NY: John Wiley & Sons), 2024.

121 Steenbarger, B.N. *Trading Psychology 2.0: From Best Practices to Best Processes*. (Hoboken, NJ: John Wiley & Sons), 2015.

122 Clear, J. *Atomic Habits: An Easy and Proven Way to Build Good Habits and Break Bad Ones*. (NY: Avery), 2018.

123 Diener, E., and Biswas-Diener, R. *Happiness: Unlocking the Mysteries of Psychological Wealth*. (Malden, MA: Blackwell), 2008 (p. 73).

124 Ibid (p. 53).

125 Gurdjieff, G.I. *Beelzebub's Tales to His Grandson: All and Everything*. (NY: Penguin), 1999.

126 Steenbarger, B.N. *Radical Renewal: Tools for Leading a Meaningful Life*. leadingrenewal.blogspot.com, 2019.

127 Williams, J. *The Mental Edge in Trading: Adapt Your Personality Traits and Control Your Emotions to Make Smarter Investments*. (NY: McGraw-Hill), 2013 (p. 188).

128 Steenbarger, B.N. *The Daily Trading Coach: 101 Lessons for Becoming Your Own Trading Psychologist*. (Hoboken, NJ: John Wiley & Sons), 2009 (p. 69).

129 Dewan, M.J, Steenbarger, B.N., and Greenberg, R.P. *The Art and Science of Brief Psychotherapies: A Practitioner's Guide, 3rd ed.* (Washington, DC: American Psychiatric Press), 2017; Dewan, M.J., Steenbarger, B.N., Greenberg, R.P., and Antshel, K. Brief Psychotherapies. In *Tasman's Psychiatry*, 5th ed., pp. 3625–3653. (NY: Springer), 2024.

130 Steenbarger, B.N. *The Daily Trading Coach: 101 Lessons for Becoming Your Own Trading Psychologist*. (Hoboken, NJ: John Wiley & Sons), 2009 (p. 217).

131 Ibid.

NOTES

132 Ibid.

133 Ibid (p. 113).

134 traderfeed.blogspot.com/2021/06/figs-focused-intensive-goal-setting.html.

135 Steenbarger, B.N. *Enhancing Trader Performance: Proven Strategies from the Cutting Edge of Trading Psychology*. (Hoboken, NJ: John Wiley & Sons), 2007 (p. 138).

136 Williams, J. *The Mental Edge in Trading: Adapt Your Personality Traits and Control Your Emotions to Make Smarter Investments*. (NY: McGraw-Hill), 2013.

137 Bellafiore, M. *The Playbook: An Inside Look at How to Think Like a Professional Trader*. (Upper Saddle River, NJ: FT Press), 2014.

138 Tendler, J. *The Mental Game of Trading: A System for Solving Problems with Greed, Fear, Anger, Confidence, and Discipline*. (Philadelphia: JT Press), 2021 (p. 309).

139 Shull, D. *Market Mind Games: A Radical Psychology of Investing, Trading, and Risk*. (NY: McGraw-Hill), 2012 (p. 59).

140 Ibid (p. 56).

141 Ibid (p. 57).

142 Dalton, J.F., Jones, E.T., and Dalton, R.B. *Mind Over Markets: Power Trading with Market Generated Information*. (Hoboken, NJ: John Wiley & Sons), 2013; Dalton, J.F., and Dalton, R.B. *Markets and Momentum: How Profiling Gives Traders an Advantage*. (Hoboken, NJ: John Wiley & Sons), 2025.

143 Dalton, J.F., Jones, E.T., and Dalton, R.B. *Mind Over Markets: Power Trading with Market Generated Information*. (Hoboken, NJ: John Wiley & Sons), 2013.

144 Basso, T. *The All-Weather Trader: Mr. Serenity's Thoughts on Trading Come Rain or Shine*. (Carson City, NV: Lioncrest), 2023.

145 Steenbarger, B.N. *Trading Psychology 2.0: From Best Practices to Best Processes*. (Hoboken, NJ: John Wiley & Sons), 2015.

146 Steenbarger, B.N. *Enhancing Trader Performance: Proven Strategies from the Cutting Edge of Trading Psychology*. (Hoboken, NJ: John Wiley & Sons), 2007.

147 Bellafiore, M. *The Playbook: An Inside Look at How to Think Like a Professional Trader*. (Upper Saddle River, NJ: FT Press), 2014 (p. 211).

148 traderfeed.blogspot.com/2024/10/why-cant-i-improve-my-trading.html.

149 Dewan, M.J., Steenbarger, B.N., Greenberg, R.P., and Antshel, K. *Brief Psychotherapies. In Tasman's Psychiatry,* 5th ed., pp. 3625–3653. (NY: Springer), 2024.

150 Compton, W.C., and Hoffman, E. *Positive Psychology: The Science of Happiness and Flourishing,* 3rd ed. (Thousand Oaks, CA: Sage), 2020 (p. 193); Kobasa, S.C. 'Stressful life events, personality, and health: An inquiry into hardiness.' *Journal of Personality and Social Psychology,* 37, pp. 1–11.

151 Zelenski, J.M. *Positive Psychology: The Science of Well-Being.* (Thousand Oaks, CA: Sage), 2020 (p. 302).

152 Ibid (p. 307).

153 Cheavens, J.S., and Feldman, D.B. *The Science and Application of Positive Psychology.* (Cambridge, UK: Cambridge University Press), 2022 (p. 131).

154 Ibid (p. 129).

155 Sawyer, R.K., and Henriksen, D. *Explaining Creativity: The Science of Human Innovation,* 3rd ed. (NY: Oxford University Press), 2024 (p. 139).

156 Ibid (p. 154).

157 Ibid (p. 265).

158 Peterson, R.L. *Inside the Investor's Brain: The Power of Mind Over Money.* (Hoboken, NJ: John Wiley & Sons), 2007 (p. 70).

159 Ibid (p. 71).

160 Diener, E., and Biswas-Diener, R. *Happiness: Unlocking the Mysteries of Psychological Wealth.* (Malden, MA: Blackwell), 2008 (p. 25).

161 Ibid (pp. 73–74).

162 Minervini, M. *Trade Like a Stock Market Wizard: How to Achieve Superperformance in Stocks in Any Market.* (NY: McGraw-Hill), 2013.

163 Minervini, M. *Think and Trade Like a Champion: The Secrets, Rules, and Blunt Truths of a Stock Market Wizard.* (Paso Robles, CA: Access Publishing), 2017.

164 Minervini, M. *Mindset Secrets for Winning: How to Bring Personal Power to Everything You Do.* (Paso Robles, CA: Access Publishing), 2019.

165 www.minervini.com.

NOTES

166 Bellafiore, M. *One Good Trade: Inside the Highly Competitive World of Proprietary Trading.* (Hoboken, NJ: John Wiley & Sons), 2010.

167 Bellafiore, M. *The Playbook: An Inside Look at How to Think Like a Professional Trader.* (Upper Saddle River, NJ: FT Press), 2014.

168 www.youtube.com/@smbcapital.

169 smbcap.com/smb-edge.

170 www.youtube.com/playlist?list=PLo5LM9g7UwiaRTiI7322qgS9K_PFrVNKP.

171 theonelanceb.com.

172 tradeciety.com.

173 tradeciety.com/trading-journal.

174 edgewonk.com/import.

175 Fisher, M.B. *The Logical Trader: Applying a Method to the Madness.* (Hoboken, NJ: John Wiley & Sons), 2002.

176 Dalton, J.F., *Markets in Profile: Profiting from the Auction Process.* (Hoboken, NJ: John Wiley & Sons), 2007.

177 Dalton, J.F., and Dalton, R.B. *Markets and Momentum: How Profiling Gives Traders an Advantage.* (Hoboken, NJ: John Wiley & Sons), 2025.

178 Shannon, B. *Technical Analysis Using Multiple Timeframes: Understanding Market Structure and Profit from Trend Alignment.* (Centennial CO: LifeVest), 2008.

179 Shannon, B. *Maximum Trading Gains with Anchored VWAP – The Perfect Combination of Price, Time, and Volume.* (AlphaTrends.net Publishing), 2023.

180 Baiynd, A. *The Trading Book: A Complete Solution to Mastering Technical Systems and Trading Psychology.* (NY: McGraw-Hill), 2011.

181 Aziz, A. *Advanced Techniques in Day Trading: A Practical Guide to High Probability Strategies and Methods.* (Vancouver, CA: Bear Bull Traders), 2018.

182 Aziz, A., and Sheehy-Kelly, C. *TradeBook: How to Build a Complete Trading System.* (Vancouver, CA: Bear Bull Traders), 2025.

183 Boboch, E., Donnelly, K., Krull, E., and Daill, K. *The Lifecycle Trade: How to Win at Trading IPOs and Super Growth Stocks.* (Westmont, IL: Blanca Graciela), 2019.

184 Basso, T. *The All-Weather Trader: Mr. Serenity's Thoughts on Trading Come Rain or Shine.* (Carson City, NV: Lioncrest), 2023 (p. 38).

185 Ibid (pp. 77–78).

186 Ibid (p. 109).

187 Raschke, L.B. *Trading Sardines: Lessons in the Markets from a Lifelong Trader.* (Wellington, FL: Daughters Press), 2018.

188 Connors, L.A., and Raschke, L.B. *Street Smarts: High Probability Short Term Trading Strategies.* (Los Angeles, CA: M. Gordon Publishing Group), 1995.

189 Schwager, J.D. *Market Wizards: Interviews with Top Traders.* (Hoboken, NJ: John Wiley & Sons), 2012.

190 Hougaard, T. *Best Loser Wins: Why Normal Thinking Never Wins the Trading Game.* (Petersfield, Hampshire UK: Harriman House), 2022.

191 Byeagee, Y. *Trading Composure: Mastering Your Mind for Trading Success.* (NY: John Wiley & Sons), 2024.

192 Goldstein, S. *Mastering the Mental Game of Trading: Harnessing the Power of the Inner Self to Fuel Trading Outperformance.* (Petersfield, Hampshire UK: Harriman House), 2024.

193 www.alpharcubed.com/trader-performance-coaching.

194 Shull, D. *Market Mind Games: A Radical Psychology of Investing, Trading, and Risk.* (NY: McGraw-Hill), 2012.

195 Tendler, J. *The Mental Game of Trading: A System for Solving Problems with Greed, Fear, Anger, Confidence, and Discipline.* (Philadelphia: JT Press), 2021.

196 Burns, S., and Burns, H. *Complete Guide to Trading Psychology.* (Gulf Breeze, FL: Stolly Media), 2022.

197 Dayton, G. *Trade Mindfully: Achieve Your Optimum Trading Performance with Mindfulness and Cutting-Edge Psychology.* (Hoboken, NJ: John Wiley & Sons), 2015.

198 Kiev, A. *Trading to Win: The Psychology of Mastering the Markets.* (NY: John Wiley & Sons), 1998.

199 Kiev, A. *Trading in the Zone: Maximizing Performance with Focus and Discipline.* (NY: John Wiley & Sons), 2001.

200 Kiev, A. *The Mental Strategies of Top Traders: The Psychological Determinants of Trading Success.* (Hoboken, NJ: John Wiley & Sons), 2010.

NOTES

201 Niederhoffer, V. *The Education of a Speculator.* (NY: John Wiley & Sons), 1997.

202 Kenner, L., and Niederhoffer, V. *Practical Speculation.* (NY: John Wiley & Sons), 2017.

203 Rand, A. *The Fountainhead.* (Indianapolis, IN: Bobbs-Merrill Company), 1943.

204 Rand, A. *The Romantic Manifesto.* (NY: New American Library), 1965.

205 Steenbarger, B.N. *The Daily Trading Coach: 101 Lessons for Becoming Your Own Trading Psychologist.* (Hoboken, NJ: John Wiley & Sons), 2009.

206 Steenbarger, B.N. *Enhancing Trader Performance: Proven Strategies from the Cutting Edge of Trading Psychology.* (Hoboken, NJ: John Wiley & Sons), 2007.

207 Steenbarger, B.N. *Trading Psychology 2.0: From Best Practices to Best Processes.* (Hoboken, NJ: John Wiley & Sons), 2015.

208 Steenbarger, B.N. *The Psychology of Trading: Tools and Techniques for Minding the Markets.* (Hoboken, NJ: John Wiley & Sons), 2003.

209 Steenbarger, B.N. *Radical Renewal: Tools for Leading a Meaningful Life.* leadingrenewal.blogspot.com, 2019.

210 Dewan, M.J, Steenbarger, B.N., and Greenberg, R.P. *The Art and Science of Brief Psychotherapies: A Practitioner's Guide, 3rd ed.* (Washington, DC: American Psychiatric Press), 2017; Dewan, M.J., Steenbarger, B.N., Greenberg, R.P., and Antshel, K. *Brief Psychotherapies. In Tasman's Psychiatry, 5th ed.*, pp. 3625–3653. (NY: Springer), 2024.

211 Steenbarger, B.N. *The Daily Trading Coach: 101 Lessons for Becoming Your Own Trading Psychologist.* (Hoboken, NJ: John Wiley & Sons), 2009.

212 Wilson, C. *G.I. Gurdjieff: The War Against Sleep* (London: Aeon), 2005 (p. 60).

213 McGonigal, K. *The Willpower Instinct: How Self-Control Works, Why It Matters, and What You Can Do to Get More of It.* (NY: Penguin), 2012 (p. 60).

214 Ibid (p. 62).

215 Ibid (pp. 66–67).

216 Rubin, G. *Better Than Before: Mastering the Habits of Our Everyday Lives.* (NY: Crown), 2015 (p. 45).

217 Tart, C. *Waking Up: Overcoming the Obstacles to Human Potential.* (Boston, MA: Shambhala), 1986 (p. 15).

218 Ratey, J.R. *A User's Guide to the Brain: Perception, Attention, and the Four Theaters of the Brain.* (NY: Vintage), 2001 (p. 146).

219 Fernandez, A., Goldberg, E., and Michelon, P. *The SharpBrains Guide to Brain Fitness: How to Optimize Brain Health and Performance at Any Age, 2nd ed.* (Lexington, KY: SharpBrains), 2013.

220 Wilson, C. *New Pathways in Psychology: Maslow and the Post-Freudian Revolution.* (NY: Taplinger), 1972 (p. 245).

221 Baumeister, R.F., & Tierney, J. *Willpower: Rediscovering the Greatest Human Strength.* (NY: Penguin), 2012.

222 Wilson, C. *New Pathways in Psychology: Maslow and the Post-Freudian Revolution.* (NY: Taplinger), 1972 (p. 251).

223 Baumeister, R.F., & Tierney, J. *Willpower: Rediscovering the Greatest Human Strength.* (NY: Penguin), 2012.

224 Seligman, M.E.P. *Flourish: A Visionary New Understanding of Happiness and Well-Being.* (NY: Simon and Schuster), 2012.

225 McGonigal, K. *The Willpower Instinct: How Self-Control Works, Why It Matters, and What You Can Do to Get More of It.* (NY: Penguin), 2012 (p. 52).

226 Ibid (p. 53).

227 Steenbarger, B.N. *The Daily Trading Coach: 101 Lessons for Becoming Your Own Trading Psychologist.* (Hoboken, NJ: John Wiley & Sons), 2009.

228 Pennebaker, J.W., and Smyth, J.M. *Opening Up by Writing It Down, 3rd ed.* (NY: Guilford), 2016.

229 Fernandez, A., Goldberg, E., and Michelon, P. *The SharpBrains Guide to Brain Fitness: How to Optimize Brain Health and Performance at Any Age, 2nd ed.* (Lexington, KY: SharpBrains), 2013 (p. 160).

230 Steenbarger, B.N. *Radical Renewal: Tools for Leading a Meaningful Life.* leadingrenewal.blogspot.com, 2019.

231 Dewan, M.J., Steenbarger, B.N., Greenberg, R.P., and Antshel, K. *Brief Psychotherapies. In Tasman's Psychiatry, 5th ed.,* pp. 3625–3653. (NY: Springer), 2024.

232 Basso, T. *The All-Weather Trader: Mr. Serenity's Thoughts on Trading Come Rain or Shine.* (Carson City, NV: Lioncrest), 2023 (p. 154).

INDEX

A
ABCD (best processes of trading), 25
acceptance of uncertainty, 105
after-action reviews (AAR), 41, 108
assessment, 117

B
Baiynd, Anne-Marie, 42–43, 45, 206
beginner's mindset, 26
behavioral stress-management skills, 146
Bellafiore, Mike, 70, 120, 195, 205
best practices, 88, 161, 185, 240, 272
Big Five personality traits, 21
Biswas-Diener, Robert, 2, 132, 204
Bollinger Bands, 74, 80
brainstorming, 75, 107
brain waves, 252, 269
breadth thrusts, 81, 263
breaks, trading, 131
breathing exercises, 141–45, 246

C
Bryan, Carlton, 233, 235, 237
business plans, 45, 47

calendar, 100
ChatGPT, 187
coaching, 38–39, 46, 68–69, 75, 98, 111, 116, 125, 188
cognitive effort, 92
cognitive fitness, 132
cognitive flexibility, 12, 19, 62
cognitive mastery, 171–72
collaboration, 121
concentration, 79, 249–52, 256
Covid crisis, 54

D
Daily Trading Coach, The (Steenbarger), 125, 150, 209
Dalton, Jim, 32, 176, 206
day trading, 14, 71–72, 82–83, 131, 196
decision making, 203
Diener, Ed, 2, 132, 204
discipline, 85, 93, 222, 246
distraction, 251, 257
diversification, 88, 114, 174, 181–82, 211
drawdowns, 30, 66, 68, 71, 76–77, 95, 98, 135, 138, 152, 154–55,

158–59, 161, 181, 188, 192, 215, 256
Drinon, Garrett, 220–21

E
edge (trading), 214
emotional experiencing, 40
emotional P/L, 66
emotional temperature, 133–34
empathy, 145, 176
entrepreneurial mindset, 26, 188, 272
entrepreneurship, 45–47, 71, 272

F
fear, 64
fear of missing out (FOMO), 2, 109, 220
Federal Reserve, 56, 63, 72, 80, 190
flow, 128, 133, 136, 142
flow (psychology), 33
Freudberg, Seth, 215–17
functional near-infrared spectroscopy (fNIRS), 267

G
global macro, 7
goal setting, 52, 167, 241, 260–61
grit, 11

H
Hasson, Ryan, 222
hedging, 57, 87, 114–15, 135
hemoencephalography (HEG), 266–67
Hougaard, Tom, 62–64, 110–11, 207
human/machine hybrid, 270

I
independence, 71
inflection points, 90
information processing, 91, 170, 173–74, 179, 189
intentional living, 257–58
interest rates, 58, 251, 255
intraday trading, 27, 197, 227–28

K
Kahneman, Daniel, 86
Kiev, Ari, 110, 118, 126, 208

L
learning environment, 244
Logical Trader, The (Fisher), 206
long/short strategies, 16
losses, handling, 62

M
market breadth, 35, 48, 74, 80–81, 86, 197, 210, 217, 227
market edges, 22, 29, 41, 45, 48, 51
market making, 14, 23
Market Mind Games (Shull), 112, 126, 208
Market Profile, 32, 176, 180, 206
Markets in Profile (Dalton), 206
Market Wizards (Schwager), 5, 10, 65, 105, 207
Mastering the Mental Game of Trading (Goldstein), 64, 103
mean reversion, 57, 74, 227
mental fatigue, 89
Mental Game of Trading, The (Tendler), 43, 208

mentoring, 10, 14, 17–18, 37, 39–41, 45, 60, 65, 116, 164, 169, 194, 199, 212–14, 223–26, 228–32, 236, 238–39, 243–44, 272
   one up, one down, 225–26, 239, 243–44, (*see also* mentoring: one up; one down)
   psychological coaching, 37, 39, 41
mindset, 45, 138, 145, 148, 163, 165–66, 174, 220, 268
mindsets, positive, 146
Minervini, Mark, 25, 67, 70, 103, 204
mission and purpose, 259
mission statements, 45–47
money management, 102, 184–85, 188
moving averages, 8, 74, 84, 162, 172, 218
muscle memory, 217, 230
Muse device, 129–30, 180, 253, 263, 267
   replacing with positive emotion, 200

N

Niederhoffer, Victor, 65, 208
NYSE TICK, 28, 35, 60, 195, 263

O

one up, one down, 228, 242
options trading, 14, 215–16
overtrading, 150, 236, 255

P

patience, 177

pattern recognition, 34, 84, 116, 130, 172–73, 176, 178, 190, 193, 210, 256, 264
peak performance, 30, 41, 50, 65, 99, 104, 137, 259, 266
peak performance psychology, 9
people management, 183–84, 187
perfectionism, 152–54
   state-dependent performance, 180
performance learning, 224
performance psychology, 31, 99–100, 245–46
personal energy management, 101–2, 106, 146, 255
personal strengths, 1, 3, 22, 30, 35
philanthropy, 159
playbooks, 19, 70, 172, 220
Playbook, The (Bellafiore), 195
portfolio construction, 114, 182, 184, 193
position sizing, 4, 30, 42, 50, 56–57, 68–69, 90–91, 113, 147, 175–76, 178, 193, 216, 218, 223, 225, 234–37
positive triggers, 136–37, 148
post-traumatic growth, 201
pre-market game plan, 218
premarket preparation, 163
price action, 48, 79, 83, 91, 102
psychological capital, 224
psychological strengths, 12

Q

quanti-mental trading, 53
quieting the mind, 128

R

Radical Renewal (Steenbarger), 62, 66, 139, 209
Raschke, Linda, 65, 70, 207
resilience, 11–12, 28, 31, 57, 66, 69, 92, 120. *see also* grit; resilience
risk-adjusted returns, 77, 114, 181–82
risk management, 7, 17, 30, 42, 50–51, 56, 64, 67–70, 76, 86, 88, 91, 93, 111, 165, 182–83, 224, 229, 233, 235–37, 243
    loss limits, 62, 113, 233–34, 237, (*see also* stop limits)
    risk reduction, 234–37
risk-taking, 57, 71, 114–16, 176, 236

S

scaling out, 90
scalping, 23
scenario rehearsal, 57
screening tools, 8, 54, 83–84
self-control, 246–48
Seykota, Ed, 10
Shannon, Brian, 32, 206
Sharpe ratio, 76–77, 235
Shull, Denise, 112, 126, 176, 208
skill development, 12, 52, 241
skills, 10, 50, 91–93, 166
sleep hygiene, 265
sleep quality, 266
social support, 19, 154, 158
solution-focused methods, 141, 163
solution-focused psychology, 99
solution-focused work, 119, 159, 161
S&P 500 Index, 27, 136, 172, 243
Spencer, Steve, 70, 205, 218–19
Spero, Justin, 228–30
state-dependent trading, 137
stock selection, 218
stocks in play, 17, 163, 172, 205
stop limits, 235
strengths, 93, 102, 165–66, 189, 272
strengths, personal, 6, 15, 21, 34, 73, 77–78, 85, 120, 135, 137, 161, 164, 171, 178, 181, 184–85, 187, 190–91, 193, 195–96, 203, 229–30, 238
stress management, 142–45, 168
study groups, 97
SUNY Upstate Medical University, 95, 123, 126, 199
sustainable happiness model, 21–22

T

talents, 9–10
team building, 108, 113, 157, 184, 186
team collaboration, 185, 188–89, 194
team communication, 185
team meetings, 72
Technical Analysis Using Multiple Timeframes (Shannon), 206
Tendler, Jared, 43, 45, 174, 208
Think and Trade Like a Champion (Minervini), 25, 67
TICK measures, 28
tilt, trading, 119, 133, 140, 148
time frames, trading, 197, 251
time management, 100–102, 121, 139
time of day, 44
trade planning, 64
trade reviews, 221–22
TraderFeed blog, 31, 36, 39, 112, 117, 167, 273

traders, 3, 8, 11–12, 14, 16–17, 22–23, 25, 34–35, 75, 176–77, 189, 194, 244, 249–50, 253, 255–56
Traders4ACause, 140, 159
trading algorithms, 23
trading as performance activity, 212
Trading Book, The (Baiynd), 42–43, 206
trading coach, 57, 169
trading communities, 11, 157, 194, 227
trading community, 238
Trading Composure (Byeagee), 207
trading journal, 260
trading mistakes, 136, 221–22
trading process, 70, 121, 196, 261
trading processes, 30, 63, 92
trading psychology, 3–4, 6, 12, 15, 19, 28–30, 41, 43, 45, 52, 56, 65, 68–69, 73, 77–78, 81, 86, 92, 96, 99, 101, 104, 109, 115–17, 119–20, 122, 126–27, 129, 131, 137, 139, 149–50, 157, 164–65, 167–71, 181, 183, 193–94, 199, 203–4, 206, 208, 211, 213, 221, 225, 228, 233, 239, 244–45, 255–57, 266, 268–69
durable trading psychology, 29
evidence-based approaches, 199
immediacy, 18, 40, 123
positive trading psychology, 70, 137, 149, 178, 204, 244, 257, 266
self-coaching, 104–5, 167
Trading Psychology 2.0 (Steenbarger), 25, 110, 129, 209
Trading Sardines (Raschke), 65, 207
trading sessions, 131
training, 92, 244
translation, 124

V

visualization, 143, 148, 154, 158, 200
volatility, 29–30, 33, 44, 54, 57–58, 62, 68, 83, 87–88, 114, 134, 193, 197, 216, 218, 251
volume weighted average price (VWAP), 32

ABOUT THE AUTHOR

Brett N. Steenbarger, Ph.D. is a clinical psychologist, trader, trading coach, and Teaching Professor of Psychiatry and Behavioral Sciences at SUNY Upstate Medical University in Syracuse, NY. He has been actively involved in coaching professional traders for over 20 years, with particular experience at hedge funds and proprietary trading firms. He is the author of the popular TraderFeed blog and has written extensively in the area of trading psychology including *Trading Psychology 2.0*, *The Daily Trading Coach*, *Enhancing Trader Performance*, *The Psychology of Trading*, and *Positive Trading Psychology*.